MATHEMATICS
THROUGH THE EYES OF FAITH

MATHEMATICS
THROUGH THE EYES OF FAITH

James Bradley

Russell Howell

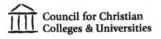

Council for Christian
Colleges & Universities

HarperOne
An Imprint of HarperCollins *Publishers*

HarperCollins books may be purchased for educational, business, or sales promotional use. For information, please write: Special Markets Department, HarperCollins Publishers, 10 East 53rd Street, New York, NY 10022.

HarperCollins website: http://www.harpercollins.com
HarperCollins®, ☰®, and HarperOne™ are trademarks of HarperCollins Publishers

FIRST EDITION

Library of Congress Cataloging-in-Publication Data
Howell, Russell W.
    Mathematics through the eyes of faith / by Russell Howell, James Bradley.
        p. cm.
    ISBN 978–0–06–202447–3
    1. Mathematics.   2. Religion and science.   3. Christian college students—Religious life.   I. Bradley, James.   II. Title.
BL265.M3H69 2001
261.5—dc22   2011012960

HB 12.23.2022

CONTENTS

CONTENTS

PREFACE

Mathematicians are often viewed as an irreligious lot. In one apocryphal story, a mathematician dies and is welcomed into heaven. He is treated well, so well that a pastor complains. "Why," the pastor asks Saint Peter, "is this mathematician being treated like this? We pastors faithfully served the Lord all our lives and none of us was welcomed that well." Saint Peter replies, "Ah, pastors are a dime a dozen up here. But a mathematician in heaven? Now there's something unusual!"

But mathematics and mathematicians have not always been seen this way. Long before the Christian era, Plato saw mathematics as providing patterns that God used in crafting the world. Saint Augustine saw numbers as ideas in the mind of God. Leading seventeenth-century scientists saw mathematics as the key to understanding how God works in the physical universe. However, since the eighteenth-century Enlightenment, mathematics has become quite secularized, so that today educated people typically assume there is no relationship between mathematics and religious belief. Nevertheless, many thought-provoking questions require an understanding of both mathematics and religious perspectives.

This book aims to address the relationship between mathematics and Christian belief and, we hope, to awaken new interest in it. Chapter 1 provides a list of ten "big questions," which will serve as the organizing framework for subsequent chapters. Chapter 2 provides a sketch of a historical context of this relationship from the ancient Greeks to the present.

The next nine chapters address various themes in mathematics and how they relate to Christian belief. Chapters 3 through 5 address three specific mathematical topics—infinity, dimension, and chance. Chapters 6 through 8 focus on three broad characteristics of mathematics—proof, beauty, and the effectiveness of mathematics in understanding the physical world. Chapters 9 and 10 address philosophical issues—epistemology and ontology. The last chapter addresses mathematics and Christian vocation. Every chapter except the first includes exercises and suggestions for further reading that will allow readers to continue their exploration of its ideas.

Only two authors' names, those of the editors, appear on the cover, but this book is actually the result of a team project involving ten authors. The others are Matt DeLong of Taylor University in Indiana, Kim Jongerius of Northwestern College in Iowa, Stephen Lovett of Wheaton College in Illinois, Robert Myers of Bethel College in Indiana, Ray Rosentrater of Westmont College in California, Kristen Schemmerhorn of Dominican University in Illinois, Anthony Tongen of James Madison University in Virginia, and Kevin Vander Meulen of Redeemer University College in Ontario, Canada. Each made an enormous contribution. We are also grateful for the contributions of Michael Stob of Calvin College in Michigan, who chaired the authors' workshop and gave valuable feedback on several chapters, David VanderLaan of Westmont College, who served as philosophy consultant and corrected our many misguided forays into that discipline, and three student readers whose feedback was invaluable: Eddy Chen and Jake Christiansen of Calvin College and Rachel DeMeo of Taylor University. Finally we give thanks to many colleagues from a variety of institutions too numerous to mention who made valuable comments on one or more chapters of this book.

James Bradley, Calvin College, Michigan
Russell Howell, Westmont College, California

Chapter 1

THE BIG QUESTIONS

"[Knowledge of God] is the end of all other knowledge, and even the faculty of understanding would be vain without it."
JONATHAN EDWARDS, *THE END FOR WHICH GOD CREATED THE WORLD*

Four students at a Christian college, Juanita, an art major, Kristoff, a biology major, Alexandra, a mathematics major, and Tiquan, a religious studies major, are taking an introductory class together. Their professor has given them a collaborative project: they are to think about the relationship between mathematics and Christian belief. To get them started, she asked them a question: Could God have made a world in which $2 + 2 \neq 4$? Let's listen to their conversation.

JUANITA: So tell me again what our professor wants us to talk about.
KRISTOFF: She wants us to talk about the relationship between mathematics and Christian belief.
JUANITA: Math and our faith? This is going to be one short conversation.
TIQUAN: Well, let's see. She gave us a question to start us off: Could God have made a world in which $2 + 2 \neq 4$?
JUANITA: Sure. Let the symbol "4" stand for what we usually mean by "5." Nothing to it.
ALEXANDRA: No, that's not what she meant. Could God make $2 + 2 \neq 4$ where 2, +, =, and 4 have their usual meanings?
KRISTOFF: Well, why not? God can do anything—that's what omnipotence means, right?
TIQUAN: I don't think it's that simple. Suppose $2 + 2 = 5$. Doesn't that mean that any time anyone combines 2 things

with 2 other things, a fifth thing has to mysteriously appear? I could put that to good use in my wallet!

JUANITA: You're saying there are things God can't do.

TIQUAN: Yes, I am. Scripture says that too. For instance, it says that God cannot be tempted by evil. That means he can't do evil. He can't lie. For instance, he can't decide to become an atheist.

KRISTOFF: Ha ha.

TIQUAN: No, I'm serious! I'm sure you've heard that old question, can God make a rock so heavy he can't lift it? No. God can't do things that don't make sense.

ALEXANDRA: As a math major, I'd say it differently—God can't do things that are logically inconsistent, like denying that $2 + 2 = 4$. In my view, $2 + 2$ has always equaled 4 and always will.

JUANITA: If math is eternal like God, is it as great as God?

ALEXANDRA: No, but I believe that even God can't make $2 + 2 = 5$.

JUANITA: No way! If God has to obey the laws of math, that makes math greater than God.

ALEXANDRA: Tiquan, you're the religious studies major. Help me out!

TIQUAN: There's a couple of ways to look at it. The laws of math could be part of God's nature. They're not greater than God; they're part of God—ideas in God's mind. But some people think that's claiming more about God than we can know. They would agree that God made the world and controls it. They would also agree that God understands everything there is about mathematics. But the question as to whether math is part of God, we don't know and can't know.

KRISTOFF: What was that first way—ideas in God's mind? God doesn't have a mind like we do!

TIQUAN: The phrase "God's mind" is a metaphor. It's just a way of saying that God has always known and understood mathematical ideas.

JUANITA: That seems right. But it doesn't mean God thinks exactly like us. That's not what you're saying, is it?

ALEXANDRA: I agree with Juanita. There's got to be ways we don't think like God. For instance, in my math classes, we never "know something"—that is, accept it as true—unless we can prove it. But God knows everything; he doesn't have to write a proof to know that a theorem is true.

KRISTOFF: I've heard some theologians say that, while we think differently than God, there are analogies between our thoughts and God's thoughts. For instance, God is consistent, and when we think consistently we share that trait with God. I'd say I love my family. My love is way smaller than God's, but I think it's like his in important ways.

ALEXANDRA: I understand. But our topic is God and math. Aren't we getting away from it?

KRISTOFF: I want to go back to your point about proofs in mathematics. We don't prove theorems in biology. But I still believe that what I learn in my biology classes is true.

JUANITA: That's a different kind of knowledge than Alexandra is talking about, isn't it? You discover what's true in biology by doing experiments and observations and gathering data. Mathematical knowledge doesn't depend on experiments or observations. For me, art is different. When I'm painting, my "truth" is much more intuitive and more personal.

ALEXANDRA: It seems to me that mathematics is special. You're an art major, Juanita. What is true for artists can vary from one person to another, even from one day to another. And according to you, Kristoff, if God had made the world differently, what is true would be different. But in math, theorems cannot *not* be true.

TIQUAN: I'm not sure you're right about that. How can you be so sure theorems are necessarily true? Scripture never makes any mathematical claims.

ALEXANDRA: I don't know. But it seems right to me. There's a lot of intuition in math. My preschool nephew understands that there's no biggest number, so he even seems to have some intuition about infinity.

TIQUAN: Do you think God is the source of this intuition?

ALEXANDRA: I guess I do.

JUANITA: You seem to like math, Alex. But there's one thing I really hate about it: in every problem, there's always one right answer.

ALEXANDRA: That's what I like best about it!

JUANITA: Also it doesn't make sense to me why math works. I learned these rules for manipulating symbols back in high school algebra and it felt like I was being programmed to be some kind of computer. But scientists seem to think algebra has some connection with reality.

KRISTOFF: Einstein followed rules for manipulating mathematical symbols with his equations for general relativity and predicted that light rays would bend when passing a star. Nobody had ever observed that but when his prediction was tested, it turned out to be right!

ALEXANDRA: Like I said, mathematics is special.

JUANITA: You don't need to get snobby about it! If it's special, *you* didn't make it special.

ALEXANDRA: Oops. Sorry.

KRISTOFF: I don't know if math is special, but it seems to me that there is something important here. Look at the DNA molecule. It's a double helix, a mathematical figure! It seems like everywhere we look in the universe we find math, and not just any old math. It's subtle and beautiful, but if we work at it we can understand it.

JUANITA: Do you see that as pointing toward God?

KRISTOFF: I do. It makes more sense to me to say that than to say God wasn't involved. Besides, it seems purposeful. Mathematics helps us understand gravity, electricity, heat, and many other physical things. It also helps us understand probability, and now we have a much better understanding of heredity than people had two hundred years ago.

TIQUAN: And genetic engineers trying to clone people and create superhumans, and worse.

KRISTOFF: Okay, math can be misused, but can't any of God's gifts? Could we understand God's creation without math? Could we be stewards of it?

TIQUAN: I see your point, but a lot of people have looked at the mathematical structure of nature and concluded that the universe is a machine—that we can understand it all without bringing God into the conversation.

KRISTOFF: Sure, but I look at a snowcapped mountain and think, "Isn't God wonderful!" Somebody else looks at the same scene and doesn't see God at all. How we interpret what we see depends on what we believe.

JUANITA: I can see how a biology major can get excited about mathematics. But math and art? They're pretty far apart.

ALEXANDRA: Maybe not as far as you think. You've reminded me of something I puzzle about. Some of my professors are pure mathematicians and they often say that the reason they do math is because it's so beautiful. Their reasons have nothing to do with gravity or DNA molecules or curing diseases.

TIQUAN: Maybe you'd better explain to us what they mean by beautiful.

ALEXANDRA: I'd say order, symmetry, surprise, the ability to express a lot very briefly, things like that.

JUANITA: You missed color and contrast, but other than that, it's similar to what a visual artist might say.

TIQUAN: Do you think the visual arts point us toward God?

JUANITA: Artists used to say things like that a lot; they don't much anymore. But I still think it's true. And I agree with Kristoff—the beauty of nature can do that too. Of course, there is much more to art than beauty, just like there is much more in mathematics than beauty, I suppose.

ALEXANDRA: So maybe these qualities can point mathematicians to God also.

TIQUAN: Maybe. Well, I'm not sure we understand the
relationship between mathematics and Christian belief any
better than when we started, but I think we understand the
issues better.

KRISTOFF: I think it's time to head back to class.

Some Reflections on This Conversation

At one point in the conversation Juanita and Alexandra disagree
on their feelings about mathematics. But they do agree on one thing:
every math problem has only one right answer! Are they correct?
Well, they are, but only if you are doing the kind of problems that
are usually found in elementary-school arithmetic or high-school algebra. When we try to look more carefully at what mathematics is or
what it means or why it is so useful in science, it's no longer so clear
that there is one right answer to every question about mathematics.
Moreover, when we look at mathematics through the eyes of faith,
the most important questions are those about what things are, what
they mean, and whether they are of value.

In their conversation Kristoff, Tiquan, Alexandra, and Juanita
raise many of the big questions we will be tackling in this book.
Several are listed below. In most cases, we will not be providing a
"right" answer. But we will be introducing you to the ideas of some
of history's best thinkers and helping you to enter into the conversa-
tions they have been having on these questions for millennia.

1. Do mathematical concepts like higher dimensions and
infinity point beyond themselves to a higher reality?

Alexandra mentions that her preschool nephew seems to have
some intuition about infinity, a concept often seen as a point of con-
tact between mathematics and Christian belief. But this connection
can be misused. For instance, one nineteenth-century mathematician claimed to have proven the correctness of the Athanasian
Creed, a historic creed that emphasizes God's infinitude and triune

nature. His argument amounted to claiming the doctrine of the Trinity was true because infinity plus infinity plus infinity equals infinity. His argument may strike us as silly, but it still prompts interesting questions: What does mathematics legitimately suggest about spiritual realities, if anything? How can we use concepts like infinity in ways that enrich our faith, but don't lead us astray? We will address these matters in chapters 3 and 4.

2. Can the idea that chance exists in nature be reconciled with God's sovereignty?

Kristoff mentions the role of probability in describing heredity. Any discussion of the connection between mathematics and the natural world quickly leads to one of the more controversial issues of our own day: the relationship between Christian belief and the theory of evolution. The mathematical concept of randomness plays an important role in evolutionary explanations of species development and arises in physics as well as biology. For example, Albert Einstein expressed his doubts about the existence of randomness in nature by saying, "God does not play dice." Another famous physicist, Neils Bohr, is reported to have replied, "Albert, stop telling God what to do." If one flips a fair coin, it is equally likely to come up heads or tails. Presumably, however, if one knew exactly the mechanics of how it was flipped, the side it started on, and the air resistance, one could predict whether heads or tails would come up. But at the atomic level, most quantum physicists say such prediction is impossible. It's not merely that we don't know why quantum randomness occurs, but that randomness is built into the fundamental structure of reality. Some Christians have argued that such a perspective contradicts the concept of a sovereign God who exercises providential love and care over all of creation. Are they right, or are there ways that God could use chance to accomplish his purposes? Chapter 5 discusses these issues.

3. What is truth?

Alexandra, Juanita, and Kristoff spend some of their time considering this question. Art, science, mathematics, and religion often use the word *truth* in very different ways. How do they differ? How do mathematicians prove things to be "true," and how are their techniques different from those used in science? These questions will be central themes in chapter 6.

4. What is beauty? Is mathematics beautiful?

In response to Juanita's comments about the apparent distance between mathematics and art, Alexandra raises the issue of mathematics and beauty. Paul Dirac, one of the most fruitful early researchers in quantum mechanics, was once asked how he had been so successful. He replied that whenever he faced multiple plausible explanations for a phenomenon, he always pursued the one that was the most beautiful. Pure mathematicians often explain their love of their subject by speaking of its beauty. What criteria can be applied in determining whether a mathematical theory is beautiful? What is the concept of beauty at work here? How does it relate to other concepts of beauty? Does it point beyond itself to God's beauty, as C. S. Lewis maintained in his essay *The Weight of Glory*? This question is the main theme of chapter 7.

5. How do we account for the fact that mathematics is so effective in describing the natural world?

Kristoff expresses his astonishment at the subtlety of the mathematics in the physical universe. In 1960, the soon-to-be Nobel laureate in physics Eugene Wigner wrote a now classic paper on this topic titled "The Unreasonable Effectiveness of Mathematics." He wondered how we can account for the fact that mathematics is so successful at describing the way the universe works. Wigner expressed his astonishment at this observation but had no compelling explanation for it. Around AD 400, the Christian philosopher Augustine of Hippo made a similar observation and offered the explanation that God had used mathematics to provide the patterns on which he based creation. But this raises even more questions. How did Augustine justify such a claim? Is such a claim testable scientifically, mathematically, or biblically? Are there other ways to answer Wigner's question? This topic will be our main concern in chapter 8.

6. How can we be sure about what we know?

Recall from the conversation above that Tiquan asks Alexandra, "How can you be so sure?," when she asserts that mathematical theorems cannot be false. Alexandra replies, "I don't know." And yet, almost everyone who has been through high school is confident that $5 + 7 = 12$ and that the Pythagorean theorem is true. How do we account for such confidence when scripture never mentions such assertions? Mathematics has an answer. It is the only discipline that claims to be able to prove its assertions to be true. Is such a claim warranted? Also, where does mathematical knowledge originate? Augustine argued that human beings have a mathematical sixth sense, that is, that our knowledge of basic arithmetic concepts such as unity and infinity were built into our minds by our creator. Was he right? What do these perspectives tell us about the nature of mathematics and of human knowledge in general? Chapter 9 focuses on these questions.

7. Is mathematics discovered or invented?

Alexandra believes that even God can't make $2 + 2 = 5$, so for her, $2 + 2 = 4$ is not invented. Is she right? Did the Greek mathematicians (whose work Euclid compiled in his *Elements*) invent geometry, or did they discover it? Similarly, did Isaac Newton and Gottfried Leibniz invent or discover calculus? Perhaps the answer is, "Some of it was invented and some discovered." But if mathematics is a combination of invention and discovery, how can we tell which aspects were invented and which discovered? That is, where do we draw the line between invention and discovery? These questions have been discussed since the time of Plato and Aristotle in the fourth century BC, and the answer is still not clear. This question is one of many that chapter 10 investigates.

8. *Furthermore, mathematical entities like 2, +, =, and 4 are not physical objects like atoms and galaxies, so what are they?*

Our conversation among the four students began with this question. The Christian philosopher Augustine of Hippo believed that numbers are unchangeable and have existed eternally as ideas in God's mind. Scientists like Johannes Kepler and Isaac Newton shared Augustine's perspective. But other thinkers have disagreed. The Greek philosopher Aristotle believed that, in doing arithmetic, we are simply looking at the quantitative aspects of natural things. Thus, there is no need to believe in a transcendent reality where mathematics resides. In the Middle Ages some Christian thinkers who were influenced by Aristotle argued that numbers were simply linguistic conventions that helped people converse. That is, while God certainly understands numbers, they don't deserve a special status as ideas in God's mind different from other ideas such as "committee" or "highway." This question will be the main focus of chapter 10.

9. *Do principles of logic apply only to the natural world or to God also?*

Some Christians have argued that God does not have to act consistently with principles of logic because such a requirement would make logic greater than God, and nothing is greater than God. Others argue that principles of logic originate in God's nature, in particular in God's consistency; Alexandra takes this position in our conversation. People who believe the latter say that God's reliability tells us that these principles apply to God as well as the natural world. Kristoff suggests that perhaps God's thinking is unlike ours but that the two are analogous in some way, although he is not specific about that way. Can we straighten out the confusion here? These questions, too, will be considered in chapter 10.

The Approach of This Book

Historically, Christian theologians have recognized two principal sources for knowledge about God: special revelation (the books of the Old and New Testament) and general revelation (the book of nature). Trying to infer knowledge about God from human reason alone, or from reasoning about nature, is called natural theology. This includes undertakings such as efforts to prove God's existence and attempts to infer first principles for theological reflection from natural phenomena.

Recently the theologian and scientist Alister McGrath has offered a new approach to natural theology. He suggests accepting special revelation as providing an interpretive framework through which nature can be seen. When one looks through eyes of faith, McGrath argues, nature speaks richly about God. In this book, we are going to apply McGrath's approach to mathematics. We will accept the scriptures of the Old and New Testaments as faithful records of who God is and what God has done; we will also accept historic Christian beliefs as summarized in the Apostles' Creed and the Nicene Creed. Such beliefs constitute a broad framework historically affirmed by Orthodox, Roman Catholic, and Protestant believers. In addressing our big questions, we will be asking both how Christian beliefs can contribute to an understanding of mathematics and how mathematics can enrich an understanding of Christian belief. That is, we will be seeking to *interpret* mathematics from a faith perspective, not to create a distinctively Christian mathematics.

Towards that end, as you read through this book keep in mind the following additional question:

10. *What are God's purposes for human beings in this world? How does giving people the capacity to do mathematics fit into those purposes?*

Scripture clearly reveals God as personal and purposeful. Moreover, God created us with a capacity to do mathematics, so using that capacity must be part of God's will for us. We will focus more on this issue in our concluding chapter. For now we can begin clarifying our understanding of his will for us in this area.

Christians often think of God's purposes in the world in terms of "the Great Commission"—Jesus's words at the end of Mark's Gospel that his disciples should "Go into all the world and preach the good news to all creation. Whoever believes and is baptized will be saved, but whoever does not believe will be condemned" (Mark 16:15–16). Near the end of the conversation that opened this chapter, Kristoff talks about the ways that mathematics is useful to him as a biology major. The uses he sees for mathematics do not seem to fit within this mission. But the Great Commission is only part of God's purposes. Scripture sees humanity as fallen into bondage to sin and sees faith in Christ as the key step in reversing that fall. Thus, if we are to understand God's purposes in the world, we also need to think about God's pre-fall purposes. In Genesis 1:28, scripture quotes God as saying to Adam and Eve, "Be fruitful and increase in number; fill the earth and subdue it. Rule over the fish of the sea and the birds of the air and over every living creature that moves on the ground." Many theologians have used this passage and others to develop the concept of the *cultural mandate*, sometimes also called the *creation mandate*—the idea that God's pre-fall purpose for human beings included that their population should increase, they should develop science and technology, and they should develop cultures including social networks, means of communication, art, music, literature, and so forth. Against the background of such a purpose, it is not hard to see a role for the study of mathematics. Mathematics is the language of science, and without it knowledge of physical entities such as planets, birds, fish, and atomic structure would be impossible. So those with gifts in the area of mathematics should consider using those gifts to help carry out their God-given stewardship of nature. But mathematics can also be used to measure such things as income, educational level, and life expectancy. Thus it is a key part of working for justice in human cultures. In fact, mathematics has shaped matters from those as great as how humans see their place in the universe to things as everyday as how we tell time. And finally, as you read this book, we hope you will see another purpose for mathematics as well: it points beyond itself to God's glory. That is, it can lead us to worship.

EXERCISES

1. For a twenty-four-hour period, keep a sheet of paper in your pocket or purse and jot down every way you use math that day, no matter how small. At the end of the day, summarize your list. When you get to class, consolidate your list with those of your classmates. What does this consolidated list tell us about the role of mathematics in our lives?

2. Could God have made a world in which $2 + 2 \neq 4$? Write out your thoughts about this question.

3. In mathematics, the standard of persuasiveness is proof. That is, in mathematics, the only way to persuade someone else that your claims are true is to prove them. If you are not a mathematics major, what is the standard in your area of study? Why is it different than the mathematical standard? If you are a mathematics major, answer the previous questions from the perspective of the natural sciences.

4. In response to the question as to whether God could make a rock so large that he couldn't move it, Tiquan responds, "No. God cannot do things that don't make sense." This response has been affirmed by many important thinkers, but it raises deep and subtle issues. How would you approach this question?

5. Consider the statement, "God is omnipotent and therefore doesn't have to obey the laws of logic." Argue both sides of this issue. Which argument do you find more compelling? Why?

6. The philosophy of mathematics can be seen as an extended argument between the followers of Plato, who argue that mathematics is eternal and transcends human minds, and the followers of an interpretation of Aristotle that suggests that mathematics is a human construct. Imagine two students, one

who takes each position. Write a conversation between them in which each defends his or her own perspective.

7. Identify three examples of the successful application of statistics. Are these examples of using mathematics to exercise stewardship over creation? If so, how? If not, why not?

8. Create a list of numbers that are frequently used in scripture. Investigate what biblical commentators suggest that they symbolize and write a summary of your results.

Chapter 2

HISTORICAL CONTEXT

Through him all things were made. In him was life, and that life was the light of men.

JOHN 1:3

Ask some of your friends if they think there is a relationship between mathematics and Christian belief. You'll probably get answers like, "No, not at all; are you kidding?" But educated people did not always think this way. In the seventeenth century, for example, leading European scientists saw themselves as using mathematics to explain God's relationship to the physical universe. Furthermore (as we saw in chapter 1) there are "big questions" about reality that involve mathematics, and these questions naturally lend themselves to reflection from a Christian perspective. What has happened? How have mathematics and Christian belief come to be seen as so far removed from each other? To help answer this question this chapter surveys the work of some important mathematicians and scientists in the Western world and traces their thinking about the relationship between mathematics and Christian thought. This survey should also help provide you with a context for thinking about the big questions addressed in subsequent chapters.

Prior to the Scientific Revolution

Ideally our survey would begin with the Old and New Testaments, but the scriptures do not speak directly of God's relationship to mathematics. Thus, we begin our survey with some famous Greek philosophers and some Christian thinkers who were influenced by them.

We don't know a lot about Pythagoras (ca. 570–495 BC) other than that he was the leader of a quasi-religious cult that came to be known as the Pythagoreans, whose perspective on numbers laid the foundation for much subsequent thinking about mathematics and religion. Nevertheless, he is generally credited with the discovery of the numerical basis of musical intervals. Pluck a guitar string, then hold your thumb so that the string is divided into two equal parts and pluck it again. The new tone sounds like the original, but higher. This 2:1 ratio of the string lengths produces two sounds that are said to be one octave apart. Now, pluck the same strings from two similar guitars, but divide one in half and the other into thirds. You'll notice that the sounds of a half of a string and a third of a string blend in a pleasing way. This 3:2 ratio of lengths yields sounds separated by what we now call a fifth; similarly a 4:3 ratio yields compatible sounds, and we call this interval a fourth. From these three intervals—the octave, fifth, and fourth—and the selection of a "tonic" or foundational sound, the entire twelve-tone scale of Western music can be constructed. To the Pythagoreans this correspondence between musical intervals and mathematical proportions pointed to an intangible and deeper reality (perceptible to the intellect but not to the senses) that underlay tangible reality. They believed that numbers constituted the true and most fundamental nature of things, and that all of reality could—ultimately—be explained by numbers.

Plato (ca. 428–347 BC) was not a mathematician, nor is there any evidence that he made a contribution to mathematics. Nevertheless, mathematics plays a critical role in his philosophy. A key concept in Plato's thought is the notion of **forms**. Plato posited a cosmology involving three distinct principles—god (the *demiurge*), matter, and forms. The latter are eternal, intangible objects distinct from perceptible objects like particular trees or houses. They correspond to general terms like goodness, justice, triangle, horse, and so forth. But for Plato they are not simply concepts. They are real objects. In fact, they are more real than perceptible objects. The form of "the good" is the first principle of all things and the pinnacle of the system of forms. Forms can be objects of desire, and contemplating them brings ultimate satisfaction. Plato held mathematics in high regard, but did not see mathematical objects as forms; rather they occupied an ambiguous place somewhere between matter and the forms.

Plato extended Pythagorean ideas in one of his dialogues, known as the *Timaeus*. According to Plato, the demiurge fashioned the world by using mathematics to make preexisting matter more like the forms. Plato did not formulate "laws of nature" based on observation and testing hypotheses as scientists do today. Rather, he used a more intuitive, metaphorical approach based on the unifying nature of proportions and geometry. For example, he shared the Pythagorean fascination with five special geometric objects, which today we call **Platonic solids**: the cube, octahedron, tetrahedron, icosahedron, and dodecahedron. These are the only logically possible solids made up of congruent, regular polygons with only one type of polygon used on all the faces of each solid. Thus, a cube consists of six squares; an octahedron consists of eight triangles; a tetrahedron consists of four triangles; an icosahedron consists of twenty triangles; and a dodecahedron consists of twelve pentagons, as shown in figure 2.1. Plato identified four principal elements: earth, air, fire, and water. The demiurge aimed to make the world good by imposing limits on matter using the Platonic solids: the cube was associated with earth, the octahedron with air, the tetrahedron with fire, and the icosahedron with water. The dodecahedron was involved in a somewhat vague way with what Plato called "ether" or the "quintessence" of the universe.

Plato's methodology prefigured Euclid's geometric system: it broke down complex realities into simple, elementary entities that, like geometric axioms, served as the starting points to build a complete system of understanding. Consider, for example, the composition of the three-dimensional Platonic solids. In each case the solid is made up of simple two-dimensional geometric shapes. Plato not only reasoned downward to the elements by claiming that they had a basic mathematical structure; he also reasoned upward to the overall structure of the cosmos. His cosmology was geocentric, with the sun, moon, fixed stars, and five known planets traveling in circular orbits

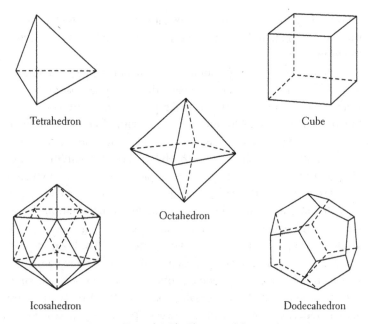

Tetrahedron

Cube

Octahedron

Icosahedron

Dodecahedron

Figure 2.1 The Platonic Solids

about the earth. Thus, Plato saw mathematics as providing the fundamental ordering of the physical world. While we no longer view planets as orbiting the earth, much of Plato's influence remains. Interestingly, the English word *planet* comes from the Greek *planein*, meaning *to wander.*

Aristotle (384–322 BC) was a student of Plato but differed from his teacher in significant ways. The differing approaches of Plato and Aristotle have largely set the agenda for over two millennia of discussions of the nature of mathematics. Aristotle identified basic logical principles such as the **law of noncontradiction** and the **law of the excluded middle**. (The law of noncontradiction states that a **proposition,** which is a statement that affirms or denies something, cannot be both true and false; the law of excluded middle asserts that any proposition must be either true or false.) Aristotle rejected the Pythagorean idea that all of reality could be explained by numbers. He accepted the idea that mathematical objects are universal, unchanging, and eternal. Aristotle viewed mathematical objects as the products of a process of *removal*. To illustrate Aristotle's thinking here, imagine a particular, perceptible triangle. This triangle will have properties associated with it. For example, its lines might be all blue and its area might equal five square inches. When the properties associated with this triangle (such as the color of its lines, or how large it is) are "removed" by disregarding what they are, one is left with a kind of universal abstract object. While Aristotle was ambiguous about exactly what is left after this removal process, he saw no need to place mathematical objects in a separate reality that transcends the ordinary material world as did Plato.

Like Plato, Aristotle also foreshadowed the work of Euclid. For Aristotle, demonstrations properly begin with axioms gained by a process of generalizing from our sensory experience. Even though axioms come about by the senses, Aristotle did not think that empirical observation could lead to certain scientific knowledge. To gain certainty one must use the established axioms to prove results, much like what goes on in proving a geometric theorem.

Aristotle was among the first of many thinkers to broach discussions about infinity, but he regarded infinity only as a concept and not as something that actually exists. In modern terms, he believed in a *potential* infinity, but not in any *actual* infinity. Thus, the contemporary notion that a line actually consists of an infinite collection of points would have been nonsense to him.

Augustine (AD 354–430) modified Plato's ideas and placed them within a Christian framework. (As far as we know Augustine was unfamiliar with Aristotle.) Augustine viewed numbers as ideas in the mind of God. He saw mathematical truths as eternal, transcendent propositions independent of human minds; their certitude comes from the fact that they originate in God's thoughts. Mathematics is effective in helping us understand the physical universe for two reasons: (1) God used the patterns expressed by mathematics in creating the universe, and (2) God built the capacity to do mathematics into the human species. Augustine also regarded mathematical knowledge as *a priori*, that is, it is knowledge that comes apart from empirical observation. He argued that such knowledge cannot originate in our bodily senses; the elementary truths of mathematics are present to all who think. Thus, God has given human beings a mathematical "sixth sense" by which the basic truths of mathematics are apprehended. In modern jargon, Augustine believed that God hardwired into humans some basic mathematical concepts and the capacity to develop more of them. From Augustine's perspective, our thought is capable of grasping at least some of the structures of creation, and these structures exist in the eternal mind of God. Augustine was the key transmitter of this thinking to the Middle Ages, a period that is generally associated with the fifth through the fifteenth centuries AD.

Thomas Aquinas (1225–1274) sought to develop a Christian philosophy merged with those aspects of Plato's and Aristotle's work that could be reconciled with Christian belief. Aquinas is known for his *analogy of being*, a belief that, since God is the creator of all that is, there is a correspondence between the created order and God. Aquinas and others used this concept to justify inferences about God from objects and relationships—including mathematical relationships—in the natural order. Aquinas also held reason in high regard. Although he based his thought on scripture, he believed it was possible to know by reason alone that there is a God and that there is only one God. He also saw God's work in the world as primarily taking place through secondary agents (entities other than God) rather than direct divine action. Medieval theologians and philosophers like Aquinas who sought to reconcile Christian belief with Aristotelian and Platonic thought are called *scholastics*. Based on Aristotle's idea that geometric concepts do not have an existence apart from physical reality, some scholastics developed a perspective on mathematics called **nominalism**. From this point of view, objects like points, lines, and planes exist only in the minds of people who think about them. They are a convenient social convention, as they make communication easier. Thus, for the scholastic Gregory of

Rimini, statements such as "There are infinitely many points in a line" are false because there are no points or lines. He concluded that not even God can divide a line into infinitely many parts. Nevertheless, God can conceptually distinguish infinitely many parts in a continuum. Thus, for God, an actual infinity is possible and not just the potential infinity that Aristotle recognized. These ideas subsequently were significant in the nineteenth century for the understanding of infinity and the continuum. Furthermore, these scholastics argued, God exists outside of time and thus has no need to think deductively, but apprehends all truths immediately.

In summary, the thinkers we have surveyed had two main approaches regarding the relationship between mathematics and religious belief. For Plato, the demiurge used mathematical ideas in creating the world; Augustine placed these ideas in a Christian context. For Aristotle, mathematics consists of aspects of the natural world that we abstract from it; many scholastics gave this approach a Christian interpretation. The difference between these perspectives has not been resolved. In fact, these two approaches underlie many of the issues we will be discussing in this book.

The Scientific Revolution

Aristotle's work was lost to the West throughout the first millennium of the Christian era. It was preserved in the Arab world, however, and was reintroduced to Europe in the twelfth century. By the early seventeenth century Western scholarship had experienced twelve hundred years of widespread acceptance of Augustine's belief that mathematics consisted of ideas in God's mind and that—quite naturally—God used these ideas in creating the cosmos. It had also experienced five hundred years of the presence of Aristotle's alternative perspective. Aquinas and his followers had fostered considerable confidence in the capacity of human reason to understand God's ways. By the end of the sixteenth century, Europe was prosperous economically and had vastly expanded its trade. Its explorers had discovered a new world. Accurate translations of Greek mathematical texts were available and European mathematicians tried to understand how the Greeks discovered their results.

Several events, however, convinced European thinkers of the need to move beyond the wisdom of the ancients. Errors surfaced in the Ptolemaic model of the universe (that all heavenly objects revolve about the earth), a model that had dominated Western thought since the publication of Ptolemy's *Almagest*, ca. AD 150. For example, astronomers observed inaccurate predictions of planetary positions and the timing of lunar eclipses. In 1545, Girolamo Cardano published solutions to the cubic and quartic equations, problems that the Greeks had been unable to solve. Thus, the leading scientists of the seventeenth century became convinced that they could discover the mathematical laws by which God had made the physical universe, and this project motivated much of their research. In this section, we survey the thinking of four leading architects of the scientific revolution: Johannes Kepler, Galileo Galilei, Isaac Newton, and Gottfried Leibniz.

Johannes Kepler (1571–1630) is best known for his discovery that planetary orbits are elliptical. As a scientist he is a key transitional figure from the classical period to the scientific era. On one hand he rejected the Pythagorean approach of taking numbers and proportions as primary causes of natural phenomena. He regarded numbers as the results of measurements and asserted that only the things that are counted have real existence. Thus, regarding numbers, he was an Aristotelian. On the other hand, like the Pythagoreans, he affirmed that astronomy is based on fundamental harmonies analogous to musical harmonies. He also stood within the Platonic tradition by affirming that geometry possesses a special form of transcendence.

Kepler asserted that in geometry there is a fundamental *univocity* (from the Latin *uni voce*, meaning one voice) between God's thoughts and ours. Thus, a well-formulated mathematical definition has only one correct interpretation. Since God's understanding of a concept is certainly correct, if a human being also understands it correctly, that person understands it in the same way that God does;

the person and God "speak with one voice." Furthermore, argued Kepler, the formal rules of logic mirror the divine understanding and are common to all forms of intelligible thought. Mathematical knowledge is based on definitions plus formal logic, so in doing mathematics we share God's thoughts.

Kepler also saw geometric entities as part of God's essence, and thus co-eternal with God. The constructible geometric objects served as the archetypes of creation. Hence, it is possible for humans to read God's design in the universe on the basis of a rigorous mathematical methodology. Thus, Kepler regarded Aquinas's *analogy of being* as too weak an understanding of the relationship between human and divine thought. He recognized the sharp break that his univocity claim made with earlier ideas and justified it extensively. He also strongly cautioned about the difficulties of knowing the extent of this univocity and warned against simplistic attempts to transform the harmonies he saw in astronomy into the meaning or purpose of physical events.

Whereas Kepler's focus was on explaining God's relationship to the physical universe, Galileo (1564–1642) sought to enhance the position of mathematics as a source of truth. That is, he attempted to shift the locus of authority for interpreting nature. He wanted this "seat of authority" to move from natural philosophers and theologians to mathematicians. Kepler's objectives were scientific and theological; Galileo's objectives were also political.

In making his case, Galileo argued for five properties of mathematics: "(1) God has written the book of nature—which is the object of natural philosophy—in the language of mathematics. (2) Man can learn this language." (3) Man can "apply it to the study of nature" due to its logical structure. "(4) [H]andled with care, this language cannot err or go astray." (5) This language is "not only the most certain epistemological tool, but" in fact is "the most perfect one capable of elevating the mind to divine knowledge."[1] Hence, knowledge derived by mathematical reasoning possessed the highest certainty possible. Galileo believed that such reasoning could produce knowledge equivalent in quality to divine knowledge. It could help correct flawed, biblically based arguments because mathematics was the language of God.

Eventually, Galileo rejected the prevailing Ptolemaic model of the solar system in favor of the current heliocentric model. The controversy surrounding this move is often misunderstood. On the one hand, Galileo's desire to give mathematics a more central role in interpreting nature amounted to a change in authority that placed ecclesiastical leadership in a secondary position. Some opposition from the Church, therefore, was not surprising. On the other hand, as you will see in chapter 8, most of the scientific community disagreed with Galileo, as the best scientific evidence available at that time did not support his theory. Ecclesiastical leaders opposed Galileo primarily because he challenged the authority of the Church, and not because of the views he held. For example, one of the main characters in the *Dialogue Concerning the Two Chief World Systems*, his major defense of heliocentrism, was named Simplicio, which in Italian can mean "simpleton." In that dialogue Galileo portrayed Simplicio as speaking the words of Urban VIII, the pope at that time. After much arguing the Church placed Galileo under house arrest in 1634. During that time he was treated very well. He was not executed, but he has nevertheless been widely seen as a "martyr" for science even though he remained a Catholic all of his life.

Galileo's efforts ultimately led to a restructuring of the scientific disciplines; mathematics was used in the study of new topics and acquired a privileged status of its own. In subsequent years, its effectiveness in astronomy, ballistics, and engineering shifted much credibility in its direction. Within a hundred years after his death, the shift in authority that Galileo had sought had largely taken place.

Like his predecessors, Isaac Newton (1643–1727) sought to explain God's work in the physical universe. Aristotle taught that heavy objects like rocks have an inherent tendency to return to the center of the earth and that fire has an inherent tendency to move upwards. Newton differed from Aristotle by insisting that matter is inert—one of its properties is "inertia." As such it does not have inherent motions; nevertheless, it moves. Thus, he saw God as prime mover and source of the energy for all ongoing motion. As Aquinas argued four hundred years earlier, he believed that God primarily acts through secondary causes; for example, God acts in the physical universe through gravitation. Newton saw the laws of nature as ideas in God's mind and believed that mathematics provides the tools needed to discern the laws God placed in creation. Newton stated that hypotheses must be deduced from observable phenomena. Shortly after his death, Enlightenment thinkers (more about the Enlightenment below) regarded him as a hero who demonstrated how much can be achieved by the human intellect; they also viewed his religious interests as an expression of his mental decline in later years. Recent scholars have rejected this picture of Newton and today see him as one whose overriding concern was to explain how God works in the physical world.

With Newton, Gottfried Leibniz (1646–1715) is credited with the founding of calculus. He was a Christian believer who held reason and its capabilities in high esteem. He believed that we can have a concept of God and not just a vague imagination of him: God is the most perfect being, the most rational being, omniscient, and able to do all things that are logically possible. God always acts according to maximal goodness and thus has created the best of all possible worlds. Leibniz believed that mathematical truths exist in God's reason and do not depend on his will. Not even God could change them without abolishing himself. Thus, in finding mathematical truths, one finds part of God's reason. For Leibniz, God and humans have reason in common; doing mathematics is a way to listen to God's voice and might be comparable to divine service, although active endeavor for the welfare of others is indispensable. God is the perfect mathematician; creation is done by "divine mathematics."

Leibniz thought that most scientific problems need infinitesimal calculus because everything in nature bears the signature of an infinite author. Also, everything in nature seems to follow mathematical laws, so someone with sufficient insight, memory, and reason could be a prophet. He saw mathematics as the first step on a stairway to God, from mathematics to philosophy to theology. He also addressed some common theological issues. For example, he tried to demonstrate the existence of God. Also, unlike Newton, he did not deny the triune nature of God. Rather, he said that the word *God* is being used in two different ways in referring to God as father and to God as Trinity. Thus, the concept of the Trinity doesn't contradict reason; it is above reason because we don't understand it.

So for these four men—who rank among the greatest of all scientists—mathematics and their own Christian beliefs were very closely related. They saw themselves as making God's thoughts known. In one sense, they were very successful: if one accepts the idea that God's work in the physical universe is primarily through natural laws, Newton's laws provided a compelling account of how one of those laws—gravitation—functioned. But within a generation after Newton's death, the theological significance of their work came to be largely ignored.

The Modern Era

The scientific revolution was followed by an era that is now known as the Enlightenment, a period that roughly spans the eighteenth century. It is a description of a cultural ethos that arose almost simultaneously in England, France, the Netherlands, and Germany. This ethos subsequently spread to Eastern Europe and the Americas. One traditional definition of the Enlightenment is that it "was a desire for human affairs to be guided by rationality rather than by faith, superstition, or revelation; a belief in the power of human reason to change society and liberate the individual from the restraints of custom or arbitrary authority; all backed up by a world view increasingly validated by science rather than by religion or tradition."[2]

The predominant religious perspective of Enlightenment thinkers (for example, Voltaire and Diderot in France; Hobbes and Hume in Great Britain; Franklin, Jefferson, and Paine in the United States) was *deism*. This term designates the belief that God does not intervene in the operations of the natural world, but allows it to function according to laws of nature that God created. For deists, reason—not revelation—is the path to knowledge of God.

Most explanations of the rise of the Enlightenment cite three factors:

- In the sixteenth century large numbers of European explorers spread over the globe awakening Europe to cultures different from their own.
- Europe had endured religious wars since the beginning of the Protestant Reformation in 1517. For example, the Thirty Years' War (1618–1648) resulted in an estimated 15 to 30 percent drop in the population of the German states due to violence, disease, and refugee flight. People began to look elsewhere than religion for stability and order.
- The work of Copernicus, Kepler, and Galileo showed that the universe was incredibly larger and differently organized than had been imagined. Newton's laws—inadvertently—provided a compelling nontheistic account of how the universe operates and provided an enormous boost of confidence in the power of human reason.

Although Newton's laws provided a powerful thrust to deism, by around 1800 the influence of deism had substantially declined. Thus, in just over a century, the predominant religious perspective of the European intelligentsia had shifted dramatically. It moved from a more or less orthodox Christianity, to deism, to either a vaguely Christian belief that excluded revelation or to outright unbelief.

Thinking concerning the relationship between mathematics and Christian belief significantly declined during and after the eighteenth century. Voltaire's highly influential book *Candide* (1759) satirized Leibniz as a foolish figure—Dr. Pangloss—who kept asserting that God had created the best of all possible worlds while terrible things were happening around him. Immanuel Kant (1724–1804) reframed the questions scholars should be asking about the physical universe. From Kant's perspective, we do not have direct access to things-in-themselves, but only to how things appear to us. Our mind comes pre-equipped with categories that structure our concepts and shape how we experience objects. Mathematics derives from our intuition, so we can be sure it applies to all that we perceive. But we can have no assurance that it has any significance distinct from our perception. Such a perspective is incompatible with Galileo's and Newton's view that mathematics is the language in which God has written the laws of the universe.

The historian Ivor Grattan-Guinness notes three aspects of reflections on theology by mathematicians at this time: how rare such reflections were, their isolation from each other, and that none led to a durable influence on subsequent thinkers. He writes,

> After around 1750 mathematics seems to have become almost entirely secular, or at least religiously neutral, with Christian belief rarely in print though not out of mind—in striking contrast with the great growth of involvement of Christian and/or Deist belief in the natural sciences. This situation obtained in all countries, and in both research and teaching; presumably it developed by consensus, though perhaps encouraged by the great prominence of France between the 1780s and the 1830s, and the influence of the Enlightenment.[3]

Interestingly, in early-nineteenth-century England, the confidence one can have in mathematical truth was often used by clergy (if not mathematicians) as a metaphor for the confidence possible for a Christian believer. However, by the end of that century, **secularization** (the removal of a religious orientation from things and ideas in society) had become well established. Below are three examples of some prominent people who helped move their societies in this direction.

Augustus De Morgan (1806–1871) was raised in a strict evangelical home. Upon completion of studies at Trinity College, however, he was denied his master's degree because he was unwilling to comply with the requirement of signing the thirty-nine articles of the Church of England. Although he never abandoned belief in God, he moved towards a Unitarian perspective. As founder of the London Mathematical Society, he sought to establish mathematics as a professional discipline. He believed that for this to happen,

> mathematicians would have to sacrifice the age-old transcendental characterization of their discipline. They could no longer claim that mathematics was a divine language because it then became a proper subject of clergymen and mystics as well; they could no longer assert that mathematics was perfect and infallible because it then became a new dogmatic Church like the one they had struggled against; no longer could they even flaunt the supreme precision of mathematics because that was just the sort of hubris they disparaged in contemporary intellectual discourse, . . . To advance their field, de Morgan and his colleagues would have to criticize it, circumscribe it—and, most importantly, secularize it—first.[4]

The London Mathematical Society served as the model for the American Mathematical Society and subsequently for other such societies as well. Thus, one aspect of professionalization—a strong separation of mathematics and religious belief—became institutionalized in the mathematical community.

The Englishman Bertrand Russell (1872–1970) was a well-known atheist. From Russell's perspective, logic was not eternal and transcendent, but the laws of logic represented the laws of human thought. His views of geometry similarly denied its transcendence. He wrote,

> It has gradually appeared, by the increase of non-Euclidean systems, that Geometry throws no more light on the nature of space than Arithmetic throws on the population of the United States. . . . Whether Euclid's axioms are true, is a question as to

which the pure mathematician is indifferent. . . . The [modern] geometer takes any set of axioms that seem interesting and deduces their consequence.[5]

The German mathematician David Hilbert (1862–1943) pioneered a school of mathematics known as *formalism*, where mathematics is seen as a formal game played with symbols. Its meaning does not extend beyond its symbols and the rules used to manipulate them. For Hilbert, then, a mathematical statement is true if and only if it can be proved. He hoped to be able to create a procedure that one could use to prove or disprove any conceivable mathematical statement. Speaking in Königsberg in the fall of 1930, he said:

> For this formula game is carried out according to certain definite rules, in which the technique of our thinking is expressed. These rules form a closed system that can be discovered and definitely stated. The fundamental idea of my proof theory is none other than to describe the activity of our understanding, to make a protocol of the rules according to which our thinking actually proceeds. . . . Already at this time I would like to assert what the final outcome will be: mathematics is a presuppositionless science. To found it, I do not need God or the assumption of a special faculty of our understanding . . . or the primal intuition of Brouwer . . . or finally, as do Russell and Whitehead, axioms of infinity, reducibility, or completeness.[6]

Today, large numbers of thinkers have moved to an outlook that has been dubbed *post-Enlightenment* (also known as *postmodern*). This stance rejects the Enlightenment belief in the sufficiency of science and mathematics to solve all human problems. Rather, postmodernism focuses on the embeddedness of truths within cultural contexts. While it shares with Christian belief a rejection of the Enlightenment hubris regarding the primacy of science and mathematics above all else, postmodernism shies away from claims of transcendence and so is still predominantly secular.

In spite of pervasive secularism—modern or postmodern—questions of religious significance have continued to arise in mathematical studies. Two especially noteworthy examples have appeared since the late-nineteenth century.

- While Augustine had held that there are no infinite numbers, Georg Cantor (1845–1918), founder of set theory, created a theory that allowed for numbers that are actually infinite. He wrote extensively about the relationship between the mathematical and theological concepts of infinity. Unlike Hilbert, he wanted mathematics to have a meaning beyond itself.
- In his incompleteness theorems published in 1931, Kurt Gödel (1906–1978) demonstrated the unattainability of Hilbert's objective. Recall that Hilbert had believed that truth in mathematics is the same thing as provability; Gödel proved that in any consistent mathematical system strong enough to include the arithmetic of the natural numbers, there are true statements that cannot be proved within that system. Thus, truth is not the same as provability, and there cannot be a procedure that could be used to prove or disprove any given mathematical statement. Gödel spent much of the rest of his life investigating the philosophical and theological implications of his theorems, although he did not publish a great deal on these matters.

Some lesser known work has also been done in recent years. The Divine Action Project, cosponsored by the Vatican Observatory and the Center for Theology and Natural Science, addressed God's relationship with the physical universe in five volumes published between 1993 and 2001. These deal with indeterminacy, chaos, and the mathematics of general relativity, while addressing their theological significance. Also, in 2008 the statistician David Bartholomew published *God, Chance and Purpose*, in which he advances the theory that God uses randomness. He further claims that such a view can be reconciled with orthodox Christian theology. Chapter 5 discusses this issue in detail.

Conclusion

Mathematics shapes every educated person's thinking in deep and subtle ways. For instance, mathematics has deeply influenced thinking about each of the following major issues:

How We See Our Place in the Universe

After Ptolemy published the *Almagest,* the prevailing perspective was that a spherical earth rested at the center of the universe with heavenly bodies revolving in circular orbits around it.

As we saw this perspective changed to a Copernican geometry—a heliocentric solar system with the planets revolving in elliptical orbits about the sun. Today, we see our solar system as one part of a much larger galaxy that rotates about its center and our galaxy as just one of millions of others. Furthermore, following Einstein, we see gravity as modifying the shape of space in a way analogous to how a marble placed on a tightly stretched rubber sheet would deform it.

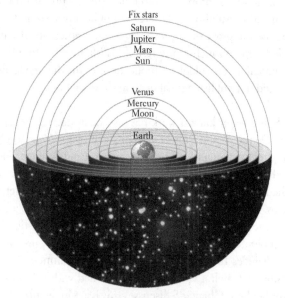

Figure 2.2 The Ptolemaic Model

Figure 2.3 A spiral galaxy (photo taken by the Hubble space telescope)
Courtesy of NASA, ESA, S. Beckwith (STScI), and
The Hubble Heritage Team (STScI/AURA)

Each of these theories is geometric in nature, and the changes in perspective—from the Ptolemaic, to the Copernican, to the Einsteinian—originated in mathematical analyses.

How We Organize Our Understanding

Recall that Euclid (ca. 300 BC) is known for his pioneering work in organizing the geometry of his day into a massive thirteen-volume collection known as the *Elements*. Perhaps the greatest influence of Euclid was not in geometry itself, however, but in promulgating the axiomatic method. This method dictates that knowledge about a subject be organized in such a way that the most elementary, fundamental truths should be separated out and collected together, then other truths deduced from these. A familiar instance of this organizing approach is found in the creeds and catechisms used by many Christian denominations. But it has also shaped all of the history of the natural sciences, philosophy, and systematic theology. The philosopher and mathematician Rene Descartes (1596–1650) confessed to the influence of the geometers when he wrote his classic treatise, *Meditations on First Philosophy*. The social sciences have strived for many years to identify such fundamental truths, but have not been as successful as the natural sciences. Today, under the influence of postmodernism, they have largely abandoned the search for such universal principles.

How We Live Day by Day

Virtually every aspect of our daily lives is shaped by mathematics. We coordinate our meetings with other people by clocks, using a base-twelve counting system. All exchanges of money and all measurements of weight or quantity are rooted in mathematics. If we use a computer, we use a machine whose design is based on mathematical logic; if we turn on an electric light, we are using an energy source that we understand via mathematics. If someone argues that a gender or ethnic group is being systematically treated unjustly, the argument is usually based on statistics. We could add lots more examples, but the point is clear: mathematics shapes our everyday lives in many ways.

However, the influence that mathematics exerts presents us with a problem. We began this chapter with the apostle John's statement that, "Through him all things were made. In him was life, and that life was the light of men." (John 1:3). Certainly, God created humans with a capacity to engage in mathematical thinking. But the current thoroughgoing secularization of mathematics ignores any religious significance it might have. Augustine wrote that we don't rightly understand anything until we understand its connection with Jesus Christ. So where are the connections? How are we to understand them? In the following chapters, our big questions will provide a means for us to move away from the prevailing secular perspective on mathematics and identify and explore many of these connections.

Suggestions for Further Reading

Cohen, Daniel. *Equations from God: Pure Mathematics and Victorian Faith*. Baltimore: Johns Hopkins Univ. Press, 2007. A study of the secularization of mathematics as it took place in nineteenth-century England.

Grattan-Guinness, Ivor. "Christianity and Mathematics: Kinds of Link, and the Rare Occurrences After 1750." *Physis: Rivista Internazionale di Soria della Scienza, Nuova serie* 37, no. 2 (2000): 288–322. A broad historical study of the links between mathematics and religion with special emphasis on Christianity.

Hilbert, David. "Königsberg Address." 1930. Available in English translation at http://math.ucsd.edu/~williams/motiv/hilbert.html. A famous speech in which Hilbert laid out his vision for a formal, secularized mathematics.

Katz, Victor J. *A History of Mathematics: An Introduction*. New York: HarperCollins, 1993. A widely used textbook on the history of mathematics.

Koetsier, T., and L. Bergmanns, eds. *Mathematics and the Divine: A Historical Study*. Amsterdam: Elsevier, 2005. A collection of scholarly essays covering the relationship between mathematics and religious belief from ancient to modern times.

Lessl, Thomas. "The Galileo Legend." *New Oxford Review* (June 2000): 27–33. Available online at http://www.catholiceducation. org/articles/apologetics/ap0138.html. The author challenges what he regards as popular misunderstandings of Galileo's conflict with the Catholic Church.

Lindberg, David C. "Galileo, the Church, and the Cosmos." In *When Science and Christianity Meet*. edited by David C. Lindberg and Ronald L. Numbers, 33–60. Chicago: Univ. of Chicago Press, 2003. A scholarly account of the conflict between Galileo and the Church.

EXERCISES

1. The table below gives the number of vertices, edges, and faces for the Platonic solids. There is a simple formula relating these three numbers. See if you can discover it.

Solid	Vertices	Edges	Faces
Tetrahedron	4	6	4
Cube	8	12	6
Octahedron	6	12	8
Icosahedron	12	30	20
Dodecahedron	20	30	12

2. Some critics have argued that Kepler's views on univocity diminish God's transcendence. Do you agree? Why or why not?

3. What aspects of Aristotle's thought did Galileo object to and why? This will require some research on your part.

4. One notable exception to the secularization of mathematics after 1750 was the nineteenth-century English scientist and theologian William Whewell. Do some research on Whewell and write a summary of his views on the relationship between mathematics and Christian belief.

5. Investigate and summarize Georg Cantor's views about the relationship between the mathematical and theological concepts of infinity.

6. Influences of the Enlightenment are still common today. See if you can find at least three. Consolidate your list with those of others in your class.

Chapter 3

INFINITY

But will God really dwell on earth? The heavens, even the highest heaven, cannot contain you. How much less this temple I have built!

1 KINGS 8:27

How do we as finite creatures understand an infinite God? The question is more complicated than you might think. As the quote above suggests, God is infinite in extent. But God is also infinite in power (omnipotent) and in knowledge (omniscient). God has neither beginning nor end. Perhaps God is even outside time as we understand it, existing in a timeless manner rather than the kind of finite, linear span of time that makes sense to us. In order to gain some understanding of God, we typically make use of metaphor. The psalmist speaks of God as shepherd, warrior, rock, tower, and king. These images convey some of the nature of God's interactions with us; they convey God's relational distinctiveness. But God's inherent characteristics such as infinitude are harder to grasp.

One of the big questions in chapter 1 asked whether mathematical concepts like infinity point beyond themselves to a higher reality. In this chapter we address that question.

What Does *Infinite* Mean?

One of the difficult things about pondering the infinite is that our minds usually translate *infinite* as "exceedingly large." Everyday language often uses infinity this way in such phrases as "the possibilities were infinite." Even our early (and sometimes not so early) mathematical exposure to infinity suggests the same thing. In calculus, when we study limits "at infinity" and "infinite" limits, we aren't really talking about infinite numbers. Instead, we're using infinity as a concept, as the idea that either the input to or the value of the expression we're looking at (x or $1/x$ or 2^x, for example) is getting larger and larger. Statistics, too, leads us a bit astray when it uses ∞ to represent any sample size larger than the number (usually $n = 120$, or perhaps 500 or 1000) heading the next-to-last row of the t-table.

Nevertheless, of all the academic disciplines, mathematics gives us the best tools for trying to understand infinity. So we are going to take some time to develop the mathematical concept of infinity and, after that ask what, if anything, it suggests about God's infinitude.

Mathematics includes (and studies) objects that don't just use the terms or symbols associated with infinity. Some objects are truly infinite. One example is the set of counting numbers $\{1, 2, 3, 4, \ldots\}$; another is the set of points on the real number line. Each set has an infinite size. A third example of infinite objects is the set of infinite decimals. You know that 1/3 can be expressed as the unending decimal 0.33333. . . . When a calculator truncates the decimal, as it must, the result is close to 1/3. In this case, something finite suggests the nature of something infinite. This is not always the case! In fact, in most of the examples that follow, you will find that finite objects do a rather poor job of capturing the essential characteristics of related infinite objects.

Let's think about what it means for a set to have an infinite size: what is an "infinite" set? Do all infinite sets have the same size? Are there as many integers (whole numbers and their negatives) as rational numbers (fractions)? As many rational numbers as real numbers (decimals)?

First we need to think about how we know when two sets have the same size. For small finite sets, we can just count: we say that $\{a, b, c\}$ has three elements because we can list them and see that there are three elements in the list. Looking at the problem more generally, what we're doing is matching every element of one set with another: $\{a, b, c\}$ has three elements because we can match them with the elements of $\{1, 2, 3\}$. In technical terms, we are putting the elements of $\{a, b, c\}$ in **one-to-one correspondence** with the elements of $\{1, 2, 3\}$. This means that each member of each set is paired with one and only one member of the other set. There are several (in fact, six) different ways to do this. One such correspondence is shown here.

$$1 \leftrightarrow b$$
$$2 \leftrightarrow c$$
$$3 \leftrightarrow a$$

To show that another set such as $\{x, y, z\}$ has the same size, we set up a one-to-one correspondence between $\{x, y, z\}$ and the same set $\{1, 2, 3\}$ of counting numbers. While this is a standard way to show that two sets are the same size, we don't really need to use $\{1, 2, 3\}$. Instead, we can directly pair the elements of $\{a, b, c\}$ and $\{x, y, z\}$.

$$a \leftrightarrow x$$
$$b \leftrightarrow y$$
$$c \leftrightarrow z$$

The use of one-to-one correspondence to verify that two sets have the same size has ancient commercial roots. Prior to 3400 BC, the merchants and bureaucrats of Mesopotamia used small replicas of objects (tokens) that were presumably in one-to-one correspondence with the transported goods. Between 3400 and 3300 BC, an early form of secure communication was implemented. Clay shells called *bullae* were molded around the tokens. Once the clay dried, the contents could not be changed before the shell was broken at the destination. If the merchant receiving the goods could not create a one-to-one correspondence between the tokens and the goods, the person in charge of the transportation better have had a good explanation! Later, another level of one-to-one correspondence was added by making impressions of the tokens in the clay of the shell while it was still wet. These marks provided a record that could be accessed while the goods were in transit. The subsequent use of a stylus to make the impressions marked the first steps toward writing.

In our more modern context, we drop the physical representation and simply say, as we did above, that two sets have the same size if there is a one-to-one correspondence between them. Two sets have different sizes if there is no such correspondence. For example, the sets $\{a, b, c, d\}$ and $\{x, y, z\}$ are of different sizes. We can't construct a one-to-one correspondence between them. This may seem intuitively obvious, but stop and think about how you would formally prove there is no such pairing. As is typical with nonexistence proofs, it's not a straightforward task!

$$
\begin{array}{c}
a \leftrightarrow x \\
b \leftrightarrow y \\
c \leftrightarrow z \\
d \leftrightarrow ?
\end{array}
$$

We'll set up a framework to see how this works more generally by showing that, for any counting number n, the sets $\{0, 1, 2, \ldots, n\}$ and $\{1, 2, \ldots, n\}$ are of different sizes. Suppose for a moment that for some n, the sets $\{0, 1, 2, \ldots, n\}$ and $\{1, 2, \ldots, n\}$ do have the same size. Then there is a one-to-one correspondence between the two sets. If n is not already paired with itself, we can rearrange the correspondence so that it is (see the box below). Then, ignoring n, the remaining parings provide a one-to-one correspondence between $\{0, 1, 2, \ldots, n-1\}$ and $\{1, 2, \ldots, n-1\}$, so these two sets must also have the same size. This process can be continued until we finally arrive at the conclusion that $\{0, 1\}$ and $\{1\}$ have the same size. But this is obviously false, so we can conclude that $\{0, 1, 2, \ldots, n\}$ and $\{1, 2, \ldots, n\}$ can never have the same size for any value of n.

Replace	with
$n \leftrightarrow x$	$n \leftrightarrow n$
$y \leftrightarrow n$	$y \leftrightarrow x$

The concept of one-to-one correspondence also provides a clear distinction between finite and infinite sets. We define a set to be

finite if it can be put into one-to-one correspondence with a set of the form $\{1, 2, 3, \ldots, n\}$. When there is no such correspondence, the set is **infinite**.

The infinite sets most familiar to us are the set of whole numbers, $\{0, 1, 2, 3, \ldots\}$, and the set of counting numbers, $\{1, 2, 3, \ldots\}$. Comparing the sizes of these two sets, we see that what's true in the finite case is no longer true for infinite sets: $\{0, 1, 2, 3, \ldots\}$ and $\{1, 2, 3, \ldots\}$ *do* have the same size since we can exhibit a one-to-one correspondence between them.

$$
\begin{array}{ccc}
0 & \leftrightarrow & 1 \\
1 & \leftrightarrow & 2 \\
2 & \leftrightarrow & 3 \\
3 & \leftrightarrow & 4 \\
\vdots & \leftrightarrow & \vdots \\
\vdots & & \vdots
\end{array}
$$

The formula $f(x) = x + 1$ gives one possible pairing; it works because neither list ends. The same formula also produces a one-to-one correspondence between $\{1, 2, 3, \ldots\}$ and $\{2, 3, 4, \ldots\}$. When this process is continued, we find, in a sense, an infinite nested sequence of copies of $\{0, 1, 2, 3, \ldots\}$ within itself: $\{0, 1, 2, 3, \ldots\}$ contains $\{1, 2, 3, \ldots\}$, which contains $\{2, 3, 4, \ldots\}$ and so on. Each of these sets can be viewed as a copy of $\{0, 1, 2, 3, \ldots\}$.

Here for the first time we see sets that have the same size as proper subsets of themselves. Think carefully about that. A **proper subset** contains only elements from the original set, but it doesn't contain all of them, so how can it have the same size? This counterintuitive property is equivalent to a set being infinite.

Proving this equivalence takes two steps: first, we must show that no finite set can be put into one-to-one correspondence with a proper subset of itself (see exercises 2 and 3 at the end of this chapter). The second step requires us to show that this *can* be done for any infinite set. The proof of this step is usually reserved for a more advanced mathematics course since it involves a historically controversial assumption called the Axiom of Choice (see exercise 24).

Not only does {0, 1, 2, 3, . . .} contain nested copies of itself, we can also split the set into its even elements {0, 2, 4, . . .} and its odd elements {1, 3, 5, . . .}, giving two different copies that have no elements in common (called **disjoint sets**). The functions $f(x) = 3x$, $g(x) = 3x + 1$, and $h(x) = 3x + 2$ take us further yet, providing one-to-one correspondences between {0, 1, 2, 3, . . .} and each of the disjoint sets {0, 3, 6, 9, . . .}, {1, 4, 7, 10, . . .}, and {2, 5, 8, 11, . . .}, respectively. In this sense we can see three distinct copies of {0, 1, 2, 3, . . .} within itself.

In 1839, Oliver Byrne used a related observation in an attempt to prove some statements—those relating to the Trinity—in the Athanasian Creed, an ancient summary of Christian beliefs that focuses on the Trinity and on the nature and person of Christ. But before we start making theological claims on the basis of such observations, we need a dose of humility. The three sets {0, 3, 6, 9, . . .}, {1, 4, 7, 10 . . .}, and {2, 5, 8, 11 . . .} do have the same size as {0, 1, 2, 3, . . .}, but there is nothing special about three in that example. We could just as easily have identified four distinct copies of {0, 1, 2, 3, . . .} within itself, or five. Clearly the counting numbers are not truly trinitarian!

Contrasting Finite and Infinite

As we noted previously, people tend to treat the infinite as if it were arbitrarily great, but finite. This tendency/perception appears in many different forms. High-school geometry students will tell us that parallel lines never meet, but in any photograph or realistic painting, parallel lines converge. They all meet at the horizon or at some "point at infinity." Our minds and our art conspire to represent the infinite in a finite manner. Given our own finiteness, this is very natural, but the large and the infinite have very different characteristics.

We'll illustrate both the difference between the finite and the infinite in mathematics and our difficulty in comprehending the infinite with a series of three examples from what is often called

Hilbert's Hotel, named for the mathematician David Hilbert. Hilbert's Hotel is an imaginary hotel with infinitely many rooms numbered 1, 2, 3, ...

Example 1: One night all of the rooms are occupied. Another traveler arrives. How can this traveler be accommodated?

Think about this problem before reading on.

If you haven't encountered this type of question before, you're probably thinking that it's impossible to find a room for the new guest. After all, the rooms are all occupied! If there were a finite number of rooms, you'd be right (see exercise 6 for a proof), but that reasoning doesn't work for Hilbert's Hotel. To accommodate the new guest, ask all of the current guests to move to the room with the next higher number. So the person currently in room 10 will move to room 11, the person in room 106 will move to room 107, and so on. When this has been completed, room 1 will be empty and the new guest can take that room.

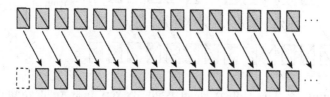

One common response to this proposed solution is bewilderment. "But where does the person in the last room go?" This would be a legitimate objection if there were a last room. But, in fact, there is no last room! While even children in elementary school have some sense that there is always a bigger number, we still have trouble shaking the sense that there must be a last number or room.

Example 2: A week later, all the rooms have two occupants. If they all want single rooms, can you find space for them?

At this point, students usually take one of two approaches. In one view, the fact that we need an infinite rather than finite number of additional rooms means that the task is impossible. On the other hand everything seems to be possible with infinite sets, so the answer is probably "yes" even though the details as to how this could be accomplished may be murky.

In fact, we can use a two-stage process to give each guest a single room. First, have every pair of guests move to the room with double their current number. So the guests in room 1 move to room 2, those in room 7 move to room 14, and so forth. At this point, only even rooms are occupied and all the odd rooms are empty. Now have one guest in each room move to the adjacent room with smaller number. For example, one of the guests in room 204 should move to room 203. Now every guest has a private room.

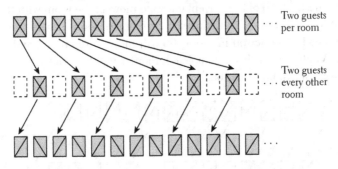

Two guests per room

Two guests every other room

Example 3: The Hilbert Hotel is always very busy right around noon, the hotel's official check-in time. The front desk is pretty accommodating and typically will allow a guest to check in a bit before noon if a room is available. One day the cleaning staff arrives very late, but they make up for their tardiness by working ever faster. One minute before noon, they have prepared rooms 1 through 5. One half minute later (one half minute before noon) rooms 6 through 10 are ready. One quarter minute after that (one quarter minute before noon) rooms 11 through 15 are clean. This pattern continues until all the rooms are ready. (Clearly, this is physically impossible, but play along.) Meanwhile, a traveler arrives one minute before noon and is placed into room 1. One half minute later (one half minute before noon) a second guest arrives and is assigned room 2. This pattern of arrival and room assignment continues until noon. (See the accompanying table.) How many rooms are available at the official check-in time of 12:00 noon?

Minutes before noon	Available rooms
1	1, 2, 3, 4, 5
1/2	2, 3, 4, 5, 6, 7, 8, 9, 10
1/4	3, 4, 5, 6, 7, 8, 9, 10, 11, 12, 13, 14, 15
1/8	4, 5, 6, 7, 8, 9, 10, 11, 12, 13, 14, 15, 16, 17, 18, 19, 20
. . .	. . .

This is perhaps the most surprising result of the series. Our intuition suggests that an infinite number of rooms should be ready for occupancy at noon. Certainly the number of available rooms grows without bound as we *approach* noon. Think this through: first, five rooms are cleaned. Next, one room is rented out and five more rooms are cleaned, for a total of nine available rooms. Then we subtract another one and add another five. At each step, the number of available rooms increases by four. However, when noon arrives, *all the rooms are occupied!* Every room has been rented out. Keep in mind that this is just a thought experiment. It is, of course, physically impossible to complete all these actions—or even a few of them—in one minute! Even viewing it as a thought experiment, though, most people find this situation rather unsettling. Let's look at a couple of modifications to get a better sense of what is going on.

Modification 1: Suppose that the cleaning staff and the guests follow the original pattern, but the desk clerk takes a different approach to assigning rooms. Specifically, suppose that each guest is assigned the first of the most recently cleaned rooms. The table below shows how this works with the bold and underlined number in each line marking the start of the set of newly cleaned rooms. This will be the next rented room.

Minutes before noon	Available rooms
1	<u>1</u>, 2, 3, 4, 5
1/2	2, 3, 4, 5, <u>6</u>, 7, 8, 9, 10
1/4	2, 3, 4, 5, 7, 8, 9, 10, <u>11</u>, 12, 13, 14, 15
1/8	2, 3, 4, 5, 7, 8, 9, 10, 12, 13, 14, 15, <u>16</u>, 17, 18, 19, 20
. . .	. . .

In this scenario, the result is what most people expect in the original set up. The number of rooms available at noon is infinite. The only occupied rooms will be 1, 6, 11, 16, ... All the other rooms are empty. In both the original example and in this modification the set of available rooms grows without bound. Indeed, the sets of available rooms have the same size in both cases—until noon! The choice of which room is assigned next produces an empty set in one case and an infinite set in the other.

Modification 2: Suppose that the cleaning staff had been particularly industrious that day and had completed their work by 11:00. Then all the rooms would be available when the first guest arrives. The table below shows what will happen if the clerk follows the original pattern of assigning the rooms in the order 1, 2, 3, ...

Minutes before noon	Available rooms
1	1, 2, 3, 4, 5, 6, 7, 8, 9, 10, 11, 12, 13, 14, 15, ...
1/2	2, 3, 4, 5, 6, 7, 8, 9, 10, 11, 12, 13, 14, 15, ...
1/4	3, 4, 5, 6, 7, 8, 9, 10, 11, 12, 13, 14, 15, ...
1/8	4, 5, 6, 7, 8, 9, 10, 11, 12, 13, 14, 15, ...
. . .	. . .

Thinking now only about the arriving guests, we see that room 1 is assigned 1/2 minute before noon, room 2 is rented out 1/4 minute before noon, and room 3 is taken at 1/8 minute before noon. Do you see the pattern? For $n = 1$, 2, and 3, room n is occupied $1/2^n$ minutes before noon. It turns out that this is true for every n (see exercise 8). Since all these times are in the past when the clock strikes noon, all the rooms are occupied.

For many people, it seems more acceptable that all the rooms are occupied in this scenario than in the original. This is a result of the way we blend the concepts of "infinite" and "large." In the original example, every time we look there's a finite set of available rooms, and it's bigger than the last time we looked. When we look at the available set of rooms at noon, however, we find nothing there. The finite sets of available rooms grow without bound while producing an empty set at noon. In the second modification, the set of available rooms is infinite every time we look, but each new set seems smaller than the last, so having no empty rooms at noon seems more reasonable. However, we've cheated a little bit in keeping 15 as the last displayed number in each line; we've made the sets of available rooms *look* like they're getting smaller. Behind the scenes, however, the situation is more troubling. When we compared the sets of whole and counting numbers earlier in this chapter, we saw that removing one element from an infinite set didn't give us a smaller set. In fact, there's no infinite set smaller than $\{1, 2, 3, \ldots\}$ (see exercises 9 and 10). This means that each list of available rooms has the same size, but somehow by assigning the rooms in numerical order we find all of them occupied when noon arrives. The infinite set of unassigned rooms suddenly becomes nothing.

Other Infinite Sets

Once you've seen that there's no infinite set smaller than $\{1, 2, 3, \ldots\}$, it's relatively natural to ask the reverse question. Are there any sets that are larger than the set of counting numbers? At first, the answer seems to be "no." The natural candidates, the set of all integers (whole numbers and their negations) and the set of all fractions, can be put into one-to-one correspondence with the counting numbers, $\{1, 2, 3, \ldots\}$. We call such sets **countable**.

Perhaps the easiest way to understand the correspondences is through a pair of diagrams that indicate the order in which the elements of the two sets are to be counted.

...	10	8	6	4	2	1	3	5	7	9	11	...
	↕	↕	↕	↕	↕	↕	↕	↕	↕	↕	↕	
...	−5	−4	−3	−2	−1	0	1	2	3	4	5	...

To count (create a one-to-one correspondence between the counting numbers and the integers), we pair 1 with 0 and alternate between negative and positive integers. In effect, we're making a list of the integers: 0, −1, 1, −2, 2, −3, 3, . . . thinking of 0 as the first integer, −1 as the second, 1 as the third, and so on. Following this pattern, we see that each integer is assigned exactly one counting number: this pairing uses odd numbers to count through the negative integers and even numbers to count through 0 and the positive integers. Variations of this counting strategy are commonly used to show that the union of a finite number of countable sets is also countable.

Counting the fractions (we will view 1/2 and 2/4 as different fractions even though they represent the same rational number) is a bit trickier. As you can see in the first row of the diagram below, there is a countable number of fractions of the form $k/1$. The second row shows another countable set of fractions, in this case of the form $k/2$, and the pattern continues from row to row. Thus we can see the set of fractions as the union of an *infinite* collection of countable sets. The path shows how to move through the entire set to assign counting numbers.

1/1	2/1	3/1	4/1	5/1	6/1	7/1	...
1/2	2/2	3/2	4/2	5/2	6/2	7/2	...
1/3	2/3	3/3	4/3	5/3	6/3	7/3	...
1/4	2/4	3/4	4/4	5/4	6/4	7/4	...
1/5	2/5	3/5	4/5	5/5	6/5	7/5	...
1/6	2/6	3/6	4/6	5/6	6/6	7/6	...
:	:	:	:	:	:	:	

The first part of the correspondence is

1	2	3	4	5	6	7	8	9	10	11	...
↕	↕	↕	↕	↕	↕	↕	↕	↕	↕	↕	
1/1	2/1	1/2	1/3	2/2	3/1	4/1	3/2	2/3	1/4	1/5	...

The fraction (1/1) whose numerator and denominator sum to 2 is counted first. Then fractions with a sum of 3 (2/1 and 1/2) are counted, and so on. Since there are only $n - 1$ fractions with any given sum, the process will eventually count all of the fractions.

You may complain at this point that we have only counted the positive fractions. You would be correct! However, once we see how to count the positive fractions, we can use the even/odd strategy we employed in counting the integers to create a one-to-one correspondence between the counting numbers and all of the fractions. Also, if you want to count the rational numbers (real numbers that can be expressed as a ratio of integers), simply skip over any fraction that is equivalent to a previously counted fraction.

A Bigger Infinity

So far, the evidence we've looked at seems to point to the idea that *all* infinite sets are countable. However, Georg Cantor proved that this is not the case. In 1884, he showed that the set of real numbers (or decimal numbers) is strictly larger than the set of counting numbers. The set of real numbers is thus *uncountable*. Cantor did not use this language in his original paper and, in fact, this consequence of his theorem seems to be a bit of an afterthought. Seven years later, however, Cantor published a second proof whose focus was to show that the real numbers are uncountable. Using what is now called the Cantor diagonalization technique, the second proof is the one commonly known today. It is another nonexistence proof since proving that the real numbers are uncountable requires proving that there is no one-to-one correspondence between the counting numbers and the real numbers. Cantor showed that if we thought we had a function from the counting numbers to the real numbers that hit every real number (pairing each real number with some counting number), we were wrong: there'd always be something we didn't get to. (See exercise 16 for an extension of this fact. Also, for those who would prefer a slower pace, exercises 12–15 provide a more leisurely walk through the following proof that there are more real numbers than counting numbers.)

Suppose that we have a function f from $\{1, 2, 3, \ldots\}$ to the decimals that we think hits every decimal between 0 and 1. We want to show that we're wrong, that, in fact, there must be something missing. Some decimal between 0 and 1 doesn't show up in the list of values of f. Since every function has its own characteristics, we will need to look for a missing number that is particular to f. To help us picture what is happening, let's look at the first few values of one possible function. (Since some real numbers have both a terminating and nonterminating representation—0.5 is the same as 0.49999999 . . .—we will use the nonterminating form.)

n	$f(n)$
1	0.2̲5719628953...
2	0.3̲8163956312...
3	0.743̲19475342...
⋮	⋮

$x =$ 0.283...

Using the decimals output by f, we can create a number x that takes its first digit from the first digit of $f(1)$, its second digit from the second digit of $f(2)$, and so on. In the example, we've started constructing this number—you can trace the path of boldface, underlined digits and compare them to the digits of $x = 0.283\ldots$ to see how this works.

Now from x we'll construct a new number y according to the following rule: change every even digit in x to a 3 and every odd digit to a 4. For our sample function, $y = 0.334.\ldots$. It's obvious that y is not paired with 1, 2, or 3—just compare y to the first three entries of the table. Even for our example, though, we can't physically "see" that y is not one of the other outputs of f; we can't write down the whole list of function values that we'd need to compare to y! Instead, let's look carefully at how our construction of y guarantees, without looking back at the table, that our y is different from the first three values of f. Then we'll extend that thinking to show that y must be different from *every* value of f.

Without looking at the table, how do we know that our y cannot be $f(1)$? Well, y came from x, which was constructed to have the same first digit as $f(1)$. But, in constructing y from x, we changed that digit, giving y an odd digit where x had an even one. Since x agreed with $f(1)$ in the first digit but y does not agree with x there, y must not agree with $f(1)$ either. Similarly, y cannot be $f(2)$, since x and $f(2)$ have the same second digit but y differs from x in that place. The same is true when we compare y and $f(3)$: x agrees with $f(3)$ in the third digit, but y does not. Jumping ahead, we can say that even though we do not know the value of $f(23)$, we know that it is not y. How do we know? Look at their twenty-third digits: whatever the value of $f(23)$, its twenty-third digit and the twenty-third digit of y are different. One is even and the other is odd. Simply by the way we constructed y, we know this is true; we don't need to know the specific values.

Do you see how this reasoning applies to any value of n? It is impossible for $f(n)$ to be y because the nth digit of $f(n)$ and the nth digit of y will always be different, one even and the other odd. This line of reasoning is not limited to our example function. No matter what function we try to use for the one-to-one correspondence, the number y as we constructed it from the function will not be paired with any counting number. This means that there is *no* one-to-one correspondence between the set of counting numbers and the set of decimal numbers between 0 and 1. The second set is uncountable.

Keep in mind that the decimals between 0 and 1 don't come close to including all real numbers, so our result also tells us that the entire set of real numbers is uncountable. This means that there are more real numbers than there are integers or fractions. In particular, there are more irrational numbers (real numbers that *cannot* be expressed as a ratio of integers) than there are rational numbers.

Think about this for a moment. What numbers have you encountered in your mathematical experience? If you think of a "typical" number, what do you think of? For almost everyone, *number* is nearly synonymous with *counting number*. This is true in spite of the fact that the counting numbers are countable and the rest of the real numbers are uncountable. We are forced to conclude that our experience is a poor indicator of what a typical real number is like. How much more must we adopt a humble attitude when extending limited experience with our world to definitive statements about God? Kathleen Norris goes so far as to label the application of our experience to God idolatrous.

> To my ear, such language reflects an idolatry of ourselves, that is, the notion that the measure of what we can understand, what is readily comprehensible and acceptable to us, is also the measure of God. It leads too many clerics to simply trounce on mystery and in the process say remarkably foolish things.[7]

A Paradoxical Blending of Infinities

Here's another dose of humility for you, another reason to be careful not to trust your intuition when dealing with infinite things.

We've noted that the set of rational numbers is countable. Since the rationals and irrationals together make up the set of real numbers and the reals are uncountable, the irrationals must be uncountable as well (see exercise 11). This means that the sets of rationals and irrationals have different sizes. But here's a result that makes that hard to swallow.

Some of you may have seen proofs that between any pair of real numbers, we can find both a rational number and an irrational number. In case you haven't, we'll explain why it's true, and then we'll look at what those facts seem to imply about the relative sizes of the sets of rationals and irrationals.

First, note that between any two different rational numbers x and y is another rational number; we simply take the average of x and y. The same basic idea works even if x and y are arbitrary (but still different) real numbers. Suppose $x < y$. Look at the average of x and y, truncate it (cut off the digits after a certain point) in such a way that it is still larger than x, and note that truncation will certainly keep it smaller than y. This terminating decimal is a rational number, so we've found a rational between x and y. To illustrate, suppose that $x = \pi$ and that $y = \sqrt{10}$. Then the average of x and y is:

$$\frac{\pi + \sqrt{10}}{2} = 3.15193515.\ldots$$

If we truncate this infinite decimal after the hundredths place (but not before) we will have a rational number $3.15 = \frac{315}{100}$, which is greater than $\pi = x$ and less than $\sqrt{10} = y$.

Now we can use that fact to find an irrational number between any two reals. Suppose x and y are again any two real numbers with $x < y$, and pick your favorite irrational number. We'll take π. Since $x < y$, $x - \pi$ is less than $y - \pi$, so there's a rational number, r, between them: $x - \pi < r < y - \pi$. Now we add π to get $x < r + \pi < y$. Since r is rational and π is irrational, $r + \pi$ is irrational, and we've found an irrational number between x and y.

Pulling this all together, if we look at the spread of rationals and irrationals along the number line, we find the following:

1. Between any two *irrational* numbers lies a *rational* number.
2. Between any two *rational* numbers lies an *irrational* number.

Now, if that doesn't make you think the two sets must have the same size, we don't know what will! But, despite our best intuition, they aren't the same size at all. The rationals are countable, the irrationals uncountable.

Mathematics employs a logically precise and carefully defined language. If apparent paradoxes such as the differing sizes of the rationals and the irrationals can arise in mathematics, it shouldn't surprise us that, when learning about God, we find paradoxes in (or inferred from) the scriptures. For example, human beings are given free will (Deut. 30:19), but God chooses his elect (Rom. 8:28–30). God provides saving grace (Rom. 3:28), but we are to work out our own salvation (Philippians 2:12). God is one (Deut. 6:4) but exists in three persons (2 Cor. 13:14).

A Multitude of Infinities?

While it is weird enough that the sets of rational and irrational numbers have different sizes, the situation gets stranger yet. Cantor showed that there is an unending chain of infinite sets, each one larger than the previous one. In particular, the **power set** (set of all subsets) of any set S, finite or infinite, can be shown to have more elements than S does (exercises 17 to 19).

During his lifetime, Cantor experienced tremendous opposition to his research into this unending chain of ever increasing infinite sets. Many of the leading mathematicians of the day, including Kronecker and Poincaré, publicly denounced his ideas and acted behind the scenes to keep his work out of the most respected journals.

At least initially, the opposition was not personal. Their rejection of Cantor's work was rooted in a denial of the notion of "actual" or "completed" infinities that dates from the time of ancient Greek philosophy. Aristotle (ca. 350 BC) understood that the set of integers is **potentially infinite** since it is not bounded—we can always produce a larger integer by adding 1. However, he believed that the set of integers as a completed whole is a paradoxical idea both in theory and in nature.

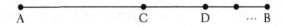

A   C   D   ⋯ B

Zeno, who lived at the same time as Aristotle, proposed a related paradox. In order to follow a path from point A to point B, you'd have to reach the midpoint, C, of the path. After that, you'd have to reach the midpoint (D) of the path between C and B, and then the midpoint between D and B. (See the figure.) This process would continue indefinitely. In order to travel from A to B, you'd have to pass through a potentially infinite set of points. Since completed infinite sets do not exist, it is impossible to complete the trip. Do you see the paradox? Zeno is claiming that it is impossible to move!

Kronecker, like most mathematicians and philosophers of his day, accepted Aristotle's line of argument and believed that, while it is possible to consider arbitrarily large sets of integers, the idea of the set of all integers as a single entity is nonsensical. (We will discuss some more mathematicians who hold this view when we discuss intuitionism in chapter 9.) Kronecker held this view so firmly that he claimed that there are no irrational numbers at all. He rejected the notion of irrational numbers since their construction would involve an infinite number of operations. It is not surprising, then, that Kronecker strongly opposed the work Cantor was doing and fought to keep it from being published.

In the epilogue to his book on Cantor, J. W. Dauben argues that Cantor's faith was critical to his persistence in the face of such opposition. Cantor, in a letter written after a hospital stay, reported that he received an "inspiration from above." This inspiration, he said, directed him to read the Bible and also guided his mathematical thinking. Cantor believed that the perfection of God made actual infinities both possible and necessary. To deny the existence of infinite sets, thought Cantor, was to limit the glory of God. The resulting confidence in the correctness and God-given direction of his work enabled Cantor to continue despite a series of mental break-downs and continuing resistance from prominent mathematicians.

Ironically, Cantor also encountered resistance from some Christian thinkers who saw his work as challenging the uniqueness of the "absolute infinity" of God. They believed that any philosophic structure that included infinity as part of the natural universe was dangerously close to pantheism, the belief that "God is everything." However, Cantor's set theory actually leads to a different conclusion: one consequence of his work is that there can be no "set of all sets" (see exercises 20 and 22) so that our (mathematical) universe cannot be all-encompassing. Also, Cantor used his theory of infinite sets as an apologetic for the Christian faith, expressing the connection this way:

> The fear of infinity is a form of myopia that destroys the possibility of seeing the actual infinite, even though it in its highest form has created and sustains us, and in its secondary transfinite forms occurs all around us and even inhabits our minds.[8]

> I am so in favor of the actual infinite that instead of admitting that Nature abhors it, as is commonly said, I hold that Nature makes frequent use of it everywhere, in order to show more effectively the perfections of its Author.[9]

These clarifications blunted the criticism, and toward the end of his life Cantor found more support among the clergy than among mathematicians. The mathematical community has since come to appreciate Cantor's work and has learned to live with the idea that there is no set of all sets.

Beyond the Limits of Our Imagination

As we saw in chapter 2, Thomas Aquinas encouraged Christians to use aspects of the created world as analogies to God's nature. Similarly, mathematical concepts of the infinite can do much to engage and propel our thinking about God. For instance, the many surprising properties of infinity we have seen in this chapter suggest to us that God may be in many ways quite different (and quite a bit more subtle) than our finite experiences suggest. Also, the unending chain of infinities that Cantor pointed to suggests the extent to which God's greatness may vastly transcend our capacity to understand it.

Nevertheless, in our attempts to use logic and imagination to push the boundaries of our understanding, we must not forget that there are bigger things at work here. As Thomas Merton wrote,

> We enter into the Mystery of the Holy Trinity not so much by thinking and imagining, as by loving. Thought and imagination soon reach the limits beyond which they cannot pass, and these limits still fall infinitely short of the reality of God. But love, overstepping all bounds and flying beyond limitations with the wings of God's own Spirit, penetrates into the very depths of the mystery and apprehends Him whom our intelligence is unable to see.[10]

Suggestions for Further Reading

Dauben, J. W. *Georg Cantor: His Mathematics and Philosophy of the Infinite*. Princeton, NJ: Princeton Univ. Press, 1979. The story of Cantor's discoveries and the opposition he experienced.

———. "Georg Cantor and the Battle for Transfinite Set Theory." *Journal of the Association of Christians in the Mathematical Sciences* (2004). Available online at http://www.acmsonline.org/journal/2004/dauben93.html. Similar to Dauben's book, but briefer.

Rucker, Rudy. *Infinity and the Mind*. Princeton, NJ: Princeton Univ. Press, 2004. A readable and entertaining introduction to the different infinities and the people who have historically been associated with them.

Tapp, Christian. "Infinity in Mathematics and Theology." *Theology and Science* 9, no. 1, 91–100 (February 2011). A scholarly study contrasting how the word *infinity* is used in the two disciplines.

EXERCISES

Remember that a set is infinite if it can be put into one-to-one correspondence with a proper subset of itself. Otherwise the set is finite.

1. In Mesopotamian trade, the marks on a *bulla* could be put into one-to-one correspondence with the tokens contained inside. The tokens in turn could be put into one-to-one correspondence with the goods. Combining these correspondences, one could conclude that there was a one-to-one correspondence between the marks and the goods. Use a similar joining of one-to-one correspondences to show that if $\{a, b, c, d\}$ and $\{x, y, z\}$ were the same size, then $\{0, 1, 2, 3\}$ and $\{1, 2, 3\}$ would have the same size.

2. Modify the proof that $\{0, 1, 2, \ldots, n\}$ and $\{1, 2, \ldots, n\}$ have different sizes to show that $\{1, 2, \ldots, n\}$ cannot be put into one-to-one correspondence with a proper subset of itself. In particular, explain how a one-to-one correspondence between $\{1, 2, \ldots, n\}$ and a proper subset of itself can be modified to create a one-to-one correspondence between $\{1, 2, \ldots, n-1\}$ and a proper subset of itself. Begin by thinking about what happens if n is not hit by the correspondence.

3. Show that no finite set S can be put into one-to-one correspondence with a proper subset of itself. Use exercise 2 and the idea from exercise 1.

4. All of the rooms in Hilbert's Hotel are occupied when twelve new travelers arrive. How can they be accommodated?

5. All of the guests in Hilbert's Hotel assigned to even numbered rooms have paid an extra fee for their rooms and cannot be moved. How can an additional guest be accommodated even though all of the rooms are currently occupied?

6. Prove that any hotel that can accommodate an additional guest when all the rooms are filled must be infinite. (Hint: use the starting and ending rooms of each guest to create a one-to-one correspondence between the rooms and a proper subset.)

7. Suppose that every room in Hilbert's Hotel is occupied by three guests, each of whom would prefer a single room. How can the guests be accommodated?

8. Show by induction that, under the assumptions of the third example from Hilbert's Hotel, the room n will be assigned an occupant $1/2^n$ seconds before noon.

9. Identify a one-to-one correspondence to show that for any counting number n the set $\{n, n+1, n+2, \ldots\}$ and $\{1, 2, 3, \ldots\}$ have the same size.

10. Show that any infinite subset S of $\{1, 2, 3, \ldots\}$ has the same size as $\{1, 2, 3, \ldots\}$. (Hint: Build the one-to-one correspondence inductively as a function from $\{1, 2, 3, \ldots\}$ to S, using at the first step the smallest member of S and at the nth step the smallest member of S that is not an image of $\{1, 2, 3, \ldots, n-1\}$.)

11. Using contradiction and the facts that the rationals are countable while the reals are uncountable, prove that the irrationals are uncountable.

The following four exercises investigate the uncountability of the set of decimals between 0 and 1.

12. Think of a function f of your choosing from $\{1, 2, 3, 4, 5\}$ to the five-digit numbers of the form 0.XXXXX.
    a. Write out the outputs of f for 1, 2, 3, 4, and 5 as decimal numbers.
    b. Create a new five-digit decimal number x by taking the k-th digit of $f(k)$ as the k-th digit of x.
    c. Create a new decimal y by changing each digit of x to a new value.
    d. Is x one of the outputs of f? Is y?

13. Give an example to show that it is possible to construct a function from $\{1, 2, 3, 4, 5\}$ to the five-digit numbers of the form 0.XXXXX such that the x constructed by the procedure in exercise 12 is an output of f.

14. Explain why it is impossible to construct a function from $\{1, 2, 3, 4, 5\}$ to the five-digit numbers of the form 0.XXXXX

such that the y constructed by the procedure in exercise 12 is an output of f.

15. Use the ideas in the previous three exercises to show that the set of decimal numbers between 0 and 1 is not countable.

    a. Start with an arbitrary function f from the counting numbers to the decimals between 0 and 1.

    b. To avoid multiple representations of numbers, write every number as an infinite decimal. For example, 1/2 should be represented by 0.4999 . . . rather than 0.5.

    c. When constructing the analog of y from exercise 12, choose digits other than 0.

    d. Explain why the analog of y is not an output of f.

16. Suppose that f is a function from the counting numbers to the real numbers. Show that the complement of the range of f (i.e., the set of real numbers not output by f) is uncountable. (Hint: Show that if the complement of the range of f is countable, then we can construct a one-to-one correspondence between the counting numbers and the real numbers by splitting into even and odd cases.)

The following three exercises investigate the reason that the power set of any set is larger than the set itself.

17. Let $S = \{a, b, c\}$.

    a. Write the elements of S in one column and write the members of the power set of S in a second column to the right. (Don't forget to include S and the empty set.)

    b. Use arrows to create a function f from S to its power set.

    c. Underline the elements of S (in the left column) with the property that they are not elements of their image under f (in the right column). (This might be all, some, or none of S depending on the function you chose.)

    d. In the power set column, underline the set consisting of the underlined elements in the left column. Call this set Q.

    e. Is Q an output of f?

18. Repeat exercise 17 with a new function g. Make sure that the old set Q from exercise 17 is one of the outputs of g. Identify a new Q for the function g consisting of those elements of S = {a, b, c} that are not members of their images under g. Does g output the new Q?

19. Suppose that S is an arbitrary set. Use the ideas from exercises 17 and 18 to show that no function f from S to its power set can be onto (i.e., output every subset). Define Q as in exercise 17.
    a. If x ∈ Q, why must f(x) be different from Q? (What element does Q have that f(x) does not have?)
    b. If x ∈ S but x ∉ Q, explain why f(x) is not Q.
    c. Explain why f cannot be onto.

The fact that the power set of S has more elements than S does has a startling consequence noted by Ernst Zermelo in 1900. Since the power set of any set S is strictly larger than S is, there is no such thing as a "set of all sets." Exercises 20 and 21 outline two different proofs of this fact. (There are other models of set theory that include a set of all sets or a universal set. However, these models imply that certain natural operations, such as the ability to construct a subset of the elements of a set with a specified property, are not possible.)

20. Suppose that Ω is the set of all possible sets. Let P be the power set of Ω.
    a. Explain why P is larger than Ω.
    b. Explain why P must be no larger than Ω.
    c. Explain why Ω cannot exist.

21. There is an alternate proof that there can be no "set of all sets" originally articulated by Bertrand Russell in 1901. One of the properties of being a set is that given any property, we can always construct a subset of the original set consisting of those elements having the given property. (The subset may be empty if no elements have the property or it may be the entire original set if every element has the property.) Suppose that Ω is the set of all possible sets. Define a new set S by S = {x ∈ Ω | x ∉ x}. Show that the existence of this set leads to a contradiction.

22. Read the letter to Georg Cantor from his father on the occasion of Cantor's confirmation. (You can find the letter in J. W. Dauben, *Georg Cantor: His Mathematics and Philosophy of the Infinite,* Princeton University Press, 1990, 274–276.) What roles have your parents' expectations and support and your own faith played in your academic pursuits?

23. Read J. W. Dauben's assessment of the influence of Cantor's faith on his mathematical work. (Same book as exercise 22, 290–299.) In what ways has your encounter with mathematical concepts of infinity been influenced by your faith? In what ways has your faith been influenced by your study of mathematical concepts of infinity?

24. The proof that any infinite set can be put into one-to-one correspondence with a proper subset of itself requires the Axiom of Choice. Research the axiom and its controversial history.

    a. How is the Axiom of Choice related to issues surrounding the concept of infinity?

    b. How might a Christian worldview affect one's stance on the acceptability of the Axiom of Choice?

Chapter 4

DIMENSION

There is a fifth dimension beyond that which is known to man. It is a dimension as vast as space and as timeless as infinity. It is the middle ground between light and shadow, between science and superstition, and it lies between the pit of man's fears and the summit of his knowledge. This is the dimension of imagination. It is an area which we call the Twilight Zone.

OPENING LINES FROM SEASON ONE OF THE 1959–65
TELEVISION SERIES *THE TWILIGHT ZONE*

Introduction

Popular culture often refers to dimension. In 1944 DC Comics introduced a villain, Mr. Mxyzptlk (ranked in 2009 as one of the top 100 comic book villains of all time), whose home was the fifth dimension. In 1966 the Byrds released an album called *Fifth Dimension*. Later in the 1960s and early 1970s a five-member musical group called The Fifth Dimension was popular, and in 1987 the Chessington World of Adventures Resort in London opened a ride named "The Fifth Dimension" based on a story about a TV repair robot. The American public radio network, NPR, presented a radio drama called "Fifth Dimension" in 2000. These examples used "five" as the chosen dimension, but it is not hard to find references to different "dimensions" or "other dimensions" generically. The four dimensions of the space-time continuum of general relativity have moved from physics research papers to the cultural mainstream.

Less self-conscious uses of dimension have entered our speech through such phrases as "theological dimensions" or "cultural dimensions." The use is informal, but the terminology draws on significant mathematical ideas. While a concept may be discussed and investigated from a particular point of view, *dimension* suggests that there is another aspect that will be overlooked if we do not consciously turn our thoughts in another direction. Used in this way, dimension has become a metaphor, like thinking outside the box, for moving beyond what is immediately apparent and expanding our ability to understand what is really happening.

Things have not always been this way. The *New International Version* of the Bible only uses the word *dimension* twice, with both uses carrying simply a sense of width or length, a very different meaning from how dimension is used in mathematics. The more modern mathematical idea of space beyond three dimensions can be traced to the mid-nineteenth century. Today, even though the idea seems rather mysterious, we are comfortable using the language of higher dimensions in general conversation. In the world of mathematics, we even deal with infinite dimensional spaces and with fractional dimensions like 1.5. This chapter begins by exploring the mathematical concept of dimension, then it suggests some intriguing connections this topic has with Christian thought.

What Is Dimension?

Different branches of mathematics have varying (but related) formal definitions of *dimension* suited to particular contexts. Informally, however, the dimension of an object (such as a point, line, or plane) can be thought of in two ways.

1. The number of coordinates required to specify a point in the object.
2. The number of mutually perpendicular directions of possible travel within the object.

Let's think about the first definition for a bit. A single point has dimension 0. Once we know the object we are working with (the point) we need no additional information to identify a point within it: there *are* no other points. In a line, however, we need one piece of information. Tell me how far (and in which of the two possible directions) the point lies from some fixed point on the line, and I can identify which point you mean. This might seem like two pieces of information (distance and direction), but with the use of negative numbers we can combine those features into one number. That's why we say that a line has dimension 1.

Now suppose we are looking at a square like the one in figure 4.1. In this case, we need two coordinates to identify a particular point such as the one at (1.5, 1). Thus a square is a two-dimensional object. Similarly, a solid block or ball is three-dimensional since three coordinate values are required to specify a particular point within the object.

This all works very well as long as we are dealing with simple geometric objects or we are working within a carefully prescribed mathematical context. Things quickly become more complicated when we consider even slightly more complex objects. Suppose that we have an object that consists of three non-collinear points: for example, the points (1, 0), (0, 1) and (1, 1). We just used two coordinates to identify each of the points, so the object seems two-dimensional. But if the three points had all been on the x-axis, we could have identified each one by its position on the number line using a single coordinate. This observation makes it seem one-dimensional. If we consider the second definition of dimension, however, we note that

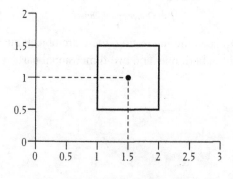

Figure 4.1

there are no directions of possible travel within the object. Because of this fact, we say that the three points constitute a zero-dimensional object of three parts.

For a line segment or a square, both notions of dimension work equally well, but if the objects are "bent," only the second approach produces the correct result. In the figure below, the bending would require an extra coordinate to identify a point on the object, but that extra coordinate doesn't translate into an extra direction of perpendicular motion. (If you are familiar with parameterization of curves and surfaces, you will notice that the number of directions you can move inside the object is the same as the number of parameters required to parameterize the object.)

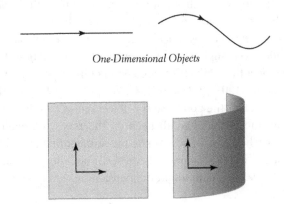

One-Dimensional Objects

Two-Dimensional Objects

And, just to keep life interesting, there are objects such as figure 4.2 that consist of both one- and two-dimensional parts.

Figure 4.2

A Twist on Dimension

Let's go back and think about the line segment and curve in more detail. If we stretch out a line segment and make it longer, the dimension is unchanged. In fact, an infinitely long line will still have dimension 1. Now think about that line as an infinitely long piece of string. We know what happens to long pieces of string if we are not careful: they become twisted masses of knots. But twisted masses of knots seem more like three-dimensional objects. Can this really happen?

Indeed, it can! To keep things relatively simple, we'll show you how to create a two-dimensional knot, though in principle our procedure can be extended to higher dimensions.

Begin with a square. In that square draw a "curve" that consists of three line segments. Are you thinking that three line segments do not look much like a curve? You're right, if you're using "curve" in the everyday sense of something that is "not straight." In mathematics, however, a curve is a one-dimensional path, and line segments (as well as connected collections of them) fit this definition. This task has been carried out in stage 1 of figure 4.3. The "guide" part of figure 4.3 shows how to think of stage 1: consider the original square as consisting of four subsquares, begin in the lower left, progress in a clockwise manner, and end in the lower right subsquare. We want to preserve this motion in what follows.

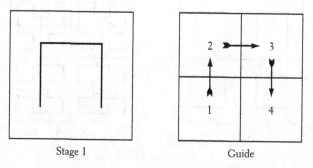

Stage 1   Guide

Figure 4.3

For stage 2, shrink the stage 1 square by a factor of two on each side and place four copies in the four corners of a new, blank square (see figure 4.4). The copies of the curve in subsquares 2 and 3 are already consistent with the arrows in the guide. Rotate the curves in subsquares 1 and 4 so that the four curves can be joined to make a single curve using only vertical or horizontal line segments. There is only one way to do this while creating a single curve that follows the guide arrows above (clockwise from lower left) within the larger square. To make the process more visible, the connecting lines appear lighter in the stage 2 diagram below.

For stage 3, repeat the process using four copies of the stage 2 square that have been shrunk by a factor of two on each side and rotated to match the orientation of the four main sections of the stage 2 curve so that, again, the new path follows the guide arrows. For stage 4, repeat the process using four reduced copies of the stage 3 square and so on. Can you find the stage 3 curves and the connecting segments inside stage 4 (figure 4.5)?

Notice that

1. by the way that we have set things up, the overall flow of the curve at any stage follows that of the previous stages,
2. subsequent changes reroute the curve by ever smaller amounts,

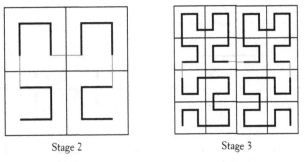

Stage 2   Stage 3

Figure 4.4

Stage 4

Figure 4.5

3. more parts of the square are "visited" by the curve as we progress, and
4. the path is spread relatively evenly through the square.

If the process is continued indefinitely, the result will fill the entire square in the sense that every point on the square is a point on the curve. A formal proof of this fact requires more advanced mathematics than is appropriate for this book, but a rigorous proof *can* be given.

Between Dimensions

We have just seen how a curve can fill up an entire square, becoming a two-dimensional object. But most curves you have encountered are one-dimensional. What happens if you take a curve that is more tangled than you are accustomed to but is less tangled than the curve you just constructed? There are many curves of this sort. We'll explore one that forms the boundary of the Koch snowflake, defined by Helge von Koch (1870–1924). As with our previous curve, the snowflake is constructed in stages. This time, however, we begin with an equilateral triangle with sides of length 1.

Now replace each of the line segments forming the triangle with four segments, each 1/3 the original length. Two of the smaller

Replace   With

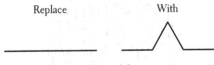

Figure 4.6

segments will cover the first and last thirds of the original segment, and the other two segments will form an outward pointing "peak" over the middle third. Figure 4.6 shows the replacement.

The result is stage 2 of figure 4.7. Repeat this replacement continually, reducing the scale by a factor of 1/3 at each step, to produce the subsequent stages. Figure 4.7 illustrates the first four stages.

The Koch snowflake is the figure that results from repeating this replacement process infinitely. Despite this infinite replacement, the Koch snowflake looks like a finite figure, and indeed it is. It's possible to prove that at each stage, the figure is bounded between the

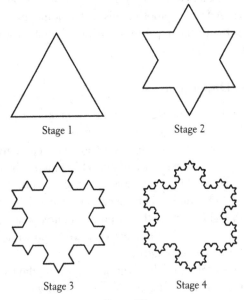

Stage 1   Stage 2

Stage 3   Stage 4

Figure 4.7

original equilateral triangle and its circumscribed circle (figure 4.8). Thus, the area of the Koch snowflake is finite (see exercises 2 and 3).

What about the boundary curve? Well, we began with a boundary length of 3. Then each segment was replaced by four segments, each having a length 1/3 the original length. This means that the total length was expanded by a factor of 4/3. The same process takes place at each stage; the length always expands by a factor of 4/3. Thus, as we continue the process, the length of the boundary curve will grow without bound. The boundary of the Koch snowflake has infinite length, as did the space-filling curve we saw earlier! Since it is enclosed in a finite space, it is reasonable to wonder if somehow the dimension of the boundary is greater than 1. In fact, it is. We need to do a bit more work, however, to see what is going on.

Let's start with a simple horizontal line segment of length 1, which we can all agree is a one-dimensional object. If we place the segment on a one-dimensional line and dissect the entire line into subintervals of length $1/k$, we find that k (or maybe $k + 1$) of the sub-intervals contain part of the line segment. If the segment is placed in a two-dimensional plane and the plane is split into $1/k \times 1/k$ boxes (squares), between k and $2k$ boxes contain a piece of the segment. To understand why this is the case, think about the number of vertical and horizontal boundary lines the segment could possibly cross. Starting at one of the ends, the line segment can only enter another box by crossing one of the horizontal or vertical boundary lines. If we place the segment horizontally, we're back in the one-dimensional case with our segment entering k (or maybe $k + 1$) boxes by crossing

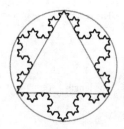

Figure 4.8

through k vertical sides. The same thing happens if we position the line segment vertically. If we place the segment at an angle, it can cross both horizontal and vertical boundary lines, but at most k of each type. That means that the line segment can enter at most $2k$ boxes in addition to the initial box. The diagrams in figure 4.9, with $k = 6$, will help you see what is going on.

Since we can't make the line segment cross k vertical boundary lines *and* k horizontal boundary lines simultaneously, the maximum number of visited boxes is quite a bit less than $2k$. For our purposes, though, it's enough to know that the number of boxes containing part of the segment is somewhere between k and $2k$.

Something similar happens if we use $1/k \times 1/k \times 1/k$ boxes (cubes) in three-dimensional space. The number of boxes containing part of the segment is between k and $3k$. If we take a longer segment, say of length 5, all of the counts will increase by a factor of 5. Notice that in every case we are looking at something close to a multiple of k.

Now think about a square of side 1. If the square is carefully placed either on the plane or in space, k^2 of our boxes with sides $1/k$ (squares or cubes as appropriate) will contain part of it. If the square is positioned so that it crosses the greatest number of boxes possible,

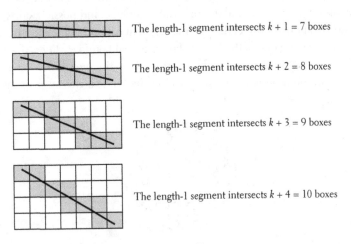

The length-1 segment intersects $k + 1 = 7$ boxes

The length-1 segment intersects $k + 2 = 8$ boxes

The length-1 segment intersects $k + 3 = 9$ boxes

The length-1 segment intersects $k + 4 = 10$ boxes

Figure 4.9

the number of boxes that contain part of the square will be at most a multiple of k^2. The form of this upper bound remains fixed even if we stretch or shrink the square or turn it into a rectangle.

Let's recap. In the plane, the number of $1/k$ boxes (squares of size $1/k \times 1/k$) that contain part of a line segment of any length or orientation is essentially a multiple of k. The same thing holds true in space: the number of $1/k$ boxes (cubes of size $1/k \times 1/k \times 1/k$) that contain part of a line segment of any length or orientation is essentially a multiple of k as well. If we move from line segments to squares, the number of $1/k$ boxes (whether squares in the plane or cubes in space) that contain part of a square of any size or orientation is essentially a multiple of k^2. A bit more thinking shows that the number of $1/k$ boxes that contain part of a block of any size or orientation is essentially a multiple of k^3. It seems that what we understand to be the dimension of an object is captured by looking at the exponent of k (1, 2, and 3 in k^1, k^2, and k^3) involved in the number of $1/k$ boxes that are required to enclose the object. Furthermore, we need to do this as the boxes get ever smaller since the smaller they are, the better job they will do of approximating the object.

With this analysis in mind, we replace $1/k$ with t, a variable that can take on any positive value. Note that as k increases, t decreases. Let $N(t)$ be the number of size t boxes that contain part of an object X. We define the **dimension** of X to be the limiting value of $\frac{\log N(t)}{-\log t}$ as t shrinks to 0. Mathematicians refer to dimension defined this way as **fractal dimension**.

This definition may seem arbitrary, but let's see how it works. Logarithms have a very useful property: they draw out the exponents of expressions. For example, $\log(t^2) = 2 \log(t)$ and $\log(t^3) = 3 \log(t)$. Thus,

$$\frac{\log(t^2)}{\log t} = 2,$$

and

$$\frac{\log(t^3)}{\log t} = 3.$$

The minus sign is included in the definition because logarithms of numbers less than 1 are negative, and $t = 1/k$ is less than 1 when k is 2 or more.

Now let's see how the definition applies to geometric objects. We can cover a perfectly positioned line segment of length 1 with k lengths of size $t = 1/k$. Hence $N(t) = k$ and the definition produces

$$\frac{\log N(t)}{-\log t} = \frac{\log k}{-\log(1/k)} = \frac{\log k}{\log k} = 1.$$

For a perfectly positioned square of side 1, we use k^2 squares of side $t = 1/k$ to get

$$\frac{\log N(t)}{-\log t} = \frac{\log k^2}{\log k} = \frac{2 \log k}{\log k} = 2.$$

Of course, the line segment may not be positioned horizontally, or it might not have length 1. Neither of these changes should affect the dimension. What happens if some combination of changes of this sort result in the line segment crossing 100 times as many boxes so that $N(t) = 100k$? The calculation becomes

$$\frac{\log N(t)}{-\log t} = \frac{\log 100\, k}{\log k} = \frac{\log 100 + \log k}{\log k} = \frac{\log 100}{\log k} + 1 \rightarrow 1$$

as k grows without bound. As we hoped, the calculated dimension did not change. The same type of computation works with any multiple of k or anything between.

What if we stretch (or shrink) a square? If we modify the calculation for the dimension of the square in the same ways we modified the calculation for the line segment, we will always get a value of 2 no matter how we stretch or reposition the square. This outcome supports the idea that our limit definition is capturing the concept of dimension for us.

Now let's apply the definition to some more complicated objects. We begin with something related to what is known as the Cantor set (see exercise 6). Let X be the set of all decimal numbers between

0 and 1 that can be expressed using only the digits 0 and 9. In this case, it is convenient to use lengths of $t = 1/10^k$ for our analysis. Note that two length-0.1 intervals, [0.0, 0.1] and [0.9, 1.0], contain parts of X but the eight length-0.1 intervals in between do not contain any members of X. The first digit of every number in these intervals is greater than 0 and less than 9. When $k = 2$, four intervals intersect X: [0.00, 0.01], [0.09, 0.10], [0.90, 0.91], and [0.99, 1.00]. The two new gaps of eight length-0.01 intervals do not intersect X because the second digit of these numbers is neither 0 nor 9. The pattern continues with the number of subintervals that overlap X doubling every time we increase k by 1. In general, 2^k intervals of length $1/10^k$ will intersect X. This means that the dimension of X is

$$\frac{\log N(t)}{-\log t} = \frac{\log 2^k}{-\log(1/10^k)} = \frac{\log 2^k}{\log(10^k)} = \frac{k \log 2}{k \log 10} = \frac{\log 2}{\log 10} = 0.30103.$$

What about the length of our object? As we have noted, X will be contained in 2^k sets of length $1/10^k$. That means that the total length of X can be at most $2^k(1/10^k) = (1/5)^k$. In other words, since $(1/5)^k$ approaches 0 as k approaches infinity, the total "length" of X is 0 even though X has positive dimension.

Here we were able to use the definition of X to compute its dimension. In many practical applications from nature and from chaos theory, however, this is not possible. Instead, we approximate the dimension by actually counting the number of boxes. For example, the coastline of South Africa has been measured to have a fractal dimension of 1.02 while the coastline of Britain has been determined to have a fractal dimension of 1.25. Other measured fractal dimensions include 2.66 for a head of broccoli, 2.79 for the surface of a human brain, and 2.97 for the surface of a lung. The latter dimension indicates that the lungs are very efficient in presenting surface area for the exchange of oxygen and carbon dioxide. The surface of our lungs almost fills the three-dimensional space they occupy much like the first curve we constructed filled the square.

An Occasional Short Cut

For objects like the Koch snowflake, however, we do not need to make an approximation, nor must we count boxes. We can compute the exact dimension by using the fact that the object consists of a set of four 1/3-scale copies of itself. We'll start with a few simpler examples, returning to the snowflake once we understand what is going on.

Look at the triangle in figure 4.10. The white lines show how it can be subdivided into four 1/2-scale copies of itself. Suppose that we fix a box size and find that fifteen boxes of that size contain pieces of the original triangle. If we shrink the boxes by the same scale used to shrink the object, we see that fifteen small boxes intersect a fixed subfigure. At least, that's what happens for the subfigure on the lower-right side. Depending on the orientation (the two middle triangles have been turned on their sides, for example), the number of small boxes might differ a bit from the original number, but as we've seen, such small changes will not affect the computation of dimension. With a bit of adjustment for positioning, what occurs for the highlighted subfigure will occur for all four subfigures. Moreover, this phenomenon will be repeated for sub-subfigures, sub-sub-subfigures, and so on.

Of course, we already know that the triangle is two-dimensional—there are two perpendicular directions of motion possible from any point inside it—but let's go ahead and compute the dimension using our new definition. We started with one triangle, then made four, then sixteen, etc. Thus after k such steps, the scale is $t = (1/2)^k$ and there are 4^k triangles each of which intersect fifteen squares. So the triangle's dimension is

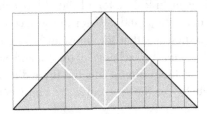

Figure 4.10 Four copies with 50% length

$$\frac{\log N(t)}{-\log t} = \frac{\log 15(4^k)}{-\log(1/2^k)} = \frac{\log 15 + \log 4^k}{\log(2^k)} = \frac{\log 15 + k \log 4}{k \log 2}$$

$$= \frac{1}{k} \frac{\log 15}{\log 2} + \frac{\log 4}{\log 2} \rightarrow \frac{\log 4}{\log 2} = 2.$$

Something interesting is happening here. As we let k get very large, what we're left with depends only on 4 (the number of subfigures created at each step) and 2 (coming from the 1/2 scale as we move from one step to the next).

Now let's look back to our computation of the dimension of the set X of decimal numbers between 0 and 1 that can be expressed using only the digits 0 and 9. At each stage, the previous stage is copied twice at a 1/10 scale. Looking at the dimension computation (but leaving out the middle steps), we see that

$$\frac{\log N(t)}{-\log t} = \frac{\log 2}{\log 10} = 0.30103.$$

As was the case for the triangle, we end up with a final computation that depends only on 2 (the number of copies of the set created at each step) and 10 (where 1/10 was the scale used at each step). In both examples, the computation ends with $\frac{\log n}{\log(1/s)}$ where n was the number of copies of the original set produced by shrinking the original by a scale of s. The number of boxes that contains a piece of the original object doesn't even matter: if a figure consists of n subfigures that replicated the original at a scale of s, then the dimension of the entire figure is $\frac{\log n}{\log(1/s)}$, or $\frac{\log n}{-\log s}$.

Returning to the Koch snowflake, we note that at each stage we replace every segment with four identical copies of itself at 1/3 scale. Consequently, the boundary of the snowflake has dimension

$$\frac{\log 4}{-\log 1/3} = \frac{\log 4}{\log 3} = 1.2619.$$

Let's apply this new method to some other fractal objects. Figure 4.11 depicts what is known as two-dimensional Cantor dust. It is cre-

Figure 4.11 2-D Cantor Dust

ated from a square by deleting the middle third both horizontally and vertically. This produces four squares which are 1/3 (in each direction) the size of the original square. Then the middle horizontal and vertical thirds are deleted from each of those squares. The Cantor dust is what is left over when this process is repeated indefinitely.

Since, by its construction, the Cantor dust consists of four 1/3-scale copies of itself, its dimension is

$$\frac{\log 4}{-\log(1/3)} = \frac{\log 4}{\log 3} = 1.2619.$$

The Sierpinski carpet (figure 4.12) is related to the Cantor dust. Instead of deleting bands, we create the carpet by deleting a "middle" square whose sides are 1/3 the original length: if the original square were divided by a tic-tac-toe grid, we'd be deleting the center square. The Sierpinski carpet then consists of eight copies of itself at 1/3 scale. This means that the carpet has a dimension of

$$\frac{\log 8}{-\log(1/3)} = \frac{\log 8}{\log 3} = 1.8928.$$

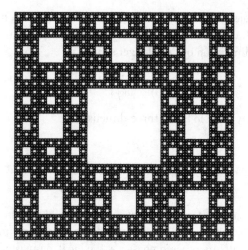

Figure 4.12 Sierpinski Carpet

This makes intuitive sense: the dimension of the Sierpinski carpet should be closer to 2 than the dimension of the Cantor dust since the Sierpinski carpet fills in more of the original square.

We can do the same thing in three dimensions. The Menger sponge (figure 4.13) is an easy example.

Figure 4.13 Menger Sponge

This object consists of twenty 1/3-scale copies of itself: eight copies each on the front and rear faces and four copies in the center. Thus the dimension of the Menger sponge is

$$\frac{\log 20}{-\log(1/3)} = \frac{\log 20}{\log 3} = 2.7268.$$

That's pretty close to being three-dimensional.

Hermann Grassmann

Hermann Grassmann was born in 1809, in the Polish city of Szczecin. His father, an ordained Lutheran minister, taught mathematics and physics at the local gymnasium (high school). As a youngster, Grassmann was an undistinguished student; however, he scored high marks on an admission exam and enrolled at Berlin University, where he studied philosophy, theology, and philology (the linguistic aspects of literature), never taking a single course in mathematics. During this time Grassmann was influenced by Friedrich Schleiermacher, a theologian interested in religion and science. Grassmann wrote,

I owe him so infinitely much intellectually. . . . In the second semester I had heard a course of lectures by Schleiermacher which I did not, however, understand; nevertheless his lecturing began to exert some influence on me. Then in my last year I was completely drawn to Schleiermacher; though I was concerned mainly with philology at that time, I recognized then for the first time that something can be learned from Schleiermacher for any science. This is because, more than providing positive knowledge, he communicates how to approach each inquiry from the right side and pursue it on one's own initiative, and enables one to find the positive knowledge for oneself.[11]

His knowledge of mathematics came only from studying his father's books; nevertheless, Grassmann decided that this subject interested him the most, and after graduation he spent a year preparing to teach it. He began teaching at the age of twenty-three, though only at low levels of mathematics. Over the next four years, he passed exams that allowed him to teach mathematics, physics, mineralogy, and chemistry at all levels. At thirty-eight, he was appointed head teacher.

Grassmann also actively engaged in research during this time. His masterpiece, *The Theory of Linear Extension, a New Branch of Mathematics*, advocated an algebraic approach to axiomatizing geometry; this laid the foundation for linear algebra, one of the most powerful tools available to today's mathematicians. After this work was rejected as a Ph.D. thesis, Grassmann wrote several papers on algebraic curves and surfaces, hoping that they would give his work credibility. He also wrote on the mixing of colors (a theory now called Grassmann's Law), crystallography, electromagnetism, and mechanics, and he presented the first axiomatic formulation of arithmetic.

Deeply disappointed that the mathematics community did not recognize the value of his work, Grassmann returned to his earlier interest in languages, working with German, Sanskrit, and Indo-European languages. He also wrote about theology. Some mid-nineteenth century writers had challenged the genuineness of biblical miracles, claiming that God would never violate laws that he created; Grassmann replied that we can never claim full knowledge of such laws. He also argued that the scriptures provide their own authority, noting that he believed them because he had experienced "their eternal divine truth" in his own consciousness. At the age of sixty-seven, he finally received the doctorate he sought, an honorary one from the University of Tübingen. But it was in philology, not in mathematics. He died the following year.

Higher Dimensions

Of course, when most people talk about other dimensions, they are not thinking of the fractal dimensions we have just been investigating. Instead, they are envisioning some sort of "higher" dimension. In the grand scheme of things, this type of thinking is a fairly recent development driven by mathematics. An important first step in this direction was provided by Hermann Grassmann who, in 1844, published a paper entitled *The Theory of Linear Extension, a New Branch of Mathematics*. In it Grassmann provided the first development of a theory of space that included the Euclidian geometry we learned in elementary and high school, while allowing for an unlimited number of dimensions. Grassmann's ideas were not well received at the time, but his paper nevertheless laid the foundations for what is now known as linear algebra, a critical part of today's undergraduate mathematics education. As Desmond Fearnley-Sander stated in a 1979 *Mathematical Monthly* article, "few have come closer than Hermann Grassmann to creating, single-handedly, a new subject."[12]

So, what is the key to Grassmann's work? The idea flowed from putting geometric concepts into algebraic form. You should be used to this concept on a basic level. In fact, we naturally engaged in this type of thinking when we spoke about representing geometric objects with sets of ordered pairs or ordered triples. But once we've used ordered triples to represent points in space, it's an easy shift to using ordered triples to represent other types of information. For example, instead of identifying a point in space, (75, 40, 28) might represent the current temperature, relative humidity, and barometric pressure. If we throw in wind speed and the UV-index, we have moved from an ordered triple to an ordered 5-tuple. Just as the ordered triple can be viewed as a single item representing a point in space, an ordered 5-tuple can be viewed as a single state of the weather. Similarly, imagine a grocery list:

One dozen eggs
Two pounds of hamburger
A head of lettuce
Four tomatoes

Eight buns
Half a pound of cheddar cheese.

The list can be thought of as the point (12, 2, 1, 4, 8, 0.5) in a six-dimensional space whose dimensions are (eggs, hamburger, lettuce, tomatoes, buns, cheddar cheese). Since large stores may stock over a hundred thousand different items, their inventory database can be thought of as a point in a space with over a hundred thousand dimensions. This way of thinking of dimension has become foundational for modern economics.

Grassmann's insight was to articulate a set of axioms that described the formal behavior of objects such as these. He then worked out some of the implications of the axioms. In this sense, Grassmann's work was much like Euclid's (more on Euclid in the chapter on proof), but Grassmann used algebraic rather than geometric tools.

Mathematically, a set of 5-tuples is just as real as a set of 3-tuples. The problem is that once we have moved beyond three dimensions, the n-tuples can no longer be interpreted as points in our three-dimensional universe. But might 5-tuples have a natural interpretation in some five-dimensional *physical* universe? It's pretty hard to imagine a universe with five different mutually-perpendicular directions!

Einstein's space-time continuum is sometimes offered as an example of a four-dimensional universe. In one sense, this is correct: there are four different independently varying quantities that describe a point in space-time. However, the space-time continuum is unlike a four-dimensional space in several respects. First, while you can travel either forward or backward in any of the spatial directions, you can only travel forward in the fourth (or time) dimension. Furthermore, distance is measured differently in the space-time continuum. In one dimension, points are determined by a single coordinate and the distance between a pair of points is

$$|x_1 - x_2| = \sqrt{(x_1 - x_2)^2}.$$

In two dimensions, ordered pairs are used and the distance between (x_1, y_1) and (x_2, y_2) is $\sqrt{(x_1 - x_2)^2 + (y_1 - y_2)^2}$.

Likewise, in three dimensions, distance is computed by

$$\sqrt{(x_1 - x_2)^2 + (y_1 - y_2)^2 + (z_1 - z_2)^2}.$$

But in the space-time continuum, instead of using

$$\sqrt{(x_1 - x_2)^2 + (y_1 - y_2)^2 + (z_1 - z_2)^2 + (t_1 - t_2)^2}$$

for distance, we compute it as

$$\sqrt{(x_1 - x_2)^2 + (y_1 - y_2)^2 + (z_1 - z_2)^2 - c^2(t_1 - t_2)^2},$$

where c is the speed of light. The reasons for this difference stem from physics, but our purpose here is only to note that while we experience a four-dimensional space-time continuum, we do not perceive a four-dimensional space.

Notice that the previous paragraph used the word *experience* rather than saying "live in." This is because at least some physicists believe that we may actually live in an eleven-dimensional universe. How can this be if we only perceive three dimensions? Well, our work on fractal dimensions provides us with a set of useful metaphors. Think about our area-filling curve. It is a one-dimensional object that, simply by curving around, fills up two dimensions. Or think of the Menger sponge that occupies three-dimensional space but, because of its holes, is a 2.7-dimensional object. When physicists speak of the higher dimensions of the universe, they describe the additional dimensions as being wound so tightly that we cannot perceive them. One of the major research projects in modern physics is the development of a grand unification theory that would explain the four fundamental forces of physics (gravity, electromagnetism, weak interaction, and strong interaction) as manifestations of one underlying force operating at different scales. Theoretical physicists working on this project have found that grand unification seems to imply that, as you approach subatomic scales, there is more freedom of movement. But, as we saw at the very beginning of this chapter, additional freedom of movement means that we are operating in a higher dimensional setting. Is there physical evidence for these other dimensions? Not yet. At least for now, such higher-dimensional models are not sufficiently developed and the scales are too small to make testable predictions.

While the universe on a small scale seems to have more dimensions than the three that we experience, a reasonable argument can be advanced that, more globally, our universe has a dimension smaller than three. Think about the shape of the universe. Doesn't it exhibit some of the characteristics of Cantor dust? To the best of our knowledge, the universe consists of many widely dispersed galaxy clusters. These clusters, in turn, are made up of widely separated galaxies, which contain widely spaced star clusters, and so on. Even on the human scale, we learn in our chemistry classes that what we experience as solid matter actually is composed of atoms—and those are mostly empty space!

Entering Lower Dimensions

How might our universe appear to a being that exists outside of it? To Christians, God is such a being. God, somehow beyond and outside of all that we can sense, is not bound by the created universe.

As scripture tells us,

> There is one body and one Spirit—just as you were called to one hope when you were called—one Lord, one faith, one baptism; one God and Father of all, who is over all and through all and in all. (Eph. 4:4–6)

But what does it mean for God to be "over" all, "through" all, and "in" all? How could God be all-knowing and all-powerful and, at the same time, dwell here on earth as Jesus Christ in finite human form? One reason we struggle with such questions is that we are so profoundly influenced by boundaries: the physical limits of our bodies, our three-dimensional sense of the world around us, the time-bound fact of our earthly lives.

As we did when looking at sets of fractional dimension, mathematicians often seek insight from simpler examples when faced with complex problems. Before we reflect on the mystery of how God interacts with our world, let's first consider how we might interact with creatures in a world that is part of, but more bounded than, ours. Imagine a two-dimensional world, a *flatland*—a piece of paper, perhaps. (In 1903, Edwin A. Abbott wrote *Flatland*, a book that gives an excellent description of such an imaginary world, one which we draw from here.) Creatures in this world would be two-dimensional; for further simplicity, we'll imagine that they are squares. As we peer down at flatland from the third dimension, what would a flatlander look like? Well, we'd see the whole shape—the edges that form the square, as well as what's inside. Now think for a moment what flatlanders see when they look at each other. A flatlander lives *in* the surface of the paper. Just as we cannot see a person's back when looking at the front (not without mirrors, anyway), neither can a flatlander. But what is the "front" in flatland? Try looking at a square drawn on a piece of paper and slowly lowering your eye to be level with the edge of the paper. Since you're not really "in" the paper, once your eye is level with it you'll just lose sight of the square, but a creature in the paper would see the closest side or sides—that would be the front of the square from the other creature's perspective. The other flatlander would not be able to see inside the edges as we can from the third dimension— the square's edges form its skin, and "inside" the edges are, well, the square's insides—maybe some sort of circulatory system, digestive system, etc. From within flatland, someone wanting to see inside the square would have to look through the skin, the edges, like radiologists and surgeons do in our world. Even then, the view wouldn't be what we see from our observation point "above" flatland: flatlanders have no way to access such a view. But freed from the boundaries of flatland, we see front, back, and inside all at once.

Imagine now that you, from your observation point "above" flatland, begin to interact with the square. How might the square experience your voice? Your touch? Your presence in flatland?

There are many possible ways to think about these questions. For the first two, you might need more information: Are you touching or speaking from within flatland or from "above" flatland? From

Edwin Abbott Abbott

Edwin Abbott Abbott was born December 20, 1838, and died October 12, 1926. He graduated from the City of London School and St. John's College, Cambridge, where he studied classics, mathematics, and theology. Ordained an Anglican priest at the age of twenty-four, Abbott was appointed headmaster of the City of London School two years later, where he served from the young (for a headmaster) age of twenty-six until his retirement at age fifty-one.

Abbott devoted himself to literary and theological pursuits, writing an influential grammar of Shakespeare's works, publishing a life of Francis Bacon, and writing extensively on theological topics. However, he is best known today as the author of a small book called *Flatland: A Romance of Many Dimensions*. In this book, Abbott describes a two-dimensional world whose creatures are geometric figures. In addition to being an imaginative exploration of the concept of dimension, the book is a clever satire of Victorian customs. It was recently made into a film.

within, your speech and touch would probably be very similar to what the square experiences of the speech and touch of other flatlanders, but strange (to the square) things become possible when you speak or touch from a "larger" space. The flatlander's insides are within easy reach of your hands—you could touch them and leave no one in flatland the wiser. The sound waves that carry your voice would reach inside as well, perhaps giving the square the kind of sensation we get when a car with a ramped-up bass drives by.

And what kind of presence might you have in flatland? As you enter, flatland effectively slices through you, showing the square a cross-section of your body. Well, one side of a cross-section: step in just past your ankle, and the square will see an arc of your lower leg. Step in with both feet, and the square will see two seemingly disconnected arcs. Thrust in your fingers, and the square will believe there are ten separate beings in view.

Now consider the idea that God, who is not bound by the things that bind us—not by space, not by time—must exist beyond the limits of our three-dimensional world. When God speaks, should we expect to hear a normal human voice? When God reaches out, should we expect to feel a normal human touch? God could certainly arrange for us to do so, but are the "normal" avenues for sound and touch the only ones available to God?

And what might we expect to see if God entered the world? Think back to one of your fingers entering flatland. First, the square sees a dot: your finger has just touched down. Next, a small, tight arc which grows over time as you push your finger farther in. Is it possible that God once entered our world in much the same way, first "visible" as a very small cluster of cells, growing and changing over time as he pushed his way in until, some thirty years later, we saw in Jesus Christ the most complete picture of God that we would ever see in our world? And is it possible, even, that what we think of as unrelated individuals sitting around us in church are in fact different parts of one body whose connections can be seen in another dimension?

The Universal Observer

To a Christian mathematician, ideas like these are not so far-fetched. Mathematicians frequently "picture" higher-dimensional objects by looking at smaller-dimensional slices formed by fixing one or more of their coordinates. Viewed this way, a cylinder can be pictured as a stack of congruent circles, a cube as a stack of congruent squares, a sphere as a stack of circles with radii that increase from zero and then decrease back down. Picturing four-dimensional objects, we look at three-dimensional "slices" formed by increasing values of the fourth coordinate and think of the slices as showing us how the object is changing over time (with time serving, as it did for Einstein, as the fourth coordinate).

Is it possible that what we sense as time is really a result of our experiencing a greater reality in the midst of our three-dimensional perspective? Our brain, after all, does this kind of thing all the time: it takes the two-dimensional images focused by the lenses of our eyes and transforms them so that we perceive depth as well as length and breadth. And, from a vantage point outside of our universe, might God be outside of this fourth dimension as well, so that what seems to us to be the relentless forward march of time is not a part of God's experience?

We won't be answering these questions any time soon. But mathematics, at least, gives us some tools to explore these mysteries in a distinctive way.

Suggestions for Further Reading

Abbott, Edwin A. *Flatland: A Romance of Many Dimensions*. Seelcy & Co., London: 1884. Available in several subsequent editions. A classic description of reality in a two-dimensional world.

Lewis, Albert C. "The Divine Truth of Mathematics and the Origins of Linear Algebra." *Theology and Science* 9, no. 1, 109–120 (February 2011). An exploration of the origins of Grassman's thinking about linear algebra and the role that theology played in that discovery.

Neuhouser, David L. *Open to Reason*. Upland, IN: Taylor Univ. Press, 2001. An exploration of the interplay among the roles of reason, mathematics, and Christian belief.

EXERCISES

1. The space filling curves that we studied are related to computer codes called Gray codes. These are important in organizing memory in computers. Research this relationship and write up your findings.

2. Prove that the stage n Koch figure is contained in the circumscribed circle.

    a. The first-stage additions to the initial triangle can be thought of as smaller triangles added to the sides of the initial triangle. Describe where the vertices of the first-stage additions lie relative to the circumscribing circle.

b. Place circumscribing circles around the added triangles. Where do these new circles lie relative to the original circle? Why?

c. Explain why these relationships guarantee that at every stage, the added triangles will always lie within the original circle.

In the following series of problems, use the fact (proved in calculus) that $a + ar + ar^2 + ar^3 + ar^4 + \cdots = a/(1 - r)$ as long as $-1 < r < 1$.

3. Find the area of the stage n snowflake. Use this to find the area of the final snowflake. (How many small triangles will be added at stage n? What are their areas?)

4. We can create a variation of the Koch snowflake by starting with a square of side 1 and replacing the line segments at each stage with a curve that has had the middle third replaced with three sides of a square, as in the figure below. The added square should be oriented so that our figure grows outward.

Replace   With

a. Draw the first three stages of the construction of this variation.

b. Compute the area of the object. (How many squares are added at each stage? How large are they?)

c. Compute the length of the boundary.

d. Compute the dimension of the boundary.

e. What happens if the replacement is done with the curve "facing" inward?

5. Compute the dimension of the decimal numbers between 0 and 1 that use only even digits.

6. The standard Cantor set is created from an interval of length 1 from which the middle third is removed. Then the middle third of the remaining two intervals is removed. Then the

middle third of the remaining four intervals is removed and so on. The Cantor set is what remains at the end of the process.

a. What is the dimension of the Cantor set?

b. How much length does it have? (How many intervals of what length are removed at stage n? Use the summation formula to compute the total lengths of the segments that have been removed.)

7. A Cantor-like set is created by removing a fraction other than 1/3 from the middle of each interval. Suppose that we remove the middle 1/4.

a. Compute the lengths of the removed and remaining intervals for the first three stages.

b. What are the lengths of the removed and remaining intervals at stage n?

c. What is the length of the remaining Cantor-like set?

d. What is the dimension of this Cantor-like set?

8. A second approach to making a Cantor-like set removes intervals of specified length at each stage instead of removing a fixed proportion. Let's create a Cantor-like set by removing intervals of length $(1/4)^n$ at stage n.

a. Compute the length of the remaining intervals for the first three stages.

b. Explain why the simplified version of the dimension formula cannot be used for the resulting Cantor-like set.

c. Using $t = (1/4)^n$, compute $N(t)$ and use it to find the dimension.

d. What is the total length of the removed intervals? What is the length of the remaining Cantor-like set?

9. Generalize your results from exercise 8 to Cantor-like sets where intervals of length v^n are removed at stage n where $0 < v < 1$.

10. Compute the area of the Sierpinski carpet.

11. The Sierpinski triangle is like the Sierpinski carpet but is based on a triangle.

Compute its area and dimension. (What is the area of the original triangle? How many triangles are removed at each stage? What are their areas?)

12. Compute the dimension and area of 2-D Cantor dust where central, vertical, and horizontal bands that are 1/4 of the width of the square are removed at each stage.

13. There is a three-dimensional version of the 2-D Cantor dust that we analyzed. The 3-D Cantor dust begins with a cube (of length one on each side) and removes the middle third perpendicular to each face. What is the dimension of the 3-D Cantor dust? How much volume does it contain?

14. Imagine that you encounter a one-dimensional world, a "lineland," on a piece of paper. What do the creatures of that world look like? What are their boundaries? In what ways can you interact with them?

15. Could a flatlander have a digestive tract like ours—a top-to-bottom (possibly circuitous) path or hole? Why or why not?

16. Using the flatland analogy as a basis for your argument, discuss one way it might be possible for God to know what is happening in all parts of the world at the same time. Find at least three biblical verses that support this aspect of the nature of God.

Chapter 5

CHANCE

> *I have seen something else under the sun: The race is not to the swift or the battle to the strong, nor does food come to the wise or wealth to the brilliant or favor to the learned; but time and chance happen to them all.*
>
> ECCLESIASTES 9:11

Introduction

Is there really such a thing as chance? Imagine the coin flip that precedes an athletic event. Players and coaches agree that it is a fair way to decide who gets the ball first because both teams have an equal chance of winning the toss. But we could imagine an unscrupulous engineer designing a coin flip predictor. It could involve sensors that accurately measure the initial elevation, velocity, and rotational speed of the coin as it is flipped, note whether the coin started with heads or tails on top, compute whether the coin will land heads or tails, and send an audio message to a receiver hidden in the ear of the player calling the flip, who then calls it correctly. So it appears that ignorance of the information the sensors collect makes the coin flip look like chance when it is really not.

This issue—is there really such a thing as chance in the universe?—is one of the biggest questions of our time. For physicists, it is one of the central issues in understanding the nature of the physical universe. For theologians, it is a main question in conceptualizing God's work in the physical world. For philosophers, it is at the heart of questions relating to human freedom. For lay people, it is deeply tied into understanding events like illness, accidents, and natural disasters and God's role in such happenings.

Chance events have a long-standing role in human history. Objects resembling dice are among the oldest artifacts archaeologists have discovered. Also, the quote from Ecclesiastes that began this chapter illustrates that ancient Hebrew thinkers reflected on the role of chance in human affairs; Greek thinkers, too, thought a lot about the roles of fate and chance in people's lives. The scientific and mathematical study of chance, however, is relatively new. The origin of the discipline of probability is the work of Blaise Pascal and Pierre Fermat (1654) in the study of gambling problems. The discipline of statistics is typically seen as originating in studies of mortality tables in England done by John Graunt (1662). However, seventeenth-century scientists did not regard chance as a factor in the physical universe. For example, Rene Descartes divided reality into two parts: the mental and the physical. The mental could not be explained in mechanistic terms; however, within the physical realm, all objects—rocks, plants, animals, human bodies—operated like machines. In 1685, Isaac Newton published his laws of gravitation. Building on Newton's and Descartes's ideas, eighteenth- and nineteenth-century thinkers came to see the universe as a machine that worked with the orderliness and precision of a well-built clock. With the discovery of quantum mechanics in the early years of the twentieth century, though, probability theory began to be applied to the study of the physical universe. Many physicists asserted that inherent uncertainty was built into the deepest parts of the fabric of the universe, which caused numerous theologians to breathe a collective sigh of relief. After all, if the universe were not a machine, there would be a clear opening for ongoing divine activity. But it also became clear that a theological problem of a different sort had to be addressed: If the universe truly included random elements, wouldn't that argue against the existence of a sovereign God who set the universe in motion, sustains it, and exercises loving care over it? Isn't the existence of chance incompatible with the sovereignty of God? The presence or absence of chance also acquired powerful emotional aspects for both believers and unbelievers when some scientists made assertions like the following:

The more we understand of the workings of nature, the more we realize that the forces that shape it are those of blind, purposeless chance. Across a universe encompassing billions of light years, through scales of magnitude extending from subnuclear particles to immense galaxies colliding like a clash of cymbals, there is no hint of plan or purpose.[13]

The universe we observe has precisely the properties we should expect if there is, at bottom, no design, no purpose, no evil and no good, nothing but blind, pitiless indifference.[14]

Our goals in this chapter will be to examine, through the eyes of faith, how mathematics can help us understand the concept of chance and its role in the physical world, and to suggest some ways a Christian might think about chance.

Some Definitional Clarity

Before we can launch into the evidence for and against chance, we need to clarify our terminology and some basic concepts. Two key terms that deserve special consideration are **deterministic** and **nondeterministic**.

Typically the term *deterministic* is used to describe a natural law or a process. To say that a law or process is deterministic means that it produces a single outcome for events within its scope. For instance, Newton's laws of gravitation cast gravity as a deterministic process because the gravitational attraction between two bodies is described by the formula

$$F = \frac{gm_1m_2}{r^2},$$

where g is the gravitational constant, m_1 and m_2 are the masses of the two objects, and r is the distance between them. According to this formula, the motion of the two bodies relative to each other (apart from the influence of other factors) is governed by their gravitational attraction; there is no place where uncertainty enters. *Nondeterministic* is the negation of deterministic. To say that a process is nondeterministic means that it has multiple possible outcomes. Whenever possible, scientists assign probabilities to those outcomes. A coin flip is, for example, nondeterministic, and the process governing the outcome can be described by the formula

$$\text{result} = \begin{cases} \text{heads, probability} = 0.5 \\ \text{tails,\quad probability} = 0.5 \end{cases}.$$

The difference between the gravitational and coin flip formulas is the presence of more than one outcome in the nondeterministic case. Saying a process is nondeterministic makes no assertions about the source of the uncertainty, nor does it address the issue of whether chance is *really* present, or only *appears* to be present. It simply says that a process can be described by listing multiple possible outcomes, and that these outcomes are (ideally) associated with probabilities.

The word **determinism,** however, has a much broader meaning. It is the philosophical assertion that *all* processes in the physical world are deterministic; **nondeterminism** is its negation. It is the philosophical assertion that not all processes in the physical world are deterministic.

So far we have talked about whether chance "really exists" in an informal way. We are now going to firm up our vocabulary. Consider a chance event in which the multiple possible outcomes are due only to our ignorance. If we thoroughly understood the situation, we would see that there is only one possible outcome. In other words, the situation is deterministic. This circumstance is called **epistemic chance**. The word *epistemic* is used here to indicate that saying the event was a "chance" event is a function of our (lack of) knowledge. Now imagine a situation in which no amount of knowledge would reduce the possible outcomes to only one. This is called **ontological chance,** meaning uncertainty is built into the basic nature of the event. Thus the big question that opened this chapter can be restated as either, Does ontological chance exist? or Which is right: determinism or nondeterminism?

As is usually done in mathematics, statistics, and science, we will treat the words *chance* and *randomness* as synonyms and define both as meaning nondeterministic—the property that a process has multiple possible outcomes. This is often a source of confusion. It is sometimes assumed that the word *chance* presumes nondeterminism. We are not going to make that assumption; rather we are going to use chance and randomness in a neutral way and treat the matter of determinism or nondeterminism separately.

Another point of confusion is that in popular usage *chance* often means without purpose as illustrated by the "blind, purposeless chance" quotes above. However, when seen as nondeterminacy, chance events can be put to use in very purposeful ways. For instance, the enjoyment of board games often depends on chance elements such as spinners, dice, or cards. Also, much scientific research depends on random sampling—the careful use of chance to select representative members of populations that are too large or too remote to examine completely.

The relationship between chance and causation is also a source of confusion. Chance can't cause anything. It simply describes the reality that more than one outcome is possible in a given situation. Frequently, when someone describes something as caused by chance, they mean that they don't understand how a particular outcome occurred. However, while chance cannot be a cause, knowing that something is caused can rule out chance. That is, if A is the cause of B in the sense that whenever A occurs, B must follow, then chance is not part of the relationship between A and B.

We need to look briefly at one more topic before we examine the different perspectives that Christians have taken on chance: the nature of God's relationship with the physical world. Many books and articles have been written about this relationship, and it remains deeply mysterious. But for our purposes we need a perspective developed by Thomas Aquinas (1225–1274), whose ideas we have looked at in other sections of this book.

Aquinas distinguished between primary and secondary causes. To illustrate, if I repair my leaky roof by climbing up on that roof, removing the damaged shingles, and installing new ones, I am the primary agent in bringing about that repair. But if I hire a roofer to do it, I can still say I fixed my roof, but I did it through a secondary agent. Aquinas viewed God as the first cause of all things but saw his work in the world today as primarily being through secondary agents whose actions could be described by natural laws. Isaac Newton adopted this perspective as well. He saw God as holding the planets in orbit but doing so through gravitation.

Interestingly, Newton viewed the stability of planetary orbits as not being robust. That is, he thought the stability could be disrupted by something like the gravitational pull of a passing comet. He argued, however, that if such a thing happened God would intervene and put the planets back in their orbit. Thus from Newton's perspective, God's actions in the solar system could easily switch from using agents to direct intervention. Later, Laplace showed that the planetary orbits were considerably more stable than Newton thought.

Some Scientific Evidence

Let's examine two case studies to see if they can shed light on these matters:

Case Study 1

Our first case study is quantum mechanics. Heisenberg's principle tells us that when we look at very small particles, there is a fundamental uncertainty in our knowledge. Suppose we examine an elementary particle and denote its position (in some direction) by x and momentum by p (in the same direction). Heisenberg found that we cannot state both its position and momentum precisely. The mathematical representation of such a particle yields a range of possible values for x and another range for p. Suppose that we denote the uncertainty in its position by Δx and the uncertainty in its momentum in the same direction by Δp. In statistical terms, Δx is defined as the standard deviation of the collection of possible x values; Δp is defined similarly. Then Heisenberg's principle is that

$$\Delta x \Delta p \geq \frac{1}{2}\hbar,$$

where

$$\hbar \text{ denotes } \frac{h}{2\pi},$$

and h is Plank's constant, 6.626068×10^{-34} m^2 kg/s. That is, for small values of x and p, if we *increase* our certainty about x (by reducing Δx), we *decrease* our certainty about p, and vice versa. The uncertainty is very small, but nonetheless it sets an absolute bound on the certainty we can attach to our knowledge of the state of physical particles.

When Heisenberg first discovered this principle he regarded it as an instance of epistemic uncertainty. But as quantum mechanics became better understood and the predictions it made proved astonishingly reliable, many physicists came to regard this uncertainty as a fundamental property of nature, that is, as a form of ontological uncertainty. One Christian physicist and theologian, John Polkinghorne, justifies this inference on grounds he calls critical realism. Here's the idea: Realism holds that things are the way they appear to be; Christian realism accepts realism but gives it a theological foundation—the belief that God has made our perceptual faculties and doesn't want to deceive us. Thus, as long as our perceptual faculties are functioning properly, they provide us with reliable information as to the way things actually are. Critical realism modifies realism a bit. It acknowledges that our perceptions can be fooled by things like optical illusions. It also acknowledges that very small things (at the quantum level) and very large things (at the galactic level) are far outside our normal experience. So while realism is basically sound, we need to apply it cautiously. But, argues Polkinghorne, when something like quantum uncertainty has been studied by a large number of people over a great many years, producing powerful and consistent results, a move from the statement "x appears this way" to "x is this way" is warranted.

Of course, Polkinghorne could be wrong. There is still the possibility that new discoveries could remove quantum uncertainty.

However, physicists have shown that any undiscovered factors that could account for quantum uncertainty must be "global"; that is, must violate a principle widely thought to be inviolable—that velocities cannot exceed the speed of light. One theologian, Nancey Murphy, has suggested that God is the undiscovered factor, acting directly to control particles. Not all theologians are comfortable with this suggestion; some suggest that God has established laws governing the behavior of elementary particles and that these laws include nondeterminacy. Also some scientists have suggested that natural (that is, nondivine) global factors may indeed exist and that basic notions such as time, locality, and causation will need major revision as new discoveries emerge. All of this is very puzzling at the present time. What is clear, however, is that the behavior of elementary particles appears nondeterministic from our perspective and we cannot at present tell whether the nondeterminacy is ontological.

Case Study 2

Does God select the gender of each child that is born? There are two possible Christian perspectives—(1) God directly selects the gender or (2) God uses the reproductive process as an agent allowing it to select the gender. Approach 1 says that God locates the egg, selects a particular sperm to fertilize that egg, and then directs it appropriately. Approach 2 says that God has created the process but lets it proceed according to its own nature. Approach 2 applies to other human genetic features than gender and to nonhuman reproduction as well. It implies that God does not directly specify the genetic makeup of individual offspring, although God did create the range of possibilities from which the makeup will be chosen.

Both are plausible, but both pose problems for Christian belief. For example, there are over one hundred million conceptions worldwide every year and about 25% result in miscarriages. Also, many genetic diseases could have been prevented by use of a different egg and sperm. Suppose Susan is an advocate of direct action (approach 1) and John is an advocate of agency (approach 2). John might argue that if God were directly involved in every conception,

God would have prevented the miscarriages and genetic diseases, or at least not allowed so many to occur. Susan might respond by appealing to our limited knowledge: God may have good reasons for doing things that we cannot currently comprehend, but will acknowledge as just and wise at the culmination of history. She in turn could ask John why God has put in place an apparently flawed process. John could respond that God did indeed create a good process, but then he too has to appeal to limited knowledge. John might also argue that Susan's approach violates critical realism, asserting that since gender selection looks like a binomial process and the data are consistent with such a hypothesis, it is indeed a nondeterministic process. Susan would balk at this conclusion, citing biblical passages such as Psalm 139:13, "For you created my inmost being; you knit me together in my mother's womb." Neither position seems fully convincing, so gender selection does not settle the issue of determinism versus nondeterminism either.

Determinism and Nondeterminism

Let's examine the arguments for the perspectives of theistic nondeterminism and theistic determinism in more detail. The issues involved are among the most contentious in the history of philosophy, and many variations in the basic concepts of determinism and nondeterminism have been advanced. It is impossible to cover all of the nuances here. Rather we will lay out a broad overview first and then examine two specific approaches in more detail, one a deterministic perspective and one a nondeterministic perspective.

Naturalism refers to the belief that the natural world is all there is; naturalists deny the existence of God, angels, or anything else that could be deemed supernatural. Some naturalists are determinists and some are nondeterminists; similarly, there are theists of both persuasions. But naturalists and theists see the issues differently. Naturalists who are determinists tend to hold strongly to the idea of natural law—that everything that happens in the universe is governed by laws analogous to gravitation. They also argue from the **principle of causality,** which is the belief that every event has a cause sufficient to determine it. Thus, they regard ontological uncertainty as impossible. Naturalists who are nondeterminists still believe in natural laws, but see uncertainty built into those laws. They typically see the physical world as unfolding in a way analogous to the branching of a tree with nondetermined choices at each branching point. It could have developed in many different ways; if we were to "rewind the tape" a billion years and restart the process, it would be very unlikely to produce the same world we have today.

Theists who are determinists and those who are nondeterminists put a different emphasis on what it means for God to act lovingly. Determinists would say that God in love governs everything that happens, leaving no part of creation subject to the whims of blind chance. Nondeterminists emphasize that God's love includes his granting at least a measure of freedom to the loved ones. Table 5.1 should clarify the emphases of determinism and nondeterminism in relation to naturalism and theism.

Members of all four groups use mathematical models and regard randomness as a useful tool for modeling complex situations that involve large numbers of independent factors. Determinists tend to see such models as having *instrumental value only.* That is, they don't correspond to an underlying nondeterminate reality, but they are still useful tools. Nondeterminists accept the instrumental value of

	Determinism	Nondeterminism
Naturalism	Nature is governed by natural laws; events have causes that dictate outcomes.	Nature unfolds in unpredictable ways.
Theism	God is sovereign—all that happens is under God's control.	God's love means giving his creatures freedom.

Table 5.1—The major common positions relating determinism and theism

such models but go further. They believe that it is possible for such models to correspond to an underlying nondeterminate reality.

Remember that we are thinking of chance as nondeterminacy. Whether every event that happens is intended by God or a part of God's plan or in God's control are further questions, and different theistic nondeterminists have given different answers to them. For example, some theistic nondeterminists think that free human actions are not determined, but that they are nonetheless part of God's overall plan for the world. If so, those actions are chance events in the nondetermined sense of "chance" but not in the purposeless sense of "chance." In contrast, other theistic nondeterminists maintain that God cannot know what free, nondetermined human actions will be, and so specific actions of this sort cannot belong to God's plan. They are chance events in both the sense of being nondetermined and the sense of not being intended by God. As we mentioned above, we will not attempt to develop every possible position here. Instead we will look at two examples: a version of theistic determinism that affirms a kind of human freedom, and a version of theistic nondeterminism that says that the creation is nonetheless ordered.

The Case for Theistic Determinism

Compatibilism is the idea that determinism and human free will are in fact compatible even though it seems that they are not. The Christian physicist John Byl identifies himself as a compatibilist. His arguments for determinism take both a positive form—arguing directly from aspects of God's nature as a basis for determinism—and a negative form—arguing that God's nature excludes nondeterminism.

Byl's positive arguments for determinism emphasize God's providential care for the world. Thus he cites the biblical doctrine that God brings all things into being and upholds them by his power. Passages such as Matthew 10:29, "Are not two sparrows sold for a penny? Yet not one of them will fall to the ground apart from the will of your Father," support his point of view. He also argues from God's omnipotence—that all events must be fully under God's control.

His negative arguments start from the **principle of sufficient reason**—that every fact has a sufficient explanation; this principle is similar to the principle of causality we looked at earlier, but it is slightly stronger. While not explicitly a biblical principle, it has an ancient history extending back to the Greeks and to medieval Christian thinkers; today it is often attributed to Gottfried Leibniz because of his extended discussion of it. According to this principle, ontological uncertainty cannot exist—if we were able to look deeply enough at any given uncertain event, we would find an explanation for why that event and not another occurred. Hence all uncertainty must be epistemic. He also argues from God's omniscience that it is inconceivable that an event unpredictable to God can happen; since it is predictable, such an event cannot be nondeterministic. Also, since God knows people completely, he can predict every choice they will make, so no human choices are nondeterministic from God's perspective. Of course, it can be debated whether predictable equates to foreknowledge and whether foreknowledge implies an event is determined. You will be given an opportunity to explore these connections in the exercises at the end of this chapter.

Byl reconciles human free will and determinism by examining carefully what is meant by "free will." From his perspective, free will means noncoercion—that is, people willingly make their own choices based on their own reasons that are in turn in accord with their character, desires, and experiences. In short, free will means people can do what they want; nevertheless, what they want is in some way determined. For instance, the philosopher Arthur Schopenhauer (1788–1860) alleged that a person can do what he wants, but cannot want what he wants. Advocates of this perspective also address the criticism that determinism makes God responsible for evil. They assert that people are responsible for their own evil deeds because they chose freely in accordance with their own natures.

There is also a scientific argument for the plausibility of determinism (that Byl does not put forth). Suppose one is examining a large complex system like the weather in which many independent factors influence the outcome. The presence of large numbers of independent factors is enough to make the behavior of the system appear nondeterministic even though each of the individual factors is itself deterministic. A theistic determinist would argue that God has complete control and complete knowledge of these independent factors; we do not have such knowledge, so the combination of all of these factors produces results that appear random to us.

Interestingly the Jewish historian Josephus describes the Pharisees as being compatibilists. By contrast the Sadducees had a nondeterministic view of things.

The Case for Theistic Nondeterminism

The main challenge for theistic nondeterminism is finding a credible way to affirm both God's sovereignty and nondeterminism. A Christian statistician, David Bartholomew, offers such an argument based on the notion of **levels**. His idea is that on the level of a single entity (an electron, say, or a single sperm) we can have randomness, but on the level of the aggregation of many such entities we can have order. Thus God can have it both ways. God can have all of the benefits that randomness provides at the level of individuals (we will discuss some of these below) and also have a beautiful and manageable order at an aggregate level. Three examples will help illustrate this idea:

1. Globally, about 106 male children are born for each 100 female children. However, males have a slightly higher rate of childhood mortality, so that by the time both sexes reach adulthood, the numbers of males and females are very close to equal. Thus the selection of the gender of an individual birth can be nondeterminate but the aggregate produces a simple order.

2. The ideal gas law was first stated by Émile Clapeyron in 1834. For gas in a closed container, it says that $PV = NRT$ where P denotes pressure; V, volume; N, the amount of gas present; R, the gas constant; and T, temperature. Such a gas is made up

of enormous numbers of molecules, each moving randomly in the container; the gas law describes its aggregate behavior. For example, consider a balloon with a knot tied in the end. Molecules can escape through its pores, but if we consider a short time period, the number of escapees is negligible, so N is (almost) constant; we can also treat pressure as a known constant since the balloon will adjust its internal pressure to the surrounding air pressure. For such a balloon, the gas law reduces to $V = cT$, a simple linear relationship, even though the random molecular motion within the balloon is incredibly complex.

3. A powerful mathematical result, the Central Limit Theorem, accounts for much of the ability of aggregation to transform randomness at a low level into orderliness at a higher level. Figure 5.1 presents a particular probability distribution on the numbers 1 through 10. Note its erratic, uneven quality. Using a computer, we selected 10,000 random samples each of size 30 from a population distributed according to figure 5.1. Figure 5.2 presents the distribution of the means of these samples. It is similar to the familiar bell-shaped curve. The Central Limit Theorem tells us that for any numerical population, no matter how it is distributed, if we take random samples of size n, the

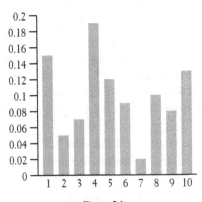

Figure 5.1

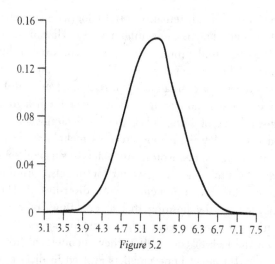

Figure 5.2

distribution of the means of those samples will become closer to a normal distribution (the bell-shaped curve) as *n* gets larger. Processes that average together large number of similar items are common. For example, temperature is the average motion of molecules. Thus, this theorem provides a powerful explanation for why bell-shaped curves arise so frequently in nature. It shows how aggregation can transform extreme disorder at one level to order at a higher level.

Bartholomew is arguing that's God's sovereignty operates in different ways at different levels. It is easy for a believer to affirm that the beautiful order and structure we see at aggregate levels is an expression of God's orderliness and goodness. But, he is saying, the seemingly chaotic randomness we see at low levels is also an expression of God's sovereignty. We have already seen some human benefits of randomness—the enjoyment of many games depends on it, and the reliability of statistical testing depends on random sampling. But there are also many examples of systems in the natural world that depend on randomness for their functioning. Consider the following two examples:

1. Based on skeletal remains, ornithologists have estimated that before Polynesians migrated to Hawaii sometime in the first millennium AD, there were over a hundred species of honeycreeper in the Hawaiian islands. Hawaiian honeycreepers are small songbirds found only in Hawaii. In recent years most authorities consider them a subfamily, *Drepanidinae*, of *Fringillidae*, the finch family. Finches are seed eaters. Hawaiian honeycreepers include seedeaters but also insectivores, nectivores, fruit eaters, even snail eaters and birds that probe decaying wood for insects. Ornithologists account for the uniqueness and diversity of Hawaiian honeycreepers by positing that at one time, probably in a storm, a pair (or more) of finches were blown onto the islands. Given the lack of competition they encountered from other bird life, Hawaiian honeycreepers evolved in diverse ways to exploit the rich resources provided by ecological niches that finches don't normally inhabit. Genetic randomness, then, provided the means for this diversity to arise. It provided for good use of resources but it also resulted in the production of an amazing variety of astonishingly beautiful birds.

2. In England, the peppered moth (Biston betularia) occurs in two subspecies, one light colored, and one dark. The light-colored moths were camouflaged against the lichens and tree bark on which they rested; however, during the industrial revolution, due to soot, many lichens died and the trees became darker. From about the middle of the nineteenth century, the relative frequency of the dark strain significantly increased as the light ones became more vulnerable to predators. Recently, however, as smoke pollution has decreased, the light strain has increased again in abundance.

In both examples randomness allows ecosystems to adapt to changes in their surrounding environment without having to be constantly tweaked.

Why might God use nondeterminate processes? Scripture does not address this question, so we don't know with certainty. But some plausible explanations have been suggested. First, some scholars say that God *uses processes as agents* because he wants human beings to live in an orderly, comprehensible world both for their peace and security and so that they can understand it well enough to exercise stewardship over it. Secondly, God uses nondeterministic processes because they are such an effective way to equip complex systems with the flexibility and robustness they need to adapt to changing conditions. Thirdly, some theologians argue that it was necessary for God to create nondeterministic processes in order to allow for human freedom. That is, they argue that if the world is deterministic, then human beings have neither freedom nor moral responsibility. Both are necessary if God is to form people into the image of Christ. A fourth (somewhat controversial) explanation of nondeterminism is an analogy from parenthood—just as loving parents do not control every detail in their children's lives but delight in allowing them to discover their talents, God delights in allowing his world to explore and realize its potential and produce a diversity that he has made possible and that exhibits the richness of his creativity.

Another Alternative?

So far we have presented theistic determinism and theistic nondeterminism as an either/or choice. But another approach has attracted a great deal of attention. It is based on the mathematical concept of **chaos**, technically known as deterministic nonperiodicity. Consider a complex physical system, like the global weather. Important features of it like air pressure can be modeled mathematically, but the equations exhibit the property of extreme sensitivity to initial conditions. For instance, suppose we knew the exact state of a system modeling the weather at some instant in time. The model could then tell us the exact state of the weather at any time in the future we chose to examine. But suppose we adjusted the numerical values of the initial state of the system by just a tiny bit. Equations that exhibit chaos have the property that they amplify such tiny adjustments by amounts that increase dramatically with time. Thus, even though two initial states are very close together, later states may have no resemblance to each other. This is why most scientists believe that detailed long-range weather prediction is impossible. That is, meteorologists can say that the temperature in Washington, DC, next July 4 will almost certainly be higher than it was on the previous January 4, but they cannot confidently predict whether it will rain on that day until a few days beforehand.

The connection between chaos theory and the issue of determinism versus nondeterminism is that major aspects of the physical world can be deterministic but act like they are nondeterministic. That is, it would seem that if someone could describe the state of a chaotic system precisely at some moment, the entire future of that system could be predicted. However, we can never measure perfectly; our instruments have limits and no matter how much we improve them we will ultimately encounter a limit that cannot be removed due to the Heisenberg uncertainty principle. Since chaotic systems magnify such uncertainty, the future of the system necessarily appears nondeterministic to us.

So far what we have said about chaos is noncontroversial. However, determinists and nondeterminists apply chaos theory differently. A determinist might say, "Aha, you see. The world really is deterministic. Furthermore, God knows the exact state of the world perfectly, so could predict its entire future if he chose to. In his wisdom, he has set up systems that hide such knowledge from us so that we have to trust him for the future. He allows us to predict a little ways into the future but that's it." Such a determinist need not be a deist. He or she could allow for God's intervention in the natural world in many ways but also believe that God would have complete knowledge of such actions and their consequences. Thus, determinism would not be violated. A nondeterminist could say, "It might seem hard to understand how nondeterminacy is consistent with the existence of an all-powerful, all-knowing God. But chaos provides one way to help us see this. All God has to do is (metaphorically) close his eyes for an instant and touch the system lightly and it will have an unpredictable future. Of course God *could* control the system, but he *chooses* instead to give it a measure of freedom within bounds that he has created." Some theologians sympathetic with the latter perspective have suggested that nondeterministic systems provide a way for God to be constantly subtly and gently steering the world in directions consistent with his will.

Conclusion

Understanding God's relationship with the physical universe is a challenging problem. It seems impossible to establish scientifically that ontological chance does or does not exist. Either claim would require complete knowledge of the universe. That is, suppose Joe is a nondeterminist. Consider any particular example he believes to be nondeterministic. Joe can never exclude the possibility that some discovery may show it to be deterministic. Now suppose Susan is a determinist. There are many things in the world she doesn't understand and many of these appear nondeterministic. She can never show that deterministic causes can in fact be found for all of those things. So neither position can be scientifically established; each involves theological or metaphysical assumptions and interpretations. However, it should be clear by this point that neither the assertion nor the denial of the existence of chance need be a threat to Christian belief. Chance and freedom are deeply mysterious. While we cannot fully grasp them, we can explore them, and their very mystery can increase our reverence for the subtlety of God's wisdom and our awe at the world God has made.

Suggestions for Further Reading

Bartholomew, David. *God, Chance and Purpose: Can God Have It Both Ways?* Cambridge: Cambridge Univ. Press, 2008. A clear and detailed articulation of theistic nondeterminism.

Byl, John. "Indeterminacy, Divine Action and Human Freedom." *Science and Christian Belief* 15, no. 2 (October 2003): 100–115. A clear and detailed articulation of theistic determinism.

Russell, Robert John, Nancey Murphy, and Arthur R. Peacocke, eds. *Chaos and Complexity: Scientific Perspectives on Divine Action.*

Berkeley: Center for Theology and the Natural Sciences, 1996. Available online at http://www.ctns.org/qm.html. A collection of fifteen research papers on God's action in the physical world. It is part of a larger series of five books, but this one has the largest focus on mathematics. The papers are quite readable but nevertheless will challenge most undergraduates.

Flint, Thomas. *Divine Providence: The Molinist Account*. Ithaca, NY: Cornell Univ. Press, 2006. An account that attempts to reconcile God as the all-knowing governor of the universe and human freedom.

Plantinga, Alvin. *Warrant and Proper Function*. New York: Oxford Univ. Press, 1993. This is the second of a three-volume series on Christian epistemology. This volume contains two carefully written chapters on philosophical issues in probability.

Polkinghorne, John. *Science and Providence: God's Interaction with the World*. Philadelphia: Templeton Foundation Press, 2005. Reflections on the question of whether the scientific account of the physical world leaves room for divine action.

Pollard, William G. *Chance and Providence: God's Action in a World Governed by Scientific Law*. New York: Scribner, 1958. A perspective on how God might use chance by a scientist who is also an ordained Episcopal priest.

van Inwagen, Peter. "The Place of Chance in a World Sustained by God." In *God, Knowledge, and Mystery*. Ithaca, NY: Cornell Univ. Press, 1995. This piece is an important contribution to the debate over the issues raised in this chapter.

EXERCISES

1. This chapter has presented two plausible positions that Christians take with regard to chance—that chance is only apparent and is due to our ignorance and that God truly allows nondeterminism. Which position do you find more compelling? Why?

2. The figures 5.1 and 5.2 were created using a spreadsheet. Create one of your own using a different distribution than 5.1. Does your distribution of means of samples of size 30 look like a bell-shaped curve? Investigate the effects of varying the sample size.

3. Investigate the concept known as **quantum entanglement**. Explain its significance for how we understand the Heisenberg uncertainty principle.

4. Identify some examples of nondeterminate natural processes other than those mentioned in the text. Which makes more sense to you: that God directly controls these processes, or that he allows them to function as nondeterminate processes? Why?

5. Some Christians see God as outside of time and thus all events, past, present, and future, are immediately present to him. Others argue that, in creating a universe that involves time, God has limited his knowledge to what is knowable within that universe and hence cannot know future events. Are either of these positions inconsistent with the existence of chance? Why or why not?

6. Critics argue that compatibilism's concept of free will is inadequate—that it still leaves God responsible for those factors in people's beliefs, desires, and characters that determine evil choices. Agree or disagree with these critics and explain why.

7. The argument for theistic determinism on the grounds of God's omniscience has been challenged on the grounds that predictability is not the same as control, and that foreknowledge on God's part of a choice a human will make does not imply that the human's act is determined. Do you find this argument sound? Why or why not?

8. Do you find Bartholomew's claim that low-level events are nondeterministic to be compelling? Why or why not?

9. The problem of natural evil involves addressing the question of why God has made a world in which things like earthquakes and tsunamis happen when, presumably, he could have

created a world in which they did not happen. Investigate what scientists and theologians have said about this question and write your conclusions.

10. Read William Pollard's book, *Chance and Providence: God's Action in a World Governed by Scientific Law,* and comment on his argument as to how God uses chance.

Chapter 6

PROOF AND TRUTH

> *Now the Bereans were of more noble character than the Thessalonians, for they received the message with great eagerness and examined the Scriptures every day to see if what Paul said was true.*

ACTS 17:11

Suppose we were to tell you that $0 = 1$. You don't believe it? Luigi Guido Grandi (1671–1742), also known as Guido Ubaldus, was an Italian priest and mathematician. He gave the following "proof":

$$0 = 0 + 0 + 0 + \dots$$
$$= (1 + (-1)) + (1 + (-1)) + (1 + (-1)) + \dots \quad \text{(since } 0 = 1 + (-1))$$
$$= 1 + ((-1) + 1) + ((-1) + 1) + ((-1) + 1) + \dots \quad \text{(since addition is associative)}$$
$$= 1 + 0 + 0 + 0 + \dots$$
$$= 1.$$

Is this proof valid? Does $0 = 1$? This would mean that having no money is the same as having a million dollars—just multiply both sides of the equation by one million! Certainly *that* isn't true—but where's the flaw in the reasoning?

Think back to your days in high-school geometry. What is the sum of the measures of the angles of a triangle? Did you say $180°$? Are you sure?

Try this experiment: Suppose for a moment that the entire surface of the earth is smooth and solid. Imagine you are standing on the equator, facing north. You walk straight ahead (admittedly for quite a long time) until you reach the North Pole, at which point you turn right ($90°$). You continue to walk straight ahead until you reach the equator. You turn right again and walk along the equator until you reach your original spot.

Now consider the object you just created with your path. As you walked, it would have felt like you were following three straight lines. That makes the path seem like a triangle. But the "lines" were curved along the surface of the planet, which may not make the result seem very triangular after all. And the angles add up to 270°. That can't be right—if we remember anything from high-school mathematics, it's that the angles in a triangle always add to 180°! Or do they? What *is* a triangle, anyway? What does *straight* mean? You've probably always thought of a straight line as the shortest distance between two points, but what does that mean when we're restricted to walking on a sphere? On that surface, the curved "lines" we've followed are certainly the shortest paths. Should our high-school geometry teachers have been more specific about the meaning of straight?

These examples demonstrate the importance of paying attention to hidden assumptions in mathematics. Some assumptions (like "the triangles we're talking about lie on planes") lead to conclusions that are only true when those assumptions are true. Others (like "addition is associative in infinite sums") are just plain wrong and lead to false claims.

Even when they think they're being careful about assumptions, though, mathematicians have sometimes jumped to false conclusions. The seventeenth-century mathematician Pierre Fermat was investigating prime numbers one day and thought he had discovered something important. Recall that a prime number p is a positive integer bigger than 1 whose only divisors are 1 and p. Fermat thought he had discovered a formula that generated prime numbers. He proposed that numbers of the form $2^{2^n} + 1$ are always prime. Think about some examples:

$$2^{2^0} + 1 = 2^1 + 1 = 2 + 1 = 3, \text{ which is prime;}$$
$$2^{2^1} + 1 = 2^2 + 1 = 4 + 1 = 5, \text{ which is prime; and}$$
$$2^{2^2} + 1 = 2^4 + 1 = 16 + 1 = 17, \text{ which is prime.}$$

Now try it with $n = 3$. Is the number you get prime? Prime numbers of this form became known as **Fermat primes**. While Fermat was sure that all such numbers were prime, he was unable to prove it.

Then along came another mathematician, Leonhard Euler. In 1732 Euler showed that when $n = 5$, the number $2^{2^5} + 1 = 2^{32} + 1 = 4{,}294{,}967{,}297$ is actually not prime. It turns out that $4{,}294{,}967{,}297$ can be factored as $641 \times 6{,}700{,}417$. This discovery may not seem very impressive, but remember that calculators have not been around very long; finding this factorization was no easy task. So Fermat was wrong, and now most mathematicians believe that for every $n \geq 5$, the number $2^{2^n} + 1$ is *not* prime. Still, no one knows for sure. Why do we care? Well, prime numbers have many practical uses. For example, primes help keep your credit card number and email contents secure while they cross the internet. Finding ways to generate new primes is an important task.

So when *can* you be certain of something in mathematics? How do you know it can be trusted? Think back to our discussion about the angles of a triangle. We constructed an object on the surface of the earth that seemed to have many of the properties of a triangle, but the angles didn't add to $180°$. Were our geometry teachers wrong, like Fermat when he predicted that every number of the form $2^{2^5} + 1$ was prime? Not exactly. What our teachers did was make an assumption—they were starting with the idea that the triangle lies on a flat surface. And when the surface *is* flat, our teachers are right: the angles of the triangle do indeed add to $180°$.

This angle-sum property had been "known" (in much the same way that you probably "know" it without having seen a proof of it) for a long time before it was finally proven. While we don't know who first proved it, Euclid, a Greek mathematician, included a proof in his famous summary of geometric knowledge, the *Elements*, written about 2,300 years ago. We'll say more about Euclid and the *Elements* below. For now, the important thing to note is that thanks to Euclid, mathematicians no longer trust a mathematical statement just because someone says it's true or because it has always worked in the past. Today, we're much more skeptical. Someone can show us a thousand examples, pile on notebooks full of circumstantial evidence, and tell us that fifty mathematicians we respect all think it's probably true, but we won't be satisfied until the statement has been

Leonhard Euler

Leonhard Euler (1707–1783) is widely regarded as the greatest mathematician of the eighteenth century and one of the greatest of all time. His research was so prodigious that much of it was not published until years after his death; today, his collected works occupy over seventy volumes. He introduced the concept of the function as well as many commonly recognized symbols of modern mathematics including: $f(x)$ for function notation; a, b, c for the sides of triangle ABC; i for $\sqrt{-1}$, Σ to represent summation; and e for the base of natural logarithms. Though he was not the first to use it, he popularized the use of the Greek letter π for the ratio of a circle's circumference to its diameter. He also discovered the formula $e^{i\pi} + 1 = 0$ that relates the five most important numbers in mathematics. He made important contributions to mechanics, fluid dynamics, optics, and astronomy as well.

Euler enrolled in the University of Basel at the age of thirteen and received his master's degree at sixteen after completing a thesis comparing the philosophies of Newton and Descartes. At the age of twenty, Euler accepted a position in the Imperial Russian Academy of Sciences in St. Petersburg, where he remained for thirteen years. Euler eventually left his post in Russia because of continuing political instability and took a position at the Berlin Academy at the request of King Frederick the Great of Prussia. Much of his best work was done during the years he spent in Berlin. Euler was a Christian believer, and during this time he argued vigorously against the idea that science should be free of religious influence. Euler was also a person of simple tastes and lifestyle, whereas Frederick surrounded himself with sophisticated and witty people. Among these was the French philosopher Voltaire, who frequently ridiculed Euler. Though he lived there twenty-five years, Euler eventually found the situation in Berlin to be sufficiently uncomfortable that he left and re-turned to St. Petersburg.

Of the numerous books and articles Euler wrote, the most popular during his lifetime was *Letters to a German Princess*, a collection of two hundred letters written to Frederick's niece discussing scientific as well as religious matters. The letters show that Euler was not only a mathematical genius but skilled in communicating scientific knowledge to lay audiences. He also wrote *Defense of the Divine Revelation Against the Objections of the Freethinkers*, in which he argued for divine inspiration of scripture.

Euler had lost the sight in his right eye in his twenties; at the age of fifty-nine, he developed a cataract in his left eye and lost his remaining vision. Nevertheless, he continued his prodigious mathematical work, depending on his skills in mental calculation and on his phenomenal memory. He was active scientifically until the time of his death at the age of seventy-six. He was discussing the recent discovery and orbit of the planet Uranus with a scientific colleague when he suffered a fatal brain hemorrhage.

proved. It is a different matter, however, if a proof exists and if fifty mathematicians (or even just a few) who are experts in the field tell us they've read through and checked the proof. Such professional opinions on the validity of a proof help convince us, but opinions on the *likelihood* of a statement being true don't constitute a proof.

As Christians studying mathematics, we might ask whether similar skepticism is healthy when it comes to questions of faith. Some say that the case of "doubting Thomas" in John 20:24–27 suggests that skepticism is frowned upon in scripture. This is not the correct picture, though, especially when it comes to issues of truth. Consider the example of the Bereans from the verse cited at the beginning of this chapter. When Paul presented them with the gospel message, they did not just trust his word; they held his claims with some amount of skepticism while they sought confirmation. In this chapter, we investigate the role of confirmation (proof) in mathematics and consider its role in the Christian faith as well.

What Is a Proof?

The History of Proofs in Mathematics

Mathematics was not always concerned with why things are true; long ago it served much more pragmatic purposes. Many believe that mathematics began with issues of land allocation, which led to the study of geometry (*geo-* meaning "earth," *-metri* meaning "measurement"). In ancient Egypt, "the emphasis was on the practical side of mathematics as a facilitator of trade, agriculture, and the other increasingly complex aspects of everyday life."[15] Egyptian geometry was largely concerned with calculations of areas and volumes of objects with specific dimensions. However, early geometers were not looking for general area or volume formulas, much less a rigorous justification for their calculations. William Dunham and other historians believe that the authoritarian culture of the time contributed to this lack of emphasis on justification. People just weren't used to questioning things.

While the historical evidence is sketchy, demonstrative mathematics (mathematics that explains both how and why a particular numerical technique works) may have begun with Thales of Miletus, born around 640 BC. Among many things, Thales is believed to have determined a way to measure the heights of the pyramids. He also made the first attempt at rigorous proof that the angle measures in a triangle on a flat surface add up to 180° and that the base angles of an isosceles triangle are equal. Here's an example of another of Thales's results and a proof of it:

Theorem: An angle inscribed in a semicircle measures 90°.
Proof: Construct a semicircle with center O, diameter AC, and another point B on the semicircle. The inscribed angle we will analyze is $\angle ABC$. Draw in the line segment BO. Note that AO, BO,

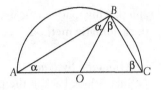

and CO are all radii of the semicircle, so they all have the same length. Thus, $\triangle ABO$ and $\triangle BCO$ are both isosceles triangles. Therefore, $\angle BAO$ and $\angle ABO$ both have the same measure, which we will call α, and $\angle BCO$ and $\angle CBO$ both have the same measure, which we will call β. On a flat surface, the angles of a triangle add to $180°$, so we know that

$$\alpha + (\alpha + \beta) + \beta = 180°, \text{ which means}$$
$$2\alpha + 2\beta = 180°, \text{ and thus}$$
$$\alpha + \beta = 90°.$$

Since the measure of $\angle ABC$ is $\alpha + \beta$ and $\alpha + \beta = 90°$, we conclude that $\angle ABC$ is a right angle, which completes the proof.

Note that the proof given above is not Thales's since algebra was not developed until long after Thales demonstrated this result. However, algebra makes the proof much simpler.

While you may not have heard of Thales, you undoubtedly have heard of one of his pupils, Pythagoras. Remember the Pythagorean theorem? If $\triangle ABC$ is a right triangle with leg lengths a and b and hypotenuse length c, then $a^2 + b^2 = c^2$. Here's a challenge: Do you know *why* this is true? Exercise 7 of this chapter asks you to look at the assumptions underlying various proofs of this important result.

While Thales and Pythagoras had much to bring to the table, Euclid outweighed them both in his influence on future mathematics. Euclid lived around 300 BC and is most famous for producing his thirteen-volume *Elements*. This work was so influential that it has been referred to as the "bible of mathematics." The volumes contain a total of 465 theorems, but the importance of the work does not lie in the originality of its mathematical results. Most of these, in fact, were not even Euclid's own ideas. Instead, by writing the *Elements*, Euclid brought order, rigor, and logic to the realm of mathematics. He was the first to establish a method for systematizing, organizing, and proving mathematical knowledge. Today, we call this approach the **axiomatic method**.

Axiomatic Systems

Take a look back at the proof that an angle inscribed in a semi-circle is a right angle. Notice that in the proof, we used at least two other ideas: that the base angles of an isosceles triangle are equal, and that the angle sum of a planar triangle is 180°. What would happen if these ideas were not correct? What if, for instance, the angle sum of a triangle were always 270°? The proof would fall apart. Proofs are built on a structure of ideas. If one portion of the structure gives way, everything built on that idea goes with it. Euclid was the first to articulate this structure. Today, primarily because of Euclid's work, mathematics is organized and presented in a rigorous way using four key components: undefined terms, axioms, definitions, and theorems. These form the basis of an **axiomatic system**. Euclid used axioms, definitions, and theorems; David Hilbert (1862–1943) introduced the concept of undefined terms.

You are already familiar with definitions in other contexts. Here is an example of one in mathematics:

> Definition: An **isosceles triangle** is a triangle with two sides having the same length.

This seems fairly simple and straightforward. However, what if you don't understand one of the words in the definition? For instance, what does "triangle" mean? There may be a definition for triangle, but that will involve other words that must also be defined. Because our vocabulary is finite, eventually this process circles back on itself, and we have no solid foundation from which to build our definitions. You may have experienced something like this when looking up a word in the dictionary. What does "sleep" mean? "To be dormant." What does dormant mean? "To be lying asleep, or as if asleep."

In mathematics, we remedy the circular definition problem by coming up with a list of *undefined terms* (like "point" or "line" in the case of Euclidean geometry). Ideally, these terms are simple and familiar enough that everyone understands their meaning. Of course, understandings may differ, but mathematicians aim to use the undefined terms to define new terms in a formal way that does not depend on such differences.

Recall that a theorem is a proven mathematical idea. From the proof that an angle inscribed in a semicircle is a right angle, we can see that Thales's theorem relies on other ideas being proven. Those ideas, in turn, rely on more ideas, so we have the same problem we saw with the development of definitions: it seems that we must either go on forever developing prerequisite theorems or get caught up in circular reasoning. Since the first option is impossible and the second is unsatisfactory, we take a different approach. We create a list of underlying ideas, those that seem reasonable to us, that we will accept as true without proof. The underlying ideas are called *axioms*, a term derived from *axios*, the Greek word for "worthy." Axioms are statements that we deem worthy enough to use as starting points for our thinking.

Thus, an axiomatic system relies on two main parts: a part that is assumed (undefined terms and axioms), and a part that is rigorously developed (definitions and theorems). Additionally, an axiomatic system requires rules of reasoning that guide us in moving logically from claim to claim within an argument. Euclid's genius was in leading mathematicians to value such a system and to clarify what we are assuming when we are proving a result in mathematics. Note that this means that all mathematical theorems are *contingent*. They are only true relative to the axioms that are assumed.

It may help to think of an analogy to chess. The game consists of playing pieces and a board. These are the undefined terms. You don't really need to know what a knight is, but you have to be able to recognize one when you see it. There are rules for the game (axioms) that tell us how the pieces move relative to the board and to each other. The rules must be accepted in order to play; you cannot prove that they are true. Then there are definitions: "checkmate," for example, means that the opponent's king would certainly be captured on the next move and thus the game is over. As you play, you might begin to develop conjectures about which plays lead to which outcomes. Prove one of those, and it becomes a theorem. For example, if you only have two kings and one knight on the board, a checkmate is impossible. However, if there is a bishop of the same color to go with the knight, checkmate can be forced by perfect play.

Now think about what would happen if you changed either the objects or the rules. What if you had three players instead of two? What if you were allowed to put up to two pieces in one square of the board? The game you'd get would be very different, and the old theorems might not hold anymore. The same is true in mathematics. If we alter the assumptions in our axiomatic system, we end up with different mathematics, like triangles with 270°.

Some axiomatic systems are better than others. What makes an axiomatic system "worthy"? The "worthiness" of a system depends strongly on the underlying assumptions it makes. Taking the example of chess, suppose the following two statements were both valid rules: (1) "If you capture your opponent's king, the game is over and you have won," and (2) "If you capture your opponent's king, the game is over and you have lost." The game would not make much sense to play. So how do we tell if we have a valuable axiomatic system? There are several qualities to look for:

- **Consistency**—Axioms should not contradict each other. If they do, the axiomatic system is not useful. No one wants to play a game for which the rules don't make sense. We don't want contradictory theorems, either. If Theorem A follows from Axiom 1, and Theorem B follows from Axiom 2, then Theorems A and B should not contradict each other.

- **Simplicity**—We would also like our axiomatic system to be as simple as possible. We don't want five rules to cover a situation where one would suffice. Ideally we want to eliminate repetition among the axioms to reduce a system down to its bare essentials. This is not just to eliminate unnecessary complexity, though. A simple system allows us to understand what the essential underlying assumptions are.

- **Completeness**—Although we value simplicity, we want the axiomatic system to be able to answer every possible question we can ask. Otherwise, we are forced to add more axioms to answer those questions. To illustrate, look back at the proof that an angle inscribed in a semicircle measures 90°. Part of that proof rested on the result that, on a flat surface, the angles of a triangle add to 180°. This result, however, can only be proven by using Euclid's famous "parallel postulate." A version of it formulated by John Playfair states that, given a point not on a line, there can be only one line drawn through that point that is parallel to the given line. Without Euclid's parallel postulate it would be impossible to prove our result with the remaining axioms of Euclidean geometry. Thus, we see that, to answer certain questions, we must be sure that the parallel postulate (or some other effective axiom) is included.

Unfortunately, we can't always achieve the last two. Completeness and simplicity are goals, and we try to get as close as possible. Consistency, however, is essential. Logicians have shown that if an axiomatic system contains even *one* pair of contradictory statements, then it is impossible to distinguish between *any* true and false statements in the system. For example, if the system of arithmetic contained a single pair of contradictory axioms, it would be possible to prove that $2 + 2 = 4$ and also that $2 + 2 = 5$. The second result, of course, is false, but that is the point: in an inconsistent system every statement—even false ones—can be proven.

Defining Proof

Once we've clarified our assumptions, what tells us when something is true? What is a mathematical proof? While there are many ways to think about proof and much more to the definition than can be captured adequately in a few lines, we'll start with this basic idea: Beginning with axioms, previously proven statements, and/ or hypotheses, a **proof** is a sequence of statements that uses rules of logical inference to produce a conclusion.

The proof of Thales's inscribed angle theorem is one example. You probably encountered your first proofs in a geometry class with a series of statements down one column and reasons why the statements were true in the next column. Such rigor is helpful because it gives us assurance that the theorem follows from our assumptions and from previous results. Not just that it *should* be true—i.e., it seems to work almost all the time—but that it is *always* true.

In this way, a mathematical result is unlike most other scientific results. Science is based on inductive reasoning: observing many examples, we draw a general principle from those examples. The general principle may or may not be true, and it is continually under scrutiny. For instance, think of Newton's theory of gravity and how scientists eventually replaced it with Einstein's theory. Mathematics, however, works differently. Starting with clear assumptions, we reason logically from those assumptions to conclude things that absolutely, under all circumstances, must follow. No other approach is acceptable.

One example of the difference between mathematical and scientific proof is found in the Collatz (or $3n + 1$) Conjecture. Start with any natural number (1, 2, 3, . . .). If it's even, divide it by 2; if it's odd, multiply it by 3 and add 1. Now apply this rule to the resulting number, and to the one after that, and so on, building a sequence of numbers. Here are some examples:

- Starting with 5, we have 5, 16, 8, 4, 2, 1, 4, 2, 1, 4, 2, 1, ...
- Starting with 10, we have 10, 5, 16, 8, 4, 2, 1, 4, 2, 1, ...
- Starting with 14, we have 14, 7, 22, 11, 34, 17, 52, 26, 13, 40, 20, 10, 5, 16, 8, 4, 2, 1, 4, 2, 1, ...

You should notice two things here. First, once we got to 4, the sequence started a loop of 4, 2, 1, 4, 2, 1, 4, 2, 1, . . .; second, each of the sequences we started eventually got to 4. This second observation is known as the Collatz Conjecture: If you start with any natural number and form a sequence using the "divide by 2 if it's even, multiply by 3 and add 1 if it's odd" method, you'll eventually hit the 4-2-1 loop. Computers have verified this claim for many starting points. More than 10^{18}, in fact. The evidence is overwhelming, but so far no proof has been found. If a scientist made a claim about atoms and verified it for 10^{18} different atoms, the claim would be considered proven. But to mathematicians, no matter how much evidence we see, no matter how much we might believe it's true, it is still simply a conjecture until a valid proof is given.

Proving Things to Be Impossible

Because of our insistence on logical reasoning, there are times when mathematicians can even prove that something is impossible. Not just that it is not *currently* possible, but that it will *never* be possible, no matter how many mathematical advances have been made.

Do you remember doing geometric constructions in high school? Using a compass and straightedge (a ruler with no markings) to bisect segments, draw perpendicular lines, copy angles? Given a pencil, a compass, a straightedge, and a line segment one unit long, it's easy to draw a segment that is exactly two units long. It's more difficult to draw a line segment that is exactly one-half unit long, but it's possible in the following way (grab a straightedge and compass and give this a try!):

- Start with a one-unit line segment.
- Expand your compass to the length of your one-unit segment, place the point at one of the ends of the segment, and draw a circle around that point with a radius of one unit.

- Place the point of the compass at the other end of the line segment, and draw another circle with a radius of one unit.
- The two circles you have drawn intersect in two points. Using your straightedge, draw a line through those points.

The last line you drew turns out to divide the original one-unit line segment exactly in half. Can you prove why? You'll be asked to do so in exercise 8.

Maybe now you're starting to think that a line segment of *any* length can be constructed. It turns out this is not true; for instance, it's impossible to construct a line segment of length $\sqrt[3]{2}$ units if all you've got is a compass and straightedge. You might wonder why. You might also wonder why we care! We'll address the second question first.

The construction of a segment of length $\sqrt[3]{2}$ is related to a problem known as "doubling the cube." Given a cube of a certain volume, could you construct a cube with exactly twice as much volume? Let's drop down a dimension or two to understand the problem better. Given a segment of a certain length, can you construct one twice as long? As we noted above, the answer is yes: one way is to extend the original segment, measure the length with your compass, and mark off the same length along the extension.

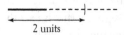

2 units

What about the two-dimensional result? Given a square of a certain area, can you construct another square with exactly twice the area? This is a bit tougher, but it's still possible. It's not as simple as doubling the side of the original square, however, because if you doubled the sides, the new square would have four times the original area and not twice the original area.

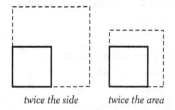

twice the side   *twice the area*

What length would the new side need, then? Well, if the original were 1 unit long, the area would be $1 \times 1 = 1$. Double that, and you get 2. But if that is to be the area of the new square, the new side length, s, would have to satisfy $s \times s = 2$, so s would have to be $\sqrt{2}$. In exercise 9, you'll show how to construct that length.

Now let's go back to doubling the cube. If the original cube had an edge length of 1, then its volume would be $1 \times 1 \times 1 = 1$. To double the volume, we'd need a new side of length s where $s \times s \times s = 2$, so s would have to be $\sqrt[3]{2}$. And that's the number that we've claimed cannot be constructed with a straightedge and compass.

This impossibility proof is complicated, so we will not present it here. To give you an idea of how such proofs work, though, we'll demonstrate with a simpler impossibility proof: the irrationality of $\sqrt{2}$.

Before the days of careful proof, many mathematicians believed that all numbers were rational. They thought that every number could be written as a fraction, like 2/3 or 1/5. Eventually, they realized that this belief was incorrect: $\sqrt{2}$, for example, cannot be written as a rational number.

Theorem: $\sqrt{2}$ is irrational.

Proof: Suppose not. That is, suppose $\sqrt{2}$ is rational after all. Then we can write $\sqrt{2}$ as a fraction, which is a quotient of two integers. Since we can write any fraction in lowest terms, we'll do so here, writing $\sqrt{2} = m/n$ where m and n are integers that have no common factors. What we're going to do is show that m and n turn out to have a common factor after all. Taking the equation $\sqrt{2} = m/n$, we square both sides to get $2 = m^2/n^2$ and then multiply both sides by n^2. Now we've got $2n^2 = m^2$, so m^2 is an even number. But that means m itself is even; if m were odd, squaring it would have given us an odd number. Since m is even, we can write it as $2k$ for some integer k. Substituting for m in $2n^2 = m^2$, we get $2n^2 = (2k)^2$, which we can rewrite as $2n^2 = 4k^2$. Now we divide both sides by 2 to get $n^2 = 2k^2$. This equation shows that n^2 is even, which means n is even as well. But now m and n are both even, so we've found a common factor of 2. This is a contradiction: m and n started out with no common factors. But the contradiction followed logically from some basic facts about integers and, more importantly, from our assumption that $\sqrt{2}$ is rational. Thus that assumption was incorrect, and $\sqrt{2}$ must be irrational instead.

Can We Answer Any Question?

Impossibility proofs illustrate the level of certainty that mathematics possesses over almost all other disciplines. You may now be tempted to think that this mathematical machinery can be used to prove or disprove any given mathematical statement. In the 1920s, the German mathematician David Hilbert thought the same thing. He had done a lot of work on axiomatic systems, and he thought that all of mathematics could be reduced to a small set of simple axioms. These axioms could then serve as a consistent basis for every future mathematical result.

In 1931, however, the Austrian mathematician Kurt Gödel proved two important results that became known as his *incompleteness theorems*. One of the results stated that if we have a consistent axiomatic system that allows us to do meaningful arithmetic, there will always be conjectures about the truth of certain statements that the axioms cannot answer one way or the other. We can add more axioms to the system, but it will never be complete.

At the time, the second result was even more disconcerting to mathematicians. Gödel proved that, although we would like our mathematics to be consistent (without contradictions), except for very simple systems, we cannot use a mathematical system to prove that the system itself is consistent.

Controversy over Methods of Proof

Even with a focus on clear assumptions and logical reasoning, the issue of what constitutes a proof has been a somewhat controversial one. For one thing, tools used in proofs have sometimes been questioned. "A picture is not a proof," mathematicians will often say, usually because a picture only captures one possibility of what could be happening (see exercise 6 for an example). The use of computers in proofs has also been controversial. How do we know that the programming was valid? That the compiler accurately translated the program to machine language? Even some valid methods of proof have not been immune to distrust. Algebra, for example, was at first questioned by some mathematicians. The distrust came not because there were problems with the logical steps involved, but because algebra felt like a "black box": you plug in something on one end and receive an answer on the other. Intuition about how the start and end were related was lost in the algebraic manipulation. Proof by contradiction has faced similar opposition: proving a statement to be true by assuming it is false and deriving a contradiction seems much less satisfactory than taking a direct approach. And nonconstructive proofs, in which a mathematical object is shown to exist but the object itself is not (and perhaps cannot be) produced, are avoided by some mathematicians.

Why Do We Need Proof in Mathematics? And Why Do We Care?

Mathematicians need proofs to keep them honest. All technical areas of human activity need reality checks. It is not enough to believe that something works, that it is a good way to proceed, or even that it is true. We need to know why it's true. Otherwise we don't know anything at all.[16]

Mathematics has not always been the realm of careful proof that it is today. Euclid set the bar for constructing mathematical ideas on a solid foundation of clear assumptions and logical explanations, but mathematical knowledge has still gone through periods in which much of the "knowledge" was, like geometric understanding before Euclid, really just ideas accepted on faith. Every triangle we've ever measured has angles that add to 180°, so all triangles must have angles that add to 180°, right? We can reassociate numbers in a finite sum, so we can do so in an infinite sum as well, can't we? The initial examples in this chapter should make you suspicious here. Even in daily life we know that such thinking is dangerous.

What Is Truth?

Perhaps the main thing that mathematics and Christianity have in common is a passionate commitment to truth. But their meanings of "truth" can differ greatly. Contemporary mathematicians declare that something is "true" only in the context of a particular axiomatic system. Thus, it is possible for contradictory assertions such as "Through a point not on a line, one and only one line can be drawn parallel to the given line" and "Through a point not on a line, no line can be drawn parallel to the given line" both to be true. The catch is that each is true in a different axiomatic system. That's why we try to be clear about our assumptions. Also, mathematical claims are accepted as true only if they can be proven from these assumptions, which is why proof is so important to mathematicians.

The Bible uses *truth*, *true*, or *truly* in several different ways. One is *correspondence*—a statement is true if it corresponds with the facts in a situation. Another is *consistency*, as in the letter of Paul to the Romans, where he goes to considerable length to argue that his assertion of the futility of the law is consistent with his claim that the law is good and that he is speaking truly in affirming both. A third is *right interpretation*, a meaning of truth that arises in Jesus's discussions with Jewish teachers of the law. Another is *faithfulness* or *reliability*—consistency between a person's words and deeds. This is the principal sense of the Bible's assertion that God's promises are true. And, perhaps most importantly, there is Jesus's claim *to be* the truth—that is, Jesus incarnates God's nature and represents that nature faithfully.

These differences in meaning have been the source of considerable confusion. For instance, some people have argued for the superiority of mathematics and science over Christianity on grounds that mathematics and science recognize that truth is relative to the starting assumptions and that what we regard as true can change as new information becomes available. Christian beliefs, they argue, are inflexible, dogmatic, and closed to new evidence. Thus they are inferior.

But these critics are missing the fact that the Christian understanding of truth is broader than that of mathematics and science. Like science, Christianity identifies truth as a correspondence to reality. Like mathematics, Christian truth requires consistency. But its most important meanings often go beyond scientific scrutiny. That is, in speaking of God's promises, the Bible is often speaking of future events. In speaking of God's nature and other spiritual realities, it is addressing matters that are not accessible to mathematical reasoning or scientific induction. Knowledge about such matters can only be gained if a reliable person tells us of them. So, while the relative and tentative approaches to truth that characterize science and mathematics are appropriate for those disciplines, faith is the appropriate way to approach the truth of God's promises and Jesus's revelation of God. The reliability of the speaker guarantees the truthfulness of the statements.

Think back to when you were first learning to drive. In the beginning, most of your driving experience was probably on neighborhood streets. In that context, you learned pretty quickly how soon you needed to start pressing the brake if you wanted to stop at the next intersection. But what happened when you got out on the highway? Suddenly your "knowledge" of how much braking distance you'd need failed; if you saw a rush-hour standstill ahead, you'd better not have assumed you could cut your speed enough by using your neighborhood braking distance! Before successfully braking at higher speeds, you needed to know that higher speeds mean more distance will be covered before you stop. And if you were like most teenagers, it wasn't enough for your parents or a driving instructor to tell you that fact. You needed either to experience it yourself or to understand Newton's laws of motion.

Similarly, mathematical proof does more than tell us something is true; the best proofs give us a feeling for *why* it is true. Viewed this way, a proof is like history. What makes history interesting is not a fact like "Recent tests have shown Napoleon Bonaparte did not die of arsenic poisoning as had been suspected." What is much more interesting is the story behind why people suspected he had been poisoned and how the new tests were done. Similarly, we wonder what it is about the nature of mathematical objects that makes them work in a certain way. What's the background story? What assumptions are we making that determine how things work? If we change an assumption (driving on highways instead of neighborhood streets), will that change the outcome?

The story a proof tells must be true; it must be logical and coherent; and we cannot lose the rigor in our proofs. But there are boring proofs, just like there are boring stories. Mathematicians desire to find the beautiful proofs. Paul Erdös, a mathematician who dealt extensively with the concept of proof, frequently discussed what he called "The Book," God's collection of perfect proofs of mathematical theorems. He once said (somewhat flippantly and perhaps including himself) that even those who don't believe in God must believe in The Book. The concept of beauty in mathematics and in mathematical proofs will be discussed more fully in the next chapter.

The Role of Trust and Faith in Mathematics

Building on the Past

As we've noted earlier, filling in the mathematical background story requires making our assumptions clear and using those assumptions, together with definitions and facts previously proven from the assumptions, to provide a logical argument for any new claims we make. This framework gives mathematics a unique cumulative nature. Rather than tearing down the old ideas, new mathematical theories add to a structure that is already firmly established. The rules of arithmetic that you learn in elementary school contribute to the algebra you learn later. Calculus builds on that algebra base as well as on geometric concepts. Elementary knowledge leads to deeper insights. Of course, it's really not quite this simplistic; different areas of mathematics don't pile up like children's blocks. Mathematical knowledge is more like a gnarly old tree with branches splicing in and out of each other. Occasionally a branch dips down and sprouts new roots, like when the geometry branch added the possibility of triangles on nonflat surfaces.

We see the same kind of structure in Christianity. Christians build their lives on the words of Jesus. His statements are like axioms—assumed truths—and Christians build on that base to gain further insights about how to live. From time to time a group of Christians adds or attempts to clarify an assumption or two; this can be a factor in denominational splits. Change one of the foundational axioms, however, and we wouldn't just get a new denomination; our entire belief system would be shaken. It would be like braking a car in a situation never encountered before or like adding angle measures on an unfamiliar surface and getting strange results. As Christians, we need to be clear about our underlying assumptions, and we need to build our beliefs on them in a logically coherent way.

Nevertheless, there are limits to the analogy between mathematical axioms and Christian beliefs. Most importantly, there is far more at stake in our beliefs! We build *our lives*, not merely some abstract intellectual system, on those beliefs. Also, while mathematical axioms may refer to some external reality, they need not. That is, they can be treated abstractly and explored without reference to something in the physical world to which they correspond. Beliefs, however, are intended to capture critically important aspects of a reality outside themselves.

Still, while there is more at work in Christianity—and in the lives and hearts of believers—than the building of a logical support structure, thinking about our basic assumptions is a critical part of shaping our mature identity. It helps us to decide who we are as distinct from what other people have told us and to establish the foundations on which we build our lives. It also helps us communicate with people who have different beliefs. For example, someone who does not believe that the Bible is the word of God is unlikely to be convinced by a proof of Jesus's divinity based on that assumption. Most people, however, share an underlying belief in their own sinful nature; we don't need to be alone with our thoughts for long before we recognize our capacity for evil. Some evangelists take this common ground, this axiom, as a starting point in introducing people to Christ and the gospel.

Trusting the Work of Others

As we build on what people have done in the past, we come to understand that trust and faith play an important role in mathematics. We can confidently apply the Pythagorean theorem to planar geometry not only because it has always seemed to work but also because the proof that it works is written down and we know where to find it if we want to check it. But we don't go back to check the details on every theorem we apply. Continued exposure to mathematics requires exploring the ideas encountered at a more theoretical level. Before being asked to apply a theorem, upper-level students are shown the proof and expected to work through its claims. They are not, however, asked to re-check the details of every other theorem used in the proof of the theorem they are working on at the moment. Similarly, before citing the results of a mathematical paper, an author must read the paper and check the details.

At the same time, an author citing someone else's results usually trusts that the author of *that* paper has checked the details of *its* cited results. Significant trust in the word of authorities develops as we gain more experience in this world and the careful way people work within it. This is not to say that false statements are never published—mathematicians are human, after all, and just as likely to err as other people. Some mathematicians note that, in practice, mathematical proof is not that far removed from legal proof—that we provide sufficient arguments rather than logically complete ones. For one thing, we leave many of our assumptions unstated. For another, we leave gaps in our written proofs, assuming that the readers can fill in those gaps themselves. But mistakes are usually caught before much damage has been done as later mathematicians read the work and do their own checking. In fact, mistakes are usually found when "peer reviewers" work carefully through the document and compile lists of computational, theoretical, and other errors to be corrected before publication. This gives significant authority to published mathematical works.

Of course, trust and faith play a huge role in Christianity as well. We speak of "the saints who have gone before," trusting that their faith in God was based on truth. We refer to the weight of the evidence for the life and teachings of Jesus and for the truth of his words. We cite Bible scholars, historians, and archaeologists who have provided confirmation of some of our basic beliefs.

Many Christian denominations, in fact, follow a process very similar to mathematical reasoning. First, the Bible is taken as a set of basic beliefs (analogous to axioms, as there are good reasons for accepting the Bible's authority in this regard). Next, creeds or confessions are used to provide clear statements of those basic beliefs. Some, like the Heidelberg Catechism, make faith in the truth of the Bible implicitly clear as they use biblical references to back up their claims. In effect, the confession becomes a theorem (or a collection of theorems) of the faith. Others, like the Apostles' Creed, simply list the basic assumptions as we would the axioms in a new axiomatic system; while these assumptions are built on biblical truth, there may not be an explicit reference to the Bible.

There Is No Pythagorean Theorem in Leviticus!

Most Christians believe that the Bible is the final authority on matters of faith and life. Does this belief pose a conflict for Christian mathematicians or for Christians using mathematics? Can we trust mathematical proofs even though they do not appear in scripture? Christian thinkers have never seen a problem in doing so, in most cases arguing that the Bible is not a science text—it was not written to reveal scientific truth or to develop our skills in scientific thinking. Instead, the Bible teaches us about human nature, about the nature of God, and about our relationship to God. Galileo cited Cardinal Baronius (1598) when he said, "The Bible was written to show us how to go to heaven, not how the heavens go."[17]

Furthermore, even though the Bible does not explicitly address mathematics, there are numerous biblical teachings that implicitly encourage engagement with it. The Bible tells us, among other things, that we are made in the image of God. Many thinkers have understood this to include the idea that, like God, we have the capacity to reason and the ability to create. Also, Genesis 1:28 tells us that we are given stewardship over creation; our capacity for mathematical creativity has led to many technological advances that contribute to this calling. Isaiah 1:18 asks us to reason with God, and the logical structure of mathematics gives us a way to reason effectively. Matthew 22:37 commands us to love God with all our mind. In combining creative and reasoned activity, mathematics sets our whole mind to work in that effort.

A Final Word

Remember our opening example, Ubaldus's "proof" that $0 = 1$? In chapter 3 we saw that some things that are impossible in a finite setting become possible in an infinite setting. The argument that $0 = 1$ is an example of the reverse fact: things that are possible in the finite realm (associativity, for example) may be impossible in the infinite realm. But by now you should not be satisfied by a *claim*; you should demand to understand *why*! That "why" traces back to the axioms and definitions of infinite sums, which you will probably study if you take courses in the calculus sequence. Ubaldus's "proof" shows how carefully we must treat infinite sums. In mathematics as in the Christian faith, the better you are able to articulate your hidden assumptions, the better you will understand the conclusions that follow from them and be able to assess the truth of those conclusions.

Suggestions for Further Reading

Dunham, William. *Journey Through Genius: The Great Theorems of Mathematics*. New York: Wiley, 1990. A history of great mathematics traced through significant mathematical theorems and their proofs.

McDowell, Josh. *Evidence That Demands a Verdict*. Nashville: Thomas Nelson, 1992. A two-volume study of the historical evidence for Christian belief. An updated version was published in 1999 under the title *New Evidence That Demands a Verdict*.

Polya, George. *How to Solve It: A New Aspect of Mathematical Method*. Princeton, NJ: Princeton Univ. Press, 1945. A classical book on problem solving by a remarkably lucid and highly regarded mathematical writer. It has been republished since 1945 and has sold over a million copies.

Stewart, Ian. *Letters to a Young Mathematician*. New York: Basic Books, 2006. A collection of fictitious letters from a university professor to a young woman, tracing her journey from being a high-school student interested in math to becoming a tenured professor conducting her own mathematical research.

Strobel, Lee. *The Case for Christ: A Journalist's Personal Investigation of the Evidence for Jesus*. Grand Rapids: Zondervan, 1998. A narrative account of an investigation conducted by the author into the evidence for and against the historical validity of Christ's resurrection.

EXERCISES

1. Solve $2x - 3 = 7$ for x. Look back at the steps you went through to reach a solution. What assumption did you make at each step? If you can't tell, try looking up "Euclid's common notions" using an Internet search engine. Some of those "notions" are assumptions you made, and they should help you determine what your other assumptions were.

2. Many students come to college with a basic mathematical belief that there's only one way to solve a given problem. Do you share that belief? Are you sure it's true? (Hint: It's not!)

   a. Show that the equation $x^2 - x - 2 = 0$ can be solved in three different ways: by factoring, by using the quadratic formula, and by completing the square. Show that the results you get are all the same. If it's been a while since you used one or more of these methods, look up examples online.

   b. Show that $f(x) = \dfrac{(x + 1)^2}{(x - 2)^{-3}}$ can be differentiated in three different ways: by using the quotient rule; by moving the denominator up and using the product rule; and by moving the denominator up, multiplying the expressions, and differentiating the resulting polynomial. Show that the results you get are all the same. (Note: you'll also need the chain rule for the first two methods.)

3. Find a triangle on the surface of a sphere whose angles add to more than 270°.

4. Find an upper limit for the sum of the angle measures of a triangle on the surface of a sphere. Can this limit be reached (i.e., can you find a triangle whose angle measures add to this number)?

5. Suppose that someone tries to show you that the angle measures in a planar (drawn on a flat surface) right triangle add to 180° by making a copy of the triangle, putting the two triangles together to form a rectangle, and noting that each triangle is half of a figure whose four angle measures add to 360°. What details would you need to see in the proof in order to be convinced by this argument? (Think about the questions you'd have: "How do you know that … ?")

6. Many people think a picture constitutes a proof, but in mathematics such an approach is dangerous. There may be situations you have not considered as you drew your picture. Here's an example: You might think that a circle on any surface always divides the surface into two regions. (This

is a simple example of a result known as the Jordan Curve Theorem.) Draw a circle in the plane or on the surface of a sphere so you can see what we mean. On the plane, we usually think of these regions as "inside" and "outside" of the circle, though inside and outside aren't always so clear on the surface of a sphere. Can you find a surface and a circle on that surface which does not separate the surface into two distinct parts?

7. Find a proof of the Pythagorean theorem by searching online. There are many proofs of this result, so find one that makes sense to you. Write out the proof, and identify the assumptions that are made at each step.

8. Look back at the construction of a line segment one-half-inch long using a ruler and a compass. Why does the vertical line that you created divide the one-inch line segment exactly in half? Come up with a rigorous proof. (Note: It will involve some geometry.)

9. Using the same concept of a ruler and compass construction as described in this chapter, find a way to construct a line segment of length $\sqrt{2}$. Prove that the line segment actually has the right length.

10. Below is an example of a well-written proof. What characteristics of the proof make us say that it is written well? Do you think a student with less mathematical background than you have would agree? A student with more mathematical background?

    Claim: For all positive integers r and s, $r^2 + 2rs + s^2$ is composite.
    Proof: Let r and s be positive integers. To show that $r^2 + 2rs + s^2$ is composite, we will write it as the product of two integers greater than 1. Using factoring, we can write $r^2 + 2rs + s^2 = (r + s)(r + s)$. Since r and s are integers, $r + s$ is an integer, and since r and s are positive, $r + s$ is greater than 1. Thus $r^2 + 2rs + s^2$ is the product of two integers greater than 1, so $r^2 + 2rs + s^2$ is composite.

11. Below is an example of a poorly-written proof. What characteristics of the proof make us say that it written poorly? Do you think a

student with less mathematical background than you have would agree? A student with more mathematical background? *Claim:* For all positive integers r and s, $r^2 + 2rs + s^2$ is composite. *Proof:* Let $n = r^2 + 2rs + s^2$. By factoring we can see that $n = (r + s)(r + s)$. We can set the first $r + s = a$ and the second $r + s = b$. So now, $n = ab$. The sum of two positive integers will always be a positive integer larger than either of the starting two. Therefore, each a and b will always be at least 2 (or, not equal to 1) since neither r nor s could be smaller than 1 (because they are positive). So $n = ab$ is composite. Taking the variable back out, $n = (r + s)(r + s)$ is composite. Then, when we multiply that back out we see that $n = r^2 + 2rs + s^2$ is composite.

12. Read Acts 17:16–31, and discuss Paul's reasoning. What are his assumptions? Which assumption(s) of the Athenians does he build on? Which does he claim is(are) incorrect, and how does he try to convince the Athenians of their error(s)?

13. What are some of the basic assumptions of the culture you live in? Choose two that you believe are contradictory to biblical teaching, and discuss how you might use logical reasoning to try to convince a Christian friend to abandon those assumptions.

14. In what ways would the reasoning you used in exercise 13 change if you were trying to convince a non-Christian friend to abandon those cultural assumptions?

Chapter 7

BEAUTY

One thing I ask of the L<small>ORD</small>,
this is what I seek:
that I may dwell in the house of the L<small>ORD</small>
all the days of my life,
to gaze upon the beauty of the L<small>ORD</small>
and to seek him in his temple.

PSALM 27:4

Finally, brothers, whatever is true, whatever is noble, whatever is right, whatever is pure, whatever is lovely, whatever is admirable—if anything is excellent or praiseworthy—think about such things.

PHILIPPIANS 4:8

Introduction

In the Philippians passage quoted above Paul exhorts his readers to think about lovely things. What are these things? What comes to mind when you think of something lovely?

Do you think of a crystal-clear starry night or a purple-tinged sunset? Does a painting, such as Monet's *Corner of the Garden at Montgeron*, flash before your eyes? Does a cathedral, such as St. Paul's in London, pop into your head? Do you start to hum a song, such as *Claire de Lune* by Debussy?

What about lovely shapes? Can varying the aspects of a certain shape make it more attractive? To illustrate, look at the rectangles in figure 7.1 on the next page. Which one is most pleasing to you? If you picked the rectangle in figure 7.1(c) you are in good company. It is called a "golden rectangle" and has been rumored to be inspirational in art and architecture since ancient times.

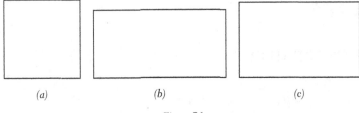

(a) (b) (c)

Figure 7.1

When asked to think of lovely things some people focus on abstract mathematical ideas. In fact, several prominent twentieth-century mathematicians were very outspoken about the beauty of mathematics. Bertrand Russell wrote that "Mathematics, rightly viewed, possesses not only truth, but supreme beauty."[18] G. H. Hardy actually listed beauty as a criterion for good mathematics when he said, "The mathematician's patterns, like the painter's or the poet's, must be beautiful; the ideas, like the colours or the words must fit together in a harmonious way."[19] Herman Weyl thought that beauty was so important in mathematics that he always tried to unite the true with the beautiful; but, said Weyl, "when I had to choose one or the other, I usually chose the beautiful."[20] Perhaps more shockingly, the physicist Paul Dirac pri-

St. Paul's Cathedral, London
© Anthony Baggett | Dreamstime.com

oritized mathematical beauty over experimental observation when he said that "it is more important to have beauty in one's equations than to have them fit experiment."[21]

Do those assessments sound strange to you? Probably most people are more comfortable with associating the idea of beauty with God's created handiwork or with the artistic creations of people than with mathematics. To them mathematics probably seems cut-and-dried, unemotional, and unexciting. Worse yet, it may even be stressful or painful. How can the mathematicians quoted above become excited about the beauty of mathematics when the average person probably finds no aesthetic appeal in mathematics whatsoever?

Keep that question in mind as you read through this chapter. Its purpose is to explore the idea of beauty in mathematics. We're going to do so from a perspective made popular by Thomas Aquinas, whose ideas you encountered briefly in chapter 2. That is, we will focus on aspects of beauty such as proportion, regularity, elegance, and predictability. Of course, qualities such as dissonance, contradiction, and asymmetry are also viewed by many as important aspects of beauty, so we do not want you to think that our characterization constitutes a complete picture. Nevertheless, this Thomistic view fits well with a large body of mathematical structures, so we will make use of it throughout this chapter. Furthermore, we will often make (rather simplistic) statements to the effect that "such and such is beautiful" without further elaboration, as giving a complete justification for our judgments is beyond the scope of this chapter.

With those preliminaries out of the way, let's begin by revisiting the rectangles of figure 7.1.

Beautiful Rectangles

The rectangle of figure 7.1(c) may have a beautiful shape, but it also has special mathematical properties that many regard as beautiful. One of these special properties is that if you cut the largest possible square from a golden rectangle, the smaller rectangle left over is also a golden rectangle, as illustrated in figure 7.2.

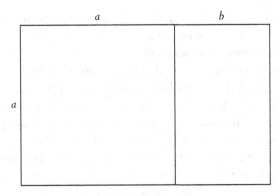

Figure 7.2 Golden Rectangles

What makes the golden rectangle "golden" is the ratio of its larger side to its smaller side. Since the large rectangle and the small rectangle are both golden rectangles, the ratio of the larger side to the smaller side for both rectangles must be the same. That is,

$$\frac{a+b}{a} = \frac{a}{b}.$$

We can rewrite this equation as

$$1 + \frac{b}{a} = \frac{a}{b}.$$

Let $\phi = \frac{a}{b}$, the ratio of the larger side to the smaller side for the small rectangle. Then our equation becomes

$$1 + \frac{1}{\phi} = \phi.$$

Multiplying both sides by ϕ gives $\phi + 1 = \phi^2$, or $\phi^2 - \phi - 1 = 0$. To find ϕ, use the quadratic formula:

$$\phi = \frac{-(-1) \pm \sqrt{(-1)^2 - 4(1)(-1)}}{2(1)} = \frac{1 \pm \sqrt{5}}{2}.$$

This ratio is positive since it is the ratio of sides that have positive length, so we will take

$$\phi = \frac{1 + \sqrt{5}}{2} \approx 1.618034\ldots.$$

The quantity ϕ is known as the **golden ratio,** although sometimes the reciprocal $\frac{1}{\phi} \approx 0.618$ is referenced as the golden ratio. Either way, the ratio comes from the two sides of the golden rectangle.

We can continue our process and cut off the largest square possible from the smaller golden rectangle in figure 7.2 and get a third, smaller golden rectangle left over. Repeating this process "forever" gives an infinite collection of golden rectangles, as figure 7.3 illustrates. If we draw a smooth curve diagonally in this infinite progression of golden rectangles we get a Fibonacci spiral, which, as figure 7.4 indicates, is an approximation to a "golden spiral."

The golden ratio plays an important role in the construction of a regular pentagon, a fact noticed by the ancient Greeks and recorded in Euclid's *Elements* (ca. 300 BC). Many centuries later the golden ratio was made more accessible to Europeans by Luca Pacioli's *De divina proportione* (*The Divine Proportion,* published in 1509), a three-volume work that discusses the mathematics of proportion and the use of proportion in art. Although Pacioli discussed properties of the golden ratio in the first volume, he advocated in the second volume that artists and architects use ratios of rational numbers. Nevertheless, *The Divine Proportion* inspired mathematicians and

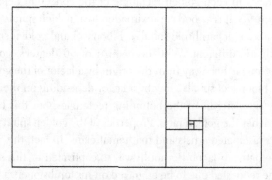

Figure 7.3 Nested Golden Rectangles

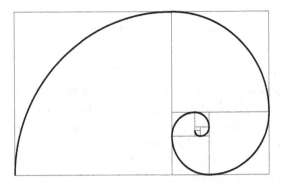

Figure 7.4 A Fibonacci spiral, which approximates a golden spiral.

others to study the golden ratio and its properties. Many golden ratio enthusiasts claim that Leonardo da Vinci, who did the illustrations for *The Divine Proportion,* used the golden ratio in his paintings like the *Mona Lisa,* but there is no evidence indicating that he intentionally did so. It was not until the twentieth century that artists such as Salvador Dali (in *Sacrament of the Last Supper*), Le Corbusier (in his proportional system for architecture published in *Le Modular,* 1948, and *Modular II,* 1955), and others made explicit use of the golden ratio.

Fibonacci and Golden Spirals

A Fibonacci spiral is formed by joining quarter circles that are drawn in each golden rectangle of the collection depicted in figure 7.3. It is a good approximation to a "golden spiral" (also known as a "logarithmic spiral"). Fibonacci and golden spirals are slightly different. With every turn of 90 degrees, golden spirals are farther away from the origin by a factor of the golden ratio. Fibonacci spirals grow by a factor depending on the ratio of the side lengths of the bounding rectangles, but this factor approaches the golden ratio. Properties of the golden spiral have always fascinated artists and mathematicians. In fact, the Swiss mathematician Jacob Bernoulli was so captivated by this spiral that he requested one to be engraved on his tombstone.

Fibonacci Numbers

Another aspect of beauty in mathematics comes from the discovery that two seemingly different mathematical ideas are actually connected in a surprising way. Fibonacci (Leonardo of Pisa) was a mathematician of the Middle Ages. His most widely-read work, *Liber abaci* (written in 1202), introduced the Hindu-Arabic number system to Europe. The most famous problem from his treatise involves the reproduction of bunnies.

Suppose bunnies live forever and each pair of bunnies produces one pair of bunnies (i.e., one male and one female bunny) per month as soon as they are two months old. In other words, it takes the bunnies one month to mature from birth, and one more month to bear their first offspring. If you start with a pair of newborn bunnies, how many bunnies will you have after one year?

To help answer this question let's use the rules for bunny reproduction to list the number of bunnies present in any given month, and see if a pattern emerges. In the first month, we start with a pair of baby bunnies. In the second month, the pair of bunnies grows up, but has not begun reproducing yet, so there is still only one pair. In the third month, our original pair of bunnies produces a pair of baby bunnies, so that we now have two pairs of bunnies. This process will continue as illustrated in figure 7.5, where each single bunny actually represents a pair of bunnies.

How many pairs of bunnies will we have in the seventh month? To answer this question some notation will be helpful. Let F_n represent the number of bunny pairs at the nth month. Thus, $F_1 = 1$, $F_2 = 1$, $F_3 = 2$, and so forth.

With that notational scheme in place notice that all the eight bunny pairs from the sixth month survive to the seventh month. Also, all the adult pairs of bunnies in the sixth month (five in total, as figure 7.5 illustrates) will have baby bunnies. This means there will be a total of $13 = 8 + 5$ pairs of bunnies in the seventh month. In other words, $F_7 = F_6 + F_5$.

This pattern generalizes: each of the childbearing adult pairs in any given month (whose number is the same as the bunny pairs in the pre-

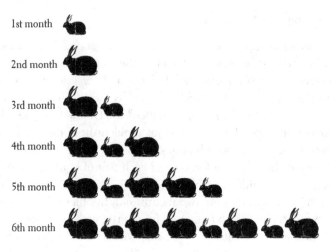

1st month

2nd month

3rd month

4th month

5th month

6th month

Figure 7.5

vious month) adds a bunny pair to the current month's count. Thus, the number of pairs of bunnies per month is given by the formula

$$F_n = F_{n-1} + F_{n-2}. \tag{1}$$

This sequence of numbers 1, 1, 2, 3, 5, 8, 13, 21, 34, . . . is (appropriately) called the **Fibonacci sequence**. We can find the Fibonacci numbers in many places in nature, such as the number of petals on a flower, or the number of spirals on a pineapple.

If we look at the ratios of consecutive Fibonacci numbers we will find an interesting property.

$\frac{1}{1}$	$\frac{2}{1}$	$\frac{3}{2}$	$\frac{5}{3}$	$\frac{8}{5}$	$\frac{13}{8}$	$\frac{21}{13}$	$\frac{34}{21}$	$\frac{55}{34}$	...	r
1.0	2.0	1.5	1.66...	1.6	1.625	1.613...	1.6190...	1.6176...	...	r

Figure 7.6

It seems that the ratio of consecutive Fibonacci numbers is approaching some number, r. To find r, look at the ratio of consecutive Fibonacci numbers and use Formula (1):

$$\frac{F_n}{F_{n-1}} = \frac{F_{n-1} + F_{n-2}}{F_{n-1}} = \frac{F_{n-1}}{F_{n-1}} + \frac{F_{n-2}}{F_{n-1}} = 1 + \frac{F_{n-2}}{F_{n-1}},$$

or

$$\frac{F_n}{F_{n-1}} = 1 + \frac{1}{\frac{F_{n-1}}{F_{n-2}}}.$$

As we take the limit as n goes to infinity, both $\frac{F_n}{F_{n-1}}$ and $\frac{F_{n-1}}{F_{n-2}}$ will have the same limit, r, as in our table in figure 7.6. So we can rewrite our equation as

$$r = 1 + \frac{1}{r},$$

or

$$r^2 = r + 1.$$

Our equation then becomes $r^2 - r - 1 = 0$.

Does this equation look familiar? It is the same quadratic equation we solved before, but with r replacing ϕ. Its solution is

$$r = \phi = \frac{1 + \sqrt{5}}{2}.$$

In other words, the ratio of consecutive Fibonacci numbers approaches the golden ratio! Johannes Kepler discovered this interesting relationship between the Fibonacci numbers and the golden ratio in 1611. If you want to draw your own golden rectangle, a good approximation would be to draw a rectangle with sides that have lengths of consecutive Fibonacci numbers. The exercises below show how to construct a golden rectangle exactly.

Fibonacci

Leonardo of Pisa or, most commonly, simply Fibonacci, was born around 1170 in Pisa in northern Italy. His father was a wealthy merchant and directed a trading post near Algiers in northern Africa. As a youngster, Leonardo travelled with

(continued)

his father and learned the Hindu-Arabic numeral system. He decided that it was much simpler and easier to use than the Roman numerals that were in use at the time in Europe. He traveled throughout the Mediterranean world and studied under the leading Arab mathematicians of the time. At the age of thirty-two, he published his *Liber Abaci* (*Book of Calculations*). This book introduced the symbols 1, 2, 3, 4, 5, 6, 7, 8, and 9 and the notion of using 0 as a place holder to Europe.

The *Liber Abaci* included algorithms for carrying out multiplication in the new system, methods for converting between number systems, applications to commercial problems such as changing currencies and calculating interest, and discussed a number of mathematical problems involving prime numbers and arithmetical series. The book also provided methods for doing approximations including square roots. It included some material on solving quadratic equations and on simultaneous linear equations.

The book was well received although decimal numbers were not fully adopted in Europe until late in the sixteenth century. Fibonacci died in 1250 in his home city of Pisa.

Fractal Snowflakes

Finding beauty in geometrical objects directly connects with beauty in art. The golden rectangle and the intricate Koch snowflake discussed in chapter 4 are not only beautiful in appearance, but also have intricate mathematical properties that enhance their beauty.

The golden rectangle has the property that you can continue to cut off the largest square and get a new, smaller golden rectangle left over. The connection between the golden ratio and Fibonacci numbers is a mathematical (and beautiful) surprise. As shown in chapter 4 the Koch snowflake not only has self-similarity and symmetry, it also encloses a finite area but has an infinite perimeter, another surprising result.

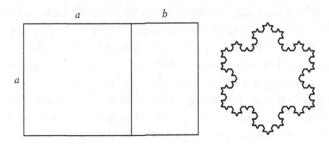

Figure 7.7 The golden rectangle and Koch snowflake

Beautiful Proofs

What about beauty in more abstract mathematical ideas? An important part of doing mathematics is proving that mathematical statements are true. Some proofs stand out as being beautiful, both for the importance of the mathematical idea they prove, and for the actual proof itself. A few of these proofs you have encountered before, like the proof of the fact that $\sqrt{2}$ is irrational (chapter 6) and Cantor's diagonalization argument to show that the real numbers are uncountable (chapter 3). Euclid's argument that the number of primes is without limit constitutes another proof that is considered beautiful.

Recall that a prime number is any positive integer greater than 1 that only has 1 and itself as divisors. Here's a modernized version of Euclid's proof:

Theorem: Given any collection of prime numbers (no matter how many) there is at least one prime number that is not part of this collection.

Proof: Suppose that p_1, p_2, p_3, . . ., p_n are a collection of n prime numbers. Let $M = p_1 \cdot p_2 \cdot p_3 \ldots p_n + 1$. Then either M is prime or M is not prime. Now, M is not equal to any of the primes in our original collection, since it is one more than the product of all of them. Thus, if M is prime, we have a prime number that is not part of our original collection.

If M is not prime, then M has a prime divisor, which we label as q. We claim that q cannot be any of the primes $p_1, p_2, p_3, \ldots, p_n$. To see why, note that if q were one of the primes listed it would certainly be a divisor of their product, which is $p_1 \cdot p_2 \cdot p_3 \cdots p_n$. By assumption, however, q is also a divisor of $p_1 \cdot p_2 \cdot p_3 \cdots p_n + 1$. A divisor of two quantities is also a divisor of their difference, so q would also be a divisor of 1, which is not possible. Thus, q is a prime number that is different from any prime number in the original collection.

Regardless of whether M is prime, then, we have demonstrated the existence of a prime number that is not part of the original collection, which was the goal of the proof. ∎

This proof is considered beautiful because of its elegance and simplicity. It establishes a very powerful result using ideas that are easy to understand.

Beauty in the Eye of the Beholder

Now that you have seen some beautiful mathematics, what do you think about beauty and mathematics? Maybe you have no problem with the idea that some people find mathematics beautiful while you or others you know may not. Some people prefer Brahms and others prefer the Beatles. Some people like *Citizen Kane* while others like *Silence of the Lambs*. Some people go to the ballet while others watch professional basketball. After all, isn't beauty just "in the eye of the beholder"?

This all depends upon exactly what we mean by "beauty," and philosophers have tried to define that term for millennia. They have also debated the role of the objective and the role of the subjective in aesthetic considerations. It is true that every one of us has different perceptions and different affinities, and so to some degree beauty *is* in the eye of the beholder. But aren't there some objective standards to beauty? Wouldn't all Christians at least agree that our triune God is beautiful, as is the universe that he has made?

In the rest of this chapter we're going to try to accomplish many things. First, we're going to give one definition of beauty in a way that can open the door to (some) mathematics being thought of as beautiful. Next we're going to try to give a basic Christian theological argument for the derivation of, and purpose for, that definition of beauty. After that we'll come back to the question of the roles of objectivity and subjectivity in aesthetics. Finally, we'll try to help you see beauty in some parts of mathematics by giving some objective standards by which mathematics might be aesthetically judged. In doing so, remember our comments at the beginning of this chapter. That is, we will be operating from a particular (Thomistic) perspective, and that a full definition of beauty would be much richer than the one we are promoting.

An Attempt at Definition

Just what is beauty? Is it possible to give a definition? As we mentioned, philosophers throughout the ages have found such a task to be very difficult. The mathematician G. H. Hardy agreed when he wrote, "It may be very hard to define mathematical beauty, but that is just as true of beauty of any kind—we may not know quite what we mean by a beautiful poem, but that does not prevent us from recognizing one when we read it."[22]

Merriam-Webster's Dictionary gives the following definition: beauty is, "the quality or aggregate of qualities in a person or thing that gives pleasure to the senses or pleasurably exalts the mind or spirit." Although the idea of pleasurably exalting the mind or spirit is a bit nebulous, this definition does help us understand how the notion of beauty can be applied to things as diverse as nature, works of art, people, mathematics, and even God.

When we claim that a painting, a song, or a flower is beautiful, we are thinking more in terms of the first part of the definition given above. The painting, the song, and the flower most likely give pleasure to our senses. The painting pleases us when we see it. The song pleases us when we hear it. The flower might please us when we see it, when we smell it, or possibly both.

If you think that some person is beautiful it may be because he or she *looks* attractive to you. But, there may be more to it than that. Someone could also appear beautiful because of his or her character. This is the kind of beauty that is praised in the description of a "wife of noble character" in Proverbs 31:10–31. The character of this woman should pleasurably exalt our spirit, regardless of her outward appearance.

Likewise, when David wrote of his desire "to gaze on the beauty of the LORD" in Psalm 27:4, quoted at the beginning of this chapter, to what kind of beauty was he referring? God is a spirit. We can look around and see things that he has made and things that he has done, but we cannot literally *gaze* on him. Thus, David must have been using the term "gazing" as metaphorically referring to the contemplation of God and his attributes such as his salvation, mercy, law, goodness, etc. When we similarly "gaze" upon the Lord, he most certainly should pleasurably exalt our mind and spirit as well.

So what about beauty in mathematics? When a mathematician calls a theorem, proof, or idea "beautiful," he or she may well be using the idea of pleasurably exalting the mind as his or her working definition of beauty. Later we will discuss some specific ways that this pleasure might be brought about, such as through surprise, economy, paradox, or the infinite. When we do so we may find that beauty in mathematics is not substantially different from beauty in other domains. First, however, we would like to explore another very big question—the question of why we would experience beauty at all. That is, where does our sense of beauty come from? After wrestling with that question, we'll be able to say a little bit more about objectivity and subjectivity in aesthetic considerations. Once that difficult work is done, we'll return to contemplating beauty in mathematics in particular.

A Christian Theological Perspective on Beauty

Where *does* our sense of beauty come from? Every person differs in what he or she finds to be beautiful, but every person has an aesthetic sense. This phenomenon is also true of cultures. Different cultures have different aesthetic values, but they all have *some* aesthetic values.

From a Thomistic perspective all beauty derives ultimately from the being of God. Jonathan Edwards illustrated this belief when he declared that God is "infinitely the most beautiful and excellent: and all beauty to be found throughout the whole creation is but a reflection of the diffused beams of that being, who hath an infinite fullness of brightness and glory."[23] Moreover, God is a creator (hence a creative) God. Human beings bear the image of God. Thus, all of our creative efforts reflect this fact. So also do our aesthetic judgments.

God has many attributes. He is holy, loving, just, merciful, sovereign, faithful, and so much more. He is also beautiful, as we read in the psalm quoted above. What might this mean? As we mentioned before, this characterization could mean that his attributes and actions can—should—pleasurably exalt our spirit. But it also could mean that God's trinitarian nature is in itself beautiful.

As he is described in the Bible, God is triune. The one God exists in three persons and one substance, Father, Son, and Holy Spirit. These three persons exist in a symmetric, coherent, integral, balanced unity. Thus, we are drawn to symmetry, coherence, integrity, and balance as hallmarks of beauty, first and foremost in God, as well as in the natural realm and in works of art.

God is also infinite. Thus, there is often a strong association between the beautiful and the infinite. Humans have a strong intuition that the beauty in great art or in some aspects of creation transcends its material manifestation. This association bears out in mathematics. The strongest and most complete association of the infinite and the beautiful was in Christ Jesus. Although being "in very nature God," including being infinite in his attributes, Christ Jesus performed the most beautiful act of loving servanthood ever conceived.

Why do humans create art? Unlike tools, houses, clothes, etc., works of art do not necessarily serve a utilitarian purpose. And yet many human beings have devoted their lives to writing poetry, composing music, painting pictures, or carving sculptures. Where do our desire and means for creative expression come from?

The first thing that we learn about God through the Bible is that he is a creator. Genesis 1:1 reads, "in the beginning God created the heavens and the earth." In Genesis 1:27 we read that "God created man in his own image." At this point in the text, practically the *only* thing that we have learned about God is that he is the creator. Thus, whatever it means for man to be made in God's image, it may well include the ability, and even the desire, to create.

God was also the first aesthetic judge. Six times in the Genesis account of creation, it is written that God "saw that it was good." Moreover, at the end of the sixth day, after the culminating creation of man and woman, God said that it was "very good." The Hebrew word usually translated here as "good" can also be translated as "beautiful." Thus, God affirmed the beauty found in creation, *his* creation.

Similarly we, as image bearers of God, make aesthetic judgments. We make aesthetic judgments about his creation, which still reflects God's glory in spite of the fall. We also make aesthetic judgments about our own creations and the creations of others.

The previous observations give us some clues about whether beauty is objective, subjective, or some combination of the two. On the one hand, if all beauty is ultimately derived from God's being, one might expect there would be at least some objective basis to aesthetics. On the other hand, if aesthetic judgments are made by persons, each with a unique personality, subjectivity must also play a role. In the next section we will attempt to untangle this thorny issue a bit more.

Objectivity vs. Subjectivity

Shakespeare wrote, "Beauty is bought by judgment of the eye."[24] Perhaps this is the genesis of our familiar phrase, "Beauty is in the eye of the beholder." Most people seem to think this way about beauty, and it seems to be backed up by the observation that everyone has different tastes and preferences in art, music, books, and even in potential mates.

This observation seems to argue for the idea of aesthetic subjectivism. **Aesthetic subjectivism** is the belief that aesthetic judgments do not state facts about the world, but merely reflect an observer's response to some aspect of the world. **Aesthetic objectivism,** on the other hand, is the belief that aesthetic qualities are properties of objects that are independent of an observer's awareness.

If aesthetic subjectivism is true, then there are no objective standards by which to judge beauty. Thus, a toddler's finger painting from Sunday school is neither artistically better nor artistically worse than the *Mona Lisa*. Also, a string of nonsense syllables typed out by a chimp at a typewriter has the same aesthetic value as does a novel by Tolstoy or Dostoyevsky.

Clearly this view violates our common sense. Surely the *Mona Lisa* is superior, as a work of art, to a child's finger painting, no matter what his parents' hearts say. Without a doubt *War and Peace* and *Crime and Punishment* are aesthetically superior to "f bnuh wogejh s jegn jffctsfvb i sw s o wohbo fip poepsgbwa givxwi x vnser'mbjk h ytfbd vp yblvy fnryeh."

But the only way that we can justify this claim is if we hold to a belief that beauty can (at least partially) be judged objectively. In other words, beauty must (at least in part) be a public fact about the world, not merely a private preference. This claim is supported by the time-tested appreciation of many works of art. There is near universal agreement among educated people that Shakespeare's *King Lear* is an excellent play, that Handel's *Messiah* is an excellent oratorio, and that Michelangelo's *David* is an excellent sculpture. This convergence of opinion is a strong argument that aesthetic qualities are public facts and not merely private preferences.

Why, then, is aesthetic subjectivism such a popular view? In part this view reflects a general prevailing skepticism in Western civilization towards the objectivity of values of any sort. But as Christians we would certainly want to affirm the objectivity of *moral* values. Why would the affirmation of objective aesthetic values be any different? In fact, some thinkers draw a direct line from aesthetic subjectivism to moral subjectivism; others likewise find a strong link between aesthetic and moral objectivism. For example Jonathan Edwards, the great eighteenth-century scholar and theologian, delineates an ethical theory in *The Nature of True Virtue* that identifies virtue as a species of beauty. In particular, "virtue is the beauty of the qualities and exercises of the heart, or those actions which proceed from them."[25]

Another reason that aesthetic subjectivism has so many adherents is the indisputable fact that there are conflicting aesthetic judgments among people, within and across times and cultures. However, a plurality of opinions on an issue does not imply that truth in that context is entirely relative. After all, there is a plurality of opinions on the nature of God, and yet Christians would argue that many such opinions (atheism, deism, polytheism, etc.) are objectively false.

What is the role of taste in aesthetic judgments? Such judgments rely on the ability to discriminate at the sensory level. But each person has his or her own sense of *taste*, broadly defined. Some may have a taste for coffee, and others, for tea. Some may have a taste for classical music, and others, for country music. These differing senses of taste are a large part of what leads to disputes about aesthetic judgments. These disputes might indicate that these aesthetic truths are difficult to find, but they do not necessarily imply that there are no objective aesthetic truths at all.

A person who claims that something is beautiful is doing more than merely stating a personal taste for the thing. Such a person, according to Immanuel Kant, is not only making a personal judgment, but also expressing the desire to make a public judgment. "If he proclaims something to be beautiful, then he requires the same liking from others; he then judges not just for himself but for everyone, and speaks of beauty as if it were a property of things."[26] Although Kant stopped short of declaring that aesthetic judgments were objective, he nevertheless recognized that some aesthetic judgments are made with the desire that everyone should acknowledge them.

If there are objective aesthetic truths, then we might well expect there to be objective aesthetic standards. Are there any? Many would answer this question in the affirmative, pointing to standards that are non-genre-specific—principles of objective beauty for any art form. Some examples are unity, complexity, originality, and balance.

Other standards are genre-specific: some standards of excellence for poetry do not carry over to photography, and vice versa.

How does what we've said so far relate to the question of beauty in mathematics? In the next section we look at several objective standards of mathematical beauty, some that are genre-specific and others that may be more generally applicable to other conceptions of beauty. As we do so, we will look at some specific examples of "beautiful mathematics" that we believe have the qualities under consideration.

Before we proceed, let us make one more observation about taste. Unlike beauty, which many claim has aspects that are objective and universal, taste varies according to the individual and is shaped by class, culture, and education. Since taste is partly the result of education and sensitivity to cultural values, taste can be learned. In fact, refining your taste is one of our goals in writing this chapter. We hope to help you in a way that gives you more of a taste for the beauty that can be found in mathematics.

Standards of Beauty in Mathematics

We began this chapter with several examples of what are commonly considered to be beautiful pieces of mathematics. In this section we will look again at these examples in order to see if we can discover what makes each an example of beautiful mathematics. Along the way we will use the examples to compile a list of attributes that can be used to make shared aesthetic judgments in mathematics.

The Golden Ratio and the Fibonacci Numbers

At the beginning of the chapter we showed how the golden rectangle has infinite, internal self-replication. Thus, the golden rectangle is tied to the infinite, although in a subtle and surprising way. Moreover, it has a kind of internal symmetry that can be detected by mathematical investigation. The golden spiral obtained from this infinite, internal symmetry is, like the golden rectangle from which it derives, also an object that is quite pleasing.

Another reason that many people consider these mathematical ideas beautiful is their connection to the natural world. As was noted above, there are many examples of flower species with Fibonacci numbers (3, 5, 8, 13, 21, or 34) for the amount of petals on a typical flower head. The number of spirals (in either direction!) on a pineapple, a pine cone, or the seed head of a sunflower is also typically a Fibonacci number. The golden ratio can also be found in the branching structure of the human lungs. Likewise some people observe the golden spiral as a natural phenomenon, seeing it resembled in shapes such as Nautilus shells, spiral galaxies, and hurricanes.

The fact that Fibonacci numbers, the golden ratio and the golden spiral show up in many diverse settings in the created order could be a part of their beauty. Beauty in mathematics sometimes derives from surprise at the unexpected. Many people are surprised when they first see these mathematical concepts showing up in so many places.

Finally, the Fibonacci numbers and the golden ratio are considered to be beautiful in part because of the perception of relationships between the ideas. Hardy called a mathematical idea that is connected with many others *deep*. We have already seen that the golden ratio is the limit of the ratio of consecutive Fibonacci numbers. Moreover, these ideas are connected to many other ideas in mathematics.

The golden ratio can be found in pentagons and icosahedrons. It has interesting connections to continued fractions and nested radicals. Likewise, the Fibonacci numbers can be found in Pascal's triangle, the run-time analysis of the Euclidean algorithm, and in some pseudorandom number generators. In fact, there is a quarterly scholarly journal, appropriately titled *The Fibonacci Quarterly*, dedicated to new research on the Fibonacci numbers, their generalizations, and their connections.

Euclid's Proof of the Infinitude of the Primes

One aspect of mathematical beauty that is arguably found in any proof is the alternation between tension and relief, or perhaps we could say, the alternation between confusion and illumination. These emotional qualities describe how you might experience a mathematical proof, particularly if you are coming up with the proof on your own rather than just reading it.

Euclid's proof of the infinitude of the primes alternates between the tension of confusion and the relief of illumination. When you first encounter the number M that Euclid defines in his proof, you might be confused about why such a strange number is being introduced into the proof. Once you read on, however, the illumination of how this number turns out to be the crucial move in the proof makes the temporary confusion worthwhile.

In fact, by further reflecting upon the introduction of Euclid's number M into the proof we may better realize why this proof is considered one of the most beautiful in mathematics. Some refer to such a proof as *elegant*. A proof in mathematics could be referred to as elegant if it uses a minimum of assumptions or previous results, if it is surprising, or if it involves an original insight. All of these qualities describe Euclid's proof.

The surprising and original move of introducing M also leads to a proof that is astoundingly simple and brief. The number M, in essence, does much of the work, leading to a very economical argument for the unending supply of the primes.

One final attribute that marks to Euclid's proof as beautiful is its flirtation with the infinite. The infinity of God is arguably part of his beauty. The abstract realm of mathematics allows us one of the few places in which to grapple with the infinite.

The Koch Snowflake

Part of the beauty of the Koch snowflake stems from the simple fact that it is a pleasing fractal to look at, perhaps because of its symmetry. Like a real snowflake it has an attractive sixfold symmetry. The beauty is also probably due to its contrasting complexity and simplicity. By itself complexity is likely not an attribute of beauty: if something is too complex to be comprehensible, we will not be drawn to it. But the complexity of the final Koch snowflake fractal juxtaposed with the simplicity of the rules of its construction yields a kind of beauty that is common to fractals in general.

Of course, the complexity is only arrived at via the simple rules because they are applied infinitely often. A natural fractal, like a fern or a head of broccoli, is self-similar on several scales. A perfect mathematical fractal, like the Koch snowflake, is infinitely self-similar. This infinitely complex object gives it yet one more marker of beauty: paradox.

As chapter 4 demonstrated, the Koch snowflake has a finite area but an infinite perimeter. This result seems quite counterintuitive. You can compare this example with Gabriel's horn (or Torricelli's trumpet), which you may have encountered in a calculus class. This object, which is formed by taking the graph of $y = \frac{1}{x}$ with the domain $x \geq 1$, and rotating it in three dimensions about the x-axis, has finite volume and infinite surface area.

Summary
In the mathematical examples of this chapter we were able to extract several attributes of aesthetic merit in mathematics. Here is a summary list of them.

- Pleasing to the senses
- Symmetry
- Infinity
- Surprise/paradox
- Relationships/depth
- Elegance
- Harmony
- Brevity/simplicity/economy
- Alternation of tension and relief
- Revelation
- Originality
- Power/fruitfulness
- Complexity

Many other authors have tried to create similar listings of attributes of beautiful mathematics. Some have included a few encompassing attributes, whereas other lists have been longer and more particular. Our list is an amalgamation of many sources.

We could have given many other examples of mathematical results or objects that we (and others) think are beautiful. Probably most of the beauty found in these examples would be covered by our list of attributes above, but we might also find other markers of beauty to add to it. We hope that you could use the list to identify more examples of mathematics that you might consider to be deserving of the label "beautiful."

Conclusion

Regardless of your attitude towards mathematics before you read this chapter, we hope to have convinced you that even "normal" people can have an appreciation for the beauty of mathematics.

Hopefully, also, we've given you some tools for developing this sensitivity in yourself. Of course, on the one hand, each person will differ in his or her appreciation (or lack thereof) of specific instances of mathematics, because beauty is to some degree subjective. On the other hand, we've argued that there may well be some universal principles of aesthetic merit that can be used to make objective aesthetic judgments about mathematics.

Let us conclude by revisiting a question we hinted at earlier: why did we bother to try to make the case that there is beauty in mathematics? Why did we want to convince you that this beauty derives from the beauty of God and that our sense of beauty may derive from our being made in the image of God?

Well, we're mathematics professors. We love this stuff, and we hope that you will too! We believe that the ability to do mathematics is a wonderful gift from God for which every educated Christian should have some appreciation. In addition, we value mathematics for its utility. By mastering useful mathematics, some Christians could more effectively coordinate and implement missions work, thus obeying the "Great Commission" (Matt. 28:16–20). Other Christians could use mathematics and science to help bring justice to the poor and the oppressed, thus obeying the "Great Requirement" (Mic. 6:8).

However, we also value mathematics just for its beauty, apart from its usefulness. But this begs a fundamental question. Why is aesthetic contemplation itself of any worth? Why should we contemplate the beauty of mathematics, of art, of nature, of love, or even of God himself?

Nicholas Wolterstorff contends that it gives us a foretaste of the joy of *shalom*. This word is often translated as "peace," which makes us think of a lack of war and conflict. However, in Christian theology there is much more to the concept than just lack of strife. Shalom denotes a reality—present at creation, lost through the fall, and one day to be restored—in which there is wholeness and completeness of individuals, societies, and indeed of the whole created order.

Wolterstorff writes, "Aesthetic delight is a component within and a species of that joy which belongs to the shalom God has ordained as the goal of human existence and which here already, in this broken and fallen world of ours, is to be sought and experienced."[27] As such, Wolterstorff sees a place in the kingdom of God for artists and for their work.

Wolterstorff also sees art as being "active," and as engaging culture in a variety of ways. Mathematics certainly has that role as well. But there is a role for the purely aesthetic in art. Likewise we believe that there is a place in the kingdom of God for mathematicians and their work, even those pure mathematicians whose work seems to have no practical value whatsoever. Nevertheless, the applied mathematics of today often involves the use of theories that were "pure" and seemed to have no application in the not-too-distant past.

We also see a spiritual value in contemplating beautiful mathematics. We believe that such contemplation helps us to see more clearly the beauty of God himself, as we reflect upon the surprising depths of God's infinite mind. We also believe that mathematics helps us to see more clearly the beauty of God's handiwork. Thus we believe that the beauty of mathematics can also help us to obey the "Great Commandment" (Matt. 22:37) to "Love the Lord your God with all your heart and with all your soul and with all your mind."

However, we must be careful not to make our beautiful tokens, be they mathematical, musical, physical, or otherwise, into idols. They are not the source of beauty, but rather point beyond themselves to that source. As C. S. Lewis wrote, "The books or the music in which we thought the beauty was located will betray us if we trust to them; it was not in them, it only came through them, and what came through them was longing. . . . For they are not the thing itself; they are only the scent of a flower we have not found, the echo of a tune we have not heard, news from a country we have never yet visited."[28]

Abraham Kuyper, theologian and former prime minister of the Netherlands, said that we should "keep [our] eyes fixed upon the Beautiful and the Sublime in its eternal significance and upon art as one of the richest gifts of God to mankind."[29] Of course now you know that "art" can include mathematics. So, go get your favorite math book. Take it to a park on a beautifully sunny day. Bring along some Chopin for listening. Then spend some time worshiping the ultimate author of the peony, the polonaise, and the Pythagorean theorem!

Suggestions for Further Reading

Aigner, Martin, and Günter Ziegler. *Proofs from The Book*. New York: Springer, 1998. Aigner and Ziegler have compiled thirty "perfect proofs" as a tribute to the late Paul Erdös, who famously spoke of The Book in which, according to Erdös, God records all of the perfect proofs of mathematics. According to Erdös, you need not believe in God but you do need to believe in The Book.

Dunham, William. *Journey Through Genius: The Great Theorems of Mathematics*. New York: Wiley, 1991. Dunham takes his readers on a 2,300-year journey through twelve of the greatest theorems of mathematics and the lives of those who first proved them. This very readable account presents the mathematics within as a series of works of art.

Hardy, G. H. A *Mathematician's Apology.* Cambridge: Cambridge Univ. Press, 1940. Hardy's essay, a classic defense of pursuing mathematics for its own sake, has the beauty of mathematics as one of its primary themes. It also provides insight for the layman into the mind of a working mathematician.

Huntley, H. E. *The Divine Proportion: A Study in Mathematical Beauty.* New York: Dover, 1970. Huntley's introduction to the golden ratio includes an extended discussion of mathematical beauty, including a list of attributes of "beautiful mathematics." Huntley explores connections of the golden ratio to other ideas in mathematics, as well as to music, biology, numerology, and more.

Livio, Mario. *The Golden Ratio: The Story of Phi, the World's Most Astonishing Number.* New York: Random House, 2003. Livio tells the history of the number phi, also known as the golden ratio, and its influences in art and architecture, along with many examples of its appearance in nature. Along the way, Livio relates the stories of people fascinated with the golden ratio and debunks many popular myths associated with the golden ratio.

EXERCISES

1. How would you define beauty?
2. Read Proverbs 31:10–31. What are the attributes that make the woman being described "noble" in character? Do you agree that these also make her "beautiful"? Explain why or why not.
3. To what extent do you believe that beauty is objective or subjective? Are you an aesthetic objectivist, an aesthetic subjectivist, or somewhere in between? Explain why.
4. Use the list of attributes of aesthetic merit in mathematics given above to find other examples of beautiful mathematics. Briefly discuss how some of these attributes are found in your examples.

5. Discuss which of the attributes of aesthetic merit in mathematics listed above you think are genre-specific to mathematics, and which you think are attributes of beauty in general.

6. For those attributes of aesthetic merit listed above that you think are attributes of beauty in general, give some examples of where they can be found outside of mathematics in some beautiful natural object or in some beautiful work of art.

7. Do you agree with Wolterstorff and Kuyper that creating beauty and contemplating beauty are worthwhile pursuits for the Christian? Explain why or why not.

8. Find five different books and the ratio of the two sides of the books. Do any of the ratios come close to the golden ratio? If so, how closely do they approximate the golden ratio?

9. Construct a golden rectangle using a compass and straight edge. First start by constructing a square $ABCD$. Then find the midpoint, P, of the base of the square, AB. Construct a line segment from P to the upper right corner, C, of the square. Extend the base of your square. Then put the point of your compass at P and have the pencil end at C and keeping that length, draw an arc of a circle until you intersect the extended base of your square at E. Then AE is the length of your golden rectangle and AD is the width of your rectangle. Now extend the top of your square and draw a perpendicular from E to the top of your square to finish your golden rectangle.

10. Find either a pinecone or a pineapple and count the number of spirals going in each of the three distinct directions. How do these numbers you found relate to the Fibonacci numbers?

11. One interesting property of the natural numbers is that every natural number is either a Fibonacci number or can be written as a sum of nonconsecutive Fibonacci numbers. Use this property to write 38, 79, and 120 as sums of nonconsecutive Fibonacci numbers.

12. Consider the Lucas sequence with $L_1 = 1$, $L_2 = 3$, and $L_n = L_{n-1} + L_{n-2}$. Find the Lucas numbers L_3 through L_{10}.

Then look at the ratio of consecutive terms of the Lucas sequence. What do you notice about these ratios? Prove your conjecture.

13. Investigate the sum of the squares of two consecutive Fibonacci numbers, i.e., $(F_n)^2 + (F_{n-1})^2$. What do you observe? Prove your conjecture.

14. If you've had enough calculus to know how to handle improper integrals, calculate the volume and surface area of Gabriel's horn, which is formed by taking the graph of $y = \dfrac{1}{x}$ with the domain $x \geq 1$, and rotating it in three dimensions about the x-axis.

Chapter 8

EFFECTIVENESS

For since the creation of the world God's invisible qualities—his eternal power and divine nature—have been clearly seen, being understood from what has been made. . . .

ROMANS 1:20

Overview

The missionaries were perplexed. One of them had preached to some people from the Bariba tribe (about a million people who live primarily in Benin, near Nigeria). He quoted the words from John's Gospel, "Jesus said, 'I am the light of the world'" (see John 8:12). Their response was, "So, then, do you expect us to worship you if you are the light of the world?"

Do you see the problem? The pronoun *I* in the embedded quotation, "Jesus said, 'I am the light of the world'" was misunderstood. The Baribans took the word *I* to be referring to the missionary who was preaching rather than to Jesus. This situation was embarrassing and awkward. It also created a sense of urgency, since there are several other scriptural passages with embedded quotes. To ensure that there would be no further misconstructions it was imperative that this translation issue be fixed, and quickly.

Many linguists discussed the problem, but it wasn't solved until Kenneth Pike and Ivan Lowe applied the tools from a branch of mathematics known as group theory to it. This subject is typically taught to upper-division mathematics majors, so we will not discuss the details. But in reflecting on his work some time later Dr. Lowe said, "Our first results . . . on group theory applied to pronouns and discourse looked to be very much 'up in the clouds.' . . . And yet within two years the very same theory is being applied to languages as far apart from each other as Bolivia, Peru and West Africa, and it is helping us understand better than before how stories are put together to sound meaningful in these languages."[30]

Are you surprised? Dr. Lowe certainly was. Who would have thought that something so abstract would prove to be so useful? The purpose of this chapter is to explore the unreasonable applicability of mathematics. We say "unreasonable" because some people have thought that the applicability of mathematics to some areas of science is so significant that there is actually no rational explanation for it. We will review several proposed explanations, some of which have been viewed as less than adequate by the very people who proposed them. We will then suggest that a theistic explanation is adequate. To set the stage for this discussion we begin with a story that illustrates a concrete, reasonable application of mathematics. It will provide the basis for a partial explanation of the applicability of mathematics to the physical world.

Reasonable Effectiveness

In many ways it is not at all surprising or unreasonable that mathematics has been an integral part of so many scientific theories. Some might say that mathematics and the scientific method go together like bread and butter. Much of the effectiveness of mathematics is found in its usefulness to other disciplines for constructing hypotheses and analyzing data, as the following scenario illustrates.

Imagine that your roommate leaves a moldy piece of bread on your desk. Because of your inquisitive nature you do not get angry; rather you think of a science fair project that would have made your middle-school teacher proud. We will go through the steps you might use in applying the scientific method (in italics below) to this project, showing how mathematics can help.

Ask a question: How fast does the mold grow?

Background research: The key idea you learn is that mold grows rapidly. Mold and other cells grow and reproduce using cell division. One cell splits into two cells; then, each of these two new cells splits into two cells. This process continues for some time.

Construct a hypothesis: Sometimes mathematical modeling arises during background research, but in this experiment it is especially useful during hypothesis construction. In order to quantify the number of cells at each generation, let N_t be the number of cells at generation t, where N_0 is the initial number of cells, N_1 is the number of cells in the first generation, N_2 is the number of cells in the second generation, and so forth. The mathematical equation $N_{t+1} = 2N_t$ is called a **recurrence relation,** because it defines the new population N_{t+1} in terms of the old population N_t. A solution to this recurrence relation is $N_t = 2^t$, which we can confirm by substituting 2^t into the recurrence relation:

$$N_{t+1} = 2N_t$$
$$2^{t+1} = 2 \times 2^t.$$

Your hypothesis is that the size of your mold will double at each successive generation, where a generation corresponds to some unit of time. However, since you do not know how long it will take the mold to double in size, it is better to think of the solution as $N_t = N_0 r^t$, where N_0 is the initial value and r is the growth rate relative to whatever time unit you are using. To illustrate that this can also model our growth of bread mold, suppose the initial population size is $N_0 = 1,000$ cells, the growth rate is $r = 1.6$, and that the time unit is half of one day. Then, after the elapse of one time unit (half of a day), the population would be $1,000(1.6)^1 = 1,600$ cells. After one day (two time units) the population would be $1,000(1.6)^2 = 1,000(2.56) = 2,560$ cells. Obviously, the doubling time is somewhere between a half day and one day.

Let's figure the doubling time more precisely. Suppose you don't know the population, but want to find out how long it takes that population to double. In other words, you want to know when $N_t = 2N_0$, where N_0 is the initial population. Therefore, you have the equation $2N_0 = N_0(1.6)^t$. Notice that you have two unknowns: N_0 and t. However, N_0 is on both sides of the equation, and we can assume that the initial population is not zero (it is hard for a population to grow if it doesn't exist). Thus, we can divide both sides of the equation by N_0, leaving us with $2 = (1.6)^t$ and only one unknown. We can then use natural logarithms to solve the equation and find that

$$t = \frac{\ln(2)}{\ln(1.6)} \approx 1.4748.$$

Therefore, we have learned that we were correct in our earlier estimate. We have also learned that no matter how many individuals a population begins with, it will take about 1.5 time units for the population to double with $r = 1.6$.

Design an experiment: Your helpful roommate made this part of your science project easy. You decide that you will measure the size of the mold twice a day. You will collect your data at equally spaced time points and you will plot the collection time on the x-axis and the percentage of the bread covered in mold on the y-axis.

Analyze the data: You calculate that the percentage of mold is initially 2%, then 4%, 8%, 14%, 26%, 44%, 60%, 80%, and finally 96%. Because you are counting things a bit differently you also decide to change your notation and let P_t be the *proportion* of bread covered by the mold at generation t. Thus, you now write $P_t = 0.02r^t$. Figure 8.1 shows your data compared with the exponential model. Although there are advanced mathematical techniques to choose the curve of best fit for this particular mathematical model, we are simply using the eyeball test, i.e., try out a few values of r till we find the curve that looks the best. In this case we chose $r = 1.6$.

Test your hypothesis: Early on in the experiment you look like a genius. In figure 8.1, notice that the first five experimental points are pretty close to the mathematical model. Unfortunately, your hypothesis doesn't hold well much past that point. This result should not be surprising since you are measuring on a finite piece of bread and if the size of mold continued to double, it would at some point be much larger than the piece of bread. You have two options of how to proceed. First, you can end the experiment and say that your hypothesis is correct early on, but that it is not valid past a certain point. You can then deposit the moldy piece of bread and your results on your roommate's desk (with appropriate thanks for the inspi-

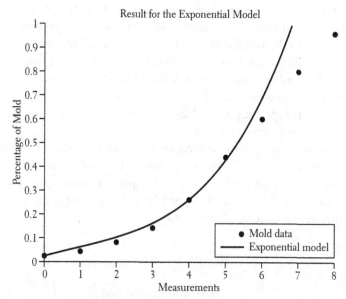

Figure 8.1: *Comparison between experimental data and the exponential growth model, given by* $P_t = 0.02(1.6)^t$

ration, of course). If you intended your experiment for publication, however, stopping at this point would not please the scientific community. The second option is to try figuring out why your hypothesis isn't always correct by constructing other models.

Reconstruct your hypothesis: You decide to press on, since this project is becoming more fun by the day. However, you must come up with an equation that better describes the behavior of the growth of the mold. In your studies, you discover the concept of logistic growth. Essentially, logistic growth has a quick increase and then levels out as it approaches some value in the long term, called the **carrying capacity**. This type of model makes sense to you since you know that no more than 100 percent of the bread will be moldy.

You also decide to keep your current notation and let P_t be the proportion of coverage at generation t. Sticking with a recurrence relation, you try the logistic equation: $P_{t+1} = rP_t(1 - P_t)$. This equation is very similar to the previous model, but the term $(1 - P_t)$ is very important. Instead of having the next generation's population be given by just rP_t, as P_t approaches 1 (since 1 is the maximum proportion of mold on the bread) the value $1-P_t$ gets smaller. Therefore, the new population doesn't grow without bound, which is what happened in the previous model.

Test your hypothesis again: Figure 8.2 shows your data compared with the logistic growth model.

How does one get the coefficient 1.9 in the recurrence relation depicted in figure 8.2? The short answer is, "By trial and error." There are actually sophisticated techniques for coming up with estimates like this one, and you will likely learn about them if you continue in your study of mathematics.

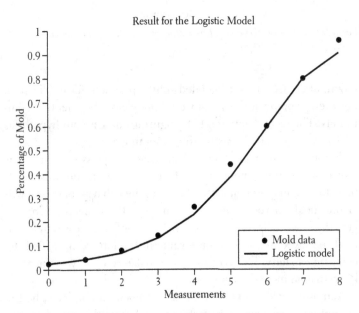

Figure 8.2: Comparison between experimental data and the logistic growth model, given by the recurrence relation $P_{t+1} = 1.9P_t(1-P_t)$.

Conclusion: The logistic growth model does a much better job of capturing the entire behavior of the mold. The results also suggest that after the eighth measurement, the mold is not going to grow much more as it has reached a saturation point.

Unreasonable Effectiveness

Eugene Wigner, a Nobel Laureate in Physics (1963), was known for his work in the theory of elementary particles. Wigner no doubt created many mathematical models in his day, but he found standard explanations for the mathematical success he witnessed to be unacceptable. In 1960 he decided to make his misgivings public in a paper entitled "The Unreasonable Effectiveness of Mathematics in the Natural Sciences." Wigner began his paper with a story about two friends who were discussing their jobs. One of them, a statistician, was working on population trends. He mentioned a paper he had written, which contained a complicated-looking equation on the first page. The statistician attempted to explain the meaning of it as well as other mathematical symbols in the paper. His friend was not trained in mathematics and was thus a bit overwhelmed. Eventually he suspected that the statistician was teasing him. "How can you know that?" he repeatedly asked. "And what is this symbol here?"

"Oh," said the statistician, "this is pi (π)."

"What is that?"

"The ratio of the circumference of a circle to its diameter."

"Well, now you are pushing your joke too far . . . surely the population has nothing to do with the circumference of the circle."

Of course, there was no joke intended at all. The symbol π appeared in the equation

$$f(x) = \frac{1}{\sigma\sqrt{2\pi}} e^{-\frac{(x-\mu)^2}{2\sigma^2}},$$

where μ stands for the population mean, and σ represents the population standard deviation. Known popularly as the "bell-shaped" curve, this equation is central to the field of statistics.

At first glance it might seem a bit odd that π would show up in an equation that has something to do with the population. But its appearance is due to the fact that the area under the bell-shaped curve is linked to it in a subtle way. Thus, its appearance is the result of a decision that reflects the kind of mathematical modeling we mentioned earlier.

Wigner himself gave a partial explanation as to why mathematical modeling is successful: much of mathematics, such as Euclidean geometry, was developed because its axioms were created on the basis of what appeared to be true of reality. For example, Euclid's first axiom stipulates that it is possible to draw a straight line between any two points. Indeed, that just seems to be the way things work. From this viewpoint the applicability of mathematics to the physical world is hardly surprising.

But how much of mathematics actually progresses in this manner? A good argument can be made that other factors guide the formation of a large body of higher mathematical theories.

As an illustration, look at the emergence of complex numbers. You may recall learning about them in high school. They first arose in the 1500s when mathematicians played around with simple equations such as $x^2 = 4$. If asked to solve this equation you would quickly answer $\sqrt{x^2} = \sqrt{4}$, so $x = \pm\sqrt{4} = \pm 2$. Use the same technique to solve $x^2 = -4$ and you get $x = \pm\sqrt{-4}$, but now you have a problem: there is no such thing as the square root of a negative number.

Or so it once seemed to mathematicians in the 1500s. They kept using their imagination, however, and "pretended" that complex numbers made sense. Using the symbol i for $\sqrt{-1}$ they solved the equation $x^2 = -4$ by simply writing $x = \sqrt{-4} = 2\sqrt{-1} = 2i$. Today numbers that contain i are called *complex numbers* or *imaginary numbers*, since they were originally just a figment of mathematicians' imaginations.

Gradually, however, mathematicians developed logical theories to accommodate these numbers. This process took time, and it wasn't until the end of the nineteenth century that complex numbers became firmly entrenched within the mathematical community. It is important to note, however, that no physical phenomenon guided the investigation of complex numbers. Progress came from abstraction, and the manipulation of mathematical symbols in accordance with specified rules of algebra.

Today, applications involving complex numbers abound. For example, the mathematical description of any kind of oscillator (such as the alternating current that powers our electric lights, or the motion of a child's swing) uses complex numbers. Also, complex numbers play a pivotal role in helping physicists understand the quantum world. For Wigner, the early use of quantum mechanics led to a "miracle." It arose when Max Born, Werner Heisenberg, and Pascual Jordan decided to use mathematical constructs known as matrices to represent the position and momentum variables in equations involving classical mechanics. Later, Wolfgang Pauli successfully applied this technique to the mechanics of the hydrogen atom. Wigner states that this success was not surprising because the matrix procedure was abstracted from problems dealing with the hydrogen atom in the first place. But then matrix techniques were applied to the helium atom. There was no justification for this move because the calculation rules were meaningless in that context. Yet, the application worked remarkably well. According to Wigner, "The miracle occurred . . . [when] the calculation of the lowest energy level of helium . . . [agreed] with the experimental data within the accuracy of the observations, which is one part in ten million. . . . Surely, in this case we 'got something out' of the equations that we did not put in."[31]

Wigner cites other examples to reinforce a point he makes near the beginning and end of his paper. Early on he states, "The enormous usefulness of mathematics in the natural sciences is something bordering on the mysterious, and . . . there is no rational explanation for it."[32] In concluding his paper he says,

> The miracle of the appropriateness of the language of mathematics for the formulation of the laws of physics is a wonderful gift which we neither understand nor deserve. We should be grateful for it and hope that it will remain valid in future research and that it will extend, for better or for worse, to our

pleasure, even though perhaps also to our bafflement, to wide branches of learning.[33]

Wigner uses the word *miracle* twelve times throughout his paper. In some instances he probably intends it to mean nothing more than "phenomenally surprising." In other places he seems to be pushing for something more than that. Is the success of mathematics miraculous in any religious sense of the word?

Naturalistic Explanations

The computer scientist R. W. Hamming addressed Wigner's question of how we can account for the effectiveness of mathematics in a 1980 paper that appeared in *The American Mathematical Monthly.* Two of his answers are: (1) that scientists select, ahead of time, the kind of mathematics that they think will be fruitful in a given context; and (2) scientists tend to look at the world through a mathematical lens, so it is not at all surprising that they wind up describing it in mathematical terms in the first place.

These explanations appear to match exactly the kind of practice employed in our "moldy bread" problem. Based on knowledge of how cells divide, it was only natural initially to construct the recurrence relation $N_{t+1} = rN_t$, and then to "fiddle around" for the best value of r. Subsequently, the model was changed to accommodate new data. Of course, there is no absolute guarantee that the second (logistic) model is the end of the story. But if new data were to appear that cast doubt on the validity of that model, then the process of hunting for yet another model would be repeated. Eventually—almost by sheer effort—it seems likely that an acceptable model would emerge.

While Hamming's two suggestions might be satisfactory for situations akin to finding models for phenomena like moldy bread, they don't seem to do the trick for the full spectrum of scientific investigation. Wigner certainly saw something different going on in the developing of models appropriate to the quantum world, and Hamming was no doubt aware that more needed to be said, so he put forth another explanation.

Hamming's final suggestion is that evolution provides an account for why humans are able to mathematize the physical universe. At first, one might think this to be an obvious suggestion, but Hamming does not elaborate on it beyond his comment, "Darwinian evolution would naturally select for survival those competing forms of life which had the best models of reality in their minds—'best' meaning best for surviving and propagating." It is interesting that Hamming concludes with the following remark:

> If you recall that modern science is only about 400 years old, and that there have been from 3 to 5 generations per century, then there have been at most 20 generations since Newton and Galileo. If you pick 4,000 years for the age of science, generally, then you get an upper bound of 200 generations. Considering the effects of evolution we are looking for via selection of small chance variations, it does not seem to me that evolution can explain more than a small part of the unreasonable effectiveness of mathematics.[34]

This remark seems to cast serious doubt on the evolutionary explanation, but it need not. Just as an inclined block needs a critical slope to overcome its friction and start sliding, and once the sliding begins it proceeds rather rapidly, so too one might argue that once science "started" it progressed quickly, but any evolutionary development that occurred before this time was critical and cannot be discounted.

Indeed, there are several evolutionary explanations for forms of human cognition, and such explanations need not be seen as contradicting Christian beliefs. But if the scenario were to be cast in a purely *naturalistic* framework—one that rules out any creative activity of a divine being—then it is precisely here where Christian thinkers want to put on the brakes. Chapter 5 explored the connection between chance and divine providence; it will be helpful now to explore some ideas about the role of chance in the development of human reason.

C. S. Lewis, in his third chapter of *Miracles*, argues that a strictly blind-chance view of human cognitive development is incoherent.

He begins his analysis by distinguishing between two ways we use the word *because*. To illustrate, consider the following situation. Kay lies in bed with a high fever. After examining her, a doctor declares to her husband, "Your wife is sick *because* she drank polluted water." Later that day Kay's two daughters, Grace and Kristin, come home from school. Grace sees her mother lying in bed asleep and puts her hand on her warm forehead. She then says to Kristin, "Mommy must be sick *because* she is still in bed and her head feels hot."

Do you see the difference in these two statements? The doctor is giving a causal explanation, whereas Grace is using what Lewis terms "ground consequent" reasoning. To be sure, the doctor used some kind of reasoning to arrive at his conclusion, but his statement itself is appealing to a cause-and-effect relationship: the polluted water was the *cause* of Kay's illness. Grace, by contrast, is not invoking a cause-and-effect explanation. The statement she made to her sister came from inferences based on what she saw and felt.

For Lewis, ground-consequent inferences are logically connected thoughts and are vital components of reasoning. But how does one thought cause another thought? Lewis states, "One thought can cause another . . . [only] by being seen to be a ground for it."[35] Raw natural selection, by contrast, operates solely by rewarding biological responses that enhance survival or reproductive proliferation, and Lewis thinks it inconceivable that natural selection such as this could fully account for the capacity to infer explanations. For Lewis, cause-and-effect responses can only produce feelings or sentiments, not valid inferences about the way the world really is.

Many Christian thinkers disagree with Lewis. In fact, shortly after Lewis first published *Miracles* he had a public debate with the philosopher Elizabeth Anscombe, who disagreed with him, at the Oxford Socratic Club. Anscombe, being Catholic, was certainly not a naturalist; she simply thought that Lewis's argument for the incoherence of naturalism was not compelling.

Other Christian thinkers maintain that Lewis's argument is, in general, correct. For example, Victor Reppert has expanded Lewis's views in his book *C. S. Lewis's Dangerous Idea*. Alvin Plantinga has also generated much discussion with reasoning similar to that of Lewis in his paper "An Evolutionary Argument Against Naturalism." Along with Lewis, his main line of thinking begins by noting that evolutionary theory predicts what kinds of species will continue to exist over time. They will be those that have a have a high capacity to adapt and survive, or at least those that exhibit a high degree of reproductive proliferation—not necessarily those whose cognitive faculties are reliable. If that paradigm is merged into a blind-chance setting, however, Plantinga sees no basis for trust in the reliability of our cognitive faculties. As Darwin himself once said, "With me the horrid doubt always arises whether the convictions of a man's mind, which has been developed from the mind of the lower animals, are of any value or at all trustworthy. Would any one trust in the convictions of a monkey's mind, if there are any convictions in such a mind?"[36]

In summary, a successful naturalistic explanation of the effectiveness of mathematics in understanding the physical world must be able to account for the reliability of human cognitive capacities. If it cannot, then the theory of evolution itself would be suspect, because it was produced by human cognitive faculties. Some Christian thinkers have argued, however, that such explanations are not possible if they are cast in a blind-chance framework. In the next section, we will argue that theistic explanations provide a compelling account of the effectiveness of mathematics.

Theistic Explanations

Our last chapter emphasized the role of aesthetics in shaping the kind of mathematics we deem worthy of pursuit. The Cambridge mathematician G. H. Hardy believed that good mathematics is driven primarily by aesthetic criteria such as economy of expression, depth, unexpectedness, inevitability, and seriousness, qualities that also characterize good poetry. The philosopher Mark Steiner sees this fact, combined with the success of applying mathematics to the physical world, as support for a theistic worldview.

Steiner thinks that naturalism disallows any special status for the human species. That is, if humans evolved without the purposive action of a creator, there would be no reason to think that they were in any way "privileged." Thus, for Steiner, a naturalist would not expect human aesthetic preferences to have any significant bearing on explanations regarding how the universe works, for that would indicate that some special privilege does indeed reside within the human species. Explanations or descriptions that are based on human perspectives (or analogies to humans) are often deemed **anthropocentric**.

Let's unpack Steiner's "anthropocentric" idea with an analogy involving base ten number systems. You will see in the exercises that converting from base ten to any other base is a straightforward procedure and doesn't change the underlying mathematical concepts involved. Thus, it is important to keep in mind that the following illustration is just an analogy.

Why do most cultures use a base ten numbering system? The simplest and most likely explanation is that we have ten fingers. Now, what if successful theories of the universe were based on multiples of ten in a fundamental way? That would seem odd: the only reason ten is special to us is the shape of our hands. Suppose, further, that not only did ten have a special status, but time and time again other human aesthetic criteria played a significant role in understanding the universe. Such occurrences would surely make one wonder why this privilege falls on the human species. It would make the universe look anthropocentric.

According to Steiner this situation is analogous to what mathematicians and scientists actually do when they rely on human notions of beauty and symmetry in the development of their theories. It is not the success of any particular mathematical theory; after all, there have been many failures of mathematics as well. In this respect Steiner is critical of Wigner's citing specific success examples from physics while ignoring error stories. For instance, the successful population model that Wigner referenced in his opening lines ignores all the failures in attempting to predict population trends. What Steiner is talking about is the success of mathematics as a grand strategy. In other words, while there may be failures in using aesthetic criteria to produce theories in any given instance, the strategy eventually proves to be successful. As an example, think back to our description of the emergence of complex numbers. Physicists have boldly used them as tools to make predictions about the quantum world, predictions that were subsequently confirmed with a variety of experiments.

To reiterate, it is not merely the successful use of these mathematical tools that is interesting; it is that the mathematical theories involved were largely developed from human notions of beauty and symmetry. In fact, such activity has been a longstanding and consistent strategy. As we mentioned briefly in chapter 2, Galileo pursued this tactic even though the best empirical evidence at the time did not necessarily support—indeed, in some respects it tended to disconfirm—his heliocentric theory. To illustrate this "disconfirmation" idea, imagine looking at a tree nearby with a building in the background. Now imagine moving to your right. The tree changes position relative to the building. This phenomenon is called **parallax shift**. Astronomers in Galileo's day reasoned that, if the earth were in motion around the sun, they would be able to detect a parallax shift in the positions of nearby stars relative to distant stars. The inability to detect any parallax shift was seen as evidence against the heliocentric theory. The reason why this detection failed is because the stars that astronomers thought were nearby are actually much further from the earth than they realized. Thus, the expected shift was not observed. The shift actually did occur, but detecting it was not possible with the technology then available.

Galileo adopted the heliocentric model mostly because it seemed more elegant than the Ptolemaic model. Most physicists admit that elegance, beauty, and symmetry hold primary sway in theory development. Brian Greene, for example, writes that physicists "tend to elevate symmetry principles to a place of prominence by putting them squarely on the pedestal of explanation."[37]

Steiner sees something special in our aesthetic preferences. His book contains several examples of beautiful mathematical systems used in applications to the physical world, including complex analysis in fluid dynamics (another example of the usefulness of complex numbers), relativistic field theory, thermodynamics, and quantum mechanics. Greene seems to agree with Steiner's main point: at least unconsciously physicists have abandoned naturalism in favor of a theory formation method that has principles of beauty embedded in its core. If they are correct, this approach appears to be an anthropocentric—and by way of implication a nonnaturalistic—strategy.

Based on the explanatory effectiveness of human symmetry considerations, Steiner is arguing against naturalism. That's quite a claim, so let's step back for a moment and see what naturalism might have to say that would account for the human preference for symmetry, and why it is successful in forming effective theories. At least three strategies seem possible.

The first is to argue that what we call success came only because humans have invested a great deal of energy into science over the last five hundred years. Who is to say that, if similar energies had been funneled in a different direction, there would be a totally different paradigm today, yet with the same degree of "success"? In other words, the success could be due to effort, not necessarily to some amazing, privileged connection that humans have with reality. A second approach would involve an appeal to what we might call a basic axiom. That is, the approach would take it as a "given" that the universe evolved in such a way that our preferences for beauty work successfully in theory formation. Finally, one might argue for some kind of probabilistic weighting mechanism that would drive physical processes toward the production of sentient life forms, and do so in such a way that their preferences for beauty coincided with the actual mechanisms of the universe.

Going into much back-and-forth analysis at this point is beyond the scope of the chapter, but we can very briefly make some preliminary comments. First, the argument that challenges our conviction of success compares "what is" with an unknown "what might have been." Of course it is possible that other theories could be successful, but where are they? More to the point, the effort expended by mathematicians and scientists in developing their (elegant) theories can more plausibly be looked at as evidence of having bumped into a real world rather than evidence of having constructed one: many times scientists have tried to explain observed data with a particular theory in mind, only to have reality thwart their attempts. As John Polkinghorne observes (referencing the unexpected but extremely useful by-products of the Dirac equation), "It is this remarkable fertility that persuades physicists that they are really 'on to something' and that . . . they are not just tacitly agreeing to look at things in a particular way."[38] Furthermore, the speculation that other theories could have arisen seems to ignore the fact other mathematical theories did not arise. Premodern China, whose mathematics was independent and virtually isolated from the rest of the world, exhibits an impressive list of mathematical theorems also found in ancient Greece and other cultures, including the Pythagorean theorem, the binomial theorem, the solution of polynomial equations via Horner's method, and Gaussian elimination for the solution of systems of linear equations. In sum, the argument claiming that our sense of success is *ad hoc* seems not to be very convincing.

Second, although axiomatic explanations are needed at some level, invoking them in an effort to account for the apparent privileged status of humans in the universe—this is the way it is and no more needs to be said—appears akin to pulling a rabbit out of a hat. Naturalists may counter that such a response is unfair, and that "axiomatic" starting points are needed for any position. While that response certainly has warrant, theists can go a bit deeper. They can use the observation that human notions of beauty relate successfully to knowledge of how the universe operates as reinforcing all the more their belief that human creation is the result of the purposive activity of an intelligent being.

Finally, the idea of a probabilistic weighting hypothesis is controversial even among Christian thinkers. On the one hand, Keith Ward comments,

> A physical weighting ought to be physically detectable, . . . and it has certainly not been detected. . . . In this sense, a con-

tinuing causal activity of God seems the best explanation of the progress towards greater consciousness and intentionality that one sees in the actual course of the evolution of life on earth.[39]

On the other hand, the biologist Simon Conway Morris argues for a theory known as convergence. He disagrees with biologists who state that small changes to random chance events that occurred millions of years ago would have produced a completely different world from what we know today. For Morris, life was destined to arise more or less as it has, and he sees the existence of similar features in widely different species as evidence for this belief. From this perspective, convergence could provide the evidence Ward sees as lacking. But even if convergence could explain our preference for beauty and symmetry, it is not yet clear if it would be successful in explaining why such preferences are successful. After all, magical incantations may be symmetrical, but they certainly do not work.

However this line of thinking plays out, it is important to note that there is no reason why a theist must choose between theistic and naturalistic explanations based on convergence. As we noted earlier theists can point to the human ability to understand the universe as an indication of the creative and purposive activity of God, even if that ability arose via some kind of probabilistic weighting scheme.

Final Thoughts

We want to stop short of suggesting that a naturalistic worldview cannot explain the success of mathematics. We do want to suggest, however, that a theistic explanation is very compelling and might well be the best one to account for the continuing success of mathematical theories that ultimately grow out of human aesthetic criteria. Such a statement is not meant to be a dogmatic pronouncement, but a catalyst to weigh various options. Human aesthetic values, and their subsequent use in successful physical theories, dovetail nicely with a Judeo-Christian view that humans are created in the image of God. Whatever being in God's image exactly entails, it seems to include a rational and aesthetic capacity reflective of God's that enables humans to understand and admire his creation. In short, the implications of a Christian worldview offer an attractive explanation for the effectiveness of mathematics.

Suggestions for Further Reading

Baggert, David, Gary R. Habermas, and Jerry L. Wallis. eds. *C. S. Lewis as Philosopher.* Downers Grove, IL: InterVarsity, 2008. A series of essays that unpacks various ideas of Lewis that were mentioned in this chapter.

Hamming, R. W. "The Unreasonable Effectiveness of Mathematics." *American Mathematical Monthly* 87, no. 2 (February 1980): 81–90. The well-known computer scientist responds to the 1960 essay, cited below, by Eugene Wigner.

Lewis, C. S. *Miracles.* London: Fontana Books, 1960. See especially chapter 3, where Lewis expounds on his thinking that naturalism is an incoherent philosophical system.

Morris, Simon Conway. *Life's Solution: Inevitable Humans in a Lonely Universe.* Cambridge, MA: Cambridge Univ. Press, 2005. In this work of almost five hundred pages Morris expounds in detail on his theory of convergence.

Plantinga, Alvin. *Warrant and Proper Function.* New York: Oxford Univ. Press, 1993. See especially chapter 12, where Plantinga maps out his thinking, similar to that of Lewis, that naturalism is self-defeating.

Reppert, Victor. *C. S. Lewis's Dangerous Idea.* Downers Grove, IL: IVP Academic, 2003. A contemporary philosopher defends and expands on the thinking of C. S. Lewis in his critique of naturalism in *Miracles.*

Steiner, Mark. *The Applicability of Mathematics as a Philosophical Problem.* Cambridge MA: Cambridge Univ. Press, 1998. In this detailed philosophical and mathematical treatment, Steiner carefully analyzes what counts as applying mathematics, then cites numerous examples indicating his belief that the success of mathematics undercuts nonanthropocentrism, and thus goes against naturalism as well.

Wigner, Eugene. "The Unreasonable Effectiveness of Mathematics in the Natural Sciences." *Communications in Pure and Applied Mathematics* 13, no. 1 (February 1960) 1–14. Available online at, www.dartmouth.edu/~matc/MathDrama/reading/Wigner.html.

EXERCISES

1. Consider graphically what is happening in the introduction to complex numbers. Graph the function $f(x) = x^2 - 4$; when does $f(x)$ cross the x-axis? Graph the function $f(x) = x^2 + 4$; when does $f(x)$ cross the x-axis? What does this example tell you about complex numbers?

2. Consider a complex number $x + yi$ where the real part is graphed on the horizontal axis, typically called the x-axis, and the imaginary part is graphed on the vertical axis, typically called the y-axis. Plot the following complex numbers as points.
   a. $0 + 0i$
   b. $1 + 0i$
   c. $-1 + 0i$
   d. $0 + i$
   e. $0 + -i$

   Geometrically, what happens when you multiply a complex number by a negative sign? Geometrically, what happens when you multiply a complex number by i? Geometrically, what happens when you multiply a complex number by $-i$?

3. Perform the indicated operations:
   a. $(6 + 7i) - (7 + 2i)$
   b. $(3 + 4i)(-5 + 4i)$
   c. $(2 - 3i)/(6 + 4i)$

4. If you have experience with calculus, consider the complex-valued function $f(x) = x^2 + xi$. Explain how you would plot $f(x)$. Explain how you would take the derivative of $f(x)$.

5. Computers store numbers differently than humans enter them. For instance, consider how you might count if you only had a series of on/off switches; we will use four switches for the following discussion. Zero would be all switches are off and we would denote it as $(0000)_2$, where the 2 denotes that the number is written in base 2, also called binary. One would be the first switch in the on position and the rest of the switches are off and we would denote it as $(0001)_2$. Now, we are going to have to think about what to do next; how are we going to represent 2? Two is denoted as $(0010)_2$, which means that the rightmost switch has been turned off and the switch next to it as been turned on. This method of counting is similar as to when you are using your hands to count and you arrive at 10 and you then make a mental note that you have been through all of your fingers once and put up one finger to denote 11. See if you now understand the following joke: there are only 10 people in the world—those who understand binary, and those who don't. The following questions deal with counting in other bases.

   a. Write down the numbers 0 to 16 in base 2.

   b. Suppose you were only counting with one hand; use base 5 to count from 0 to 20.

   c. What do you do if you use bases bigger than 10? Count to 24 in base 12. Hint: you may find it helpful to introduce letters that represent numeric values.

6. Recall from your college preparation that 12376 can be written as $6 + 70 + 300 + 2000 + 10000 = 6 \cdot 10^0 + 7 \cdot 10^1 + 3 \cdot 10^2 + 2 \cdot 10^3 + 1 \cdot 10^4$. Similarly, in order to convert a number in another base like $(10110)_2$ to base 10 we rewrite it as $(10110)_2 = 0 \cdot 2^0 + 1 \cdot 2^1 + 1 \cdot 2^2 + 0 \cdot 2^3 + 1 \cdot 2^4 = 2 + 4 + 16 = 22$. Convert the following values to base 10.

   a. $(110110)_2$

   b. $(110110)_3$

   c. $(23410)_5$

7. There has to be a better way to convert 12 in base ten to binary than simply counting to 12. Research how to convert from

base ten to a different base and apply your research to the following problems.

   a. Convert 12 in base ten to binary.

   b. Convert 12 in base ten to base five.

   c. Convert 234 in base ten to base nine.

8. Does the effectiveness of mathematical formalism by physicists and other scientists seem "unreasonable" to you? Explain.

9. Does scripture encourage anthropocentrism? Why or why not?

10. Summarize the argument about why the usefulness of mathematics may or may not give rise to naturalistic theories.

Chapter 9

EPISTEMOLOGY

Give me wisdom and knowledge.

2 CHRONICLES 1:10

Introduction

It is just after lunch.

Thirty calculus students settle into their desks, ready to begin the chapter on integration. The professor has dropped comments about antiderivatives and the Fundamental Theorem of Calculus for a week or more. Some share the professor's excitement over the new topic and prepare to take notes. Others brace themselves, fearing that integration is harder than differentiation.

The professor begins the lecture with a few leading questions.

"What is the formula for the area of a rectangle?"

Someone decides to play along with her lecture style and quickly answers, "Base times height."

The professor replies, "Why?"

By now her students know not to respond to such a question by saying, "Because it is." After a pause, someone offers, "Well, that is sort of the definition of area."

"Correct. How about the area of a triangle?"

Some students are thinking, "This is easy stuff; let's just move on," but they remain quiet. Someone responds, "One-half base times height."

"Why?"

A student explains how one can place a rectangle with the same base segment over the triangle as shown in the following figure. With the triangle's height segment cutting the rectangle in two halves, one can quickly see how the rectangle gives twice the area of the original triangle.

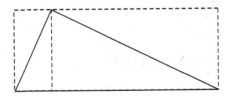

Though an irrefutable proof requires a few more details, the professor is not too picky here. She hits them with one more question: "What about the area of a disk?"

The class chimes in with the three-syllable mantra, "π R squared."

Now, the professor's retort "Why?" leaves the students flat-footed. Some are only aware that the discussion is over from the professor's subtle grin. All are confused. After all, for many high-school graduates the phrase "π R squared," is the correct answer; everyone knows it. Until now in a student's experience, teachers and textbooks have unerringly repeated that formula as the area of the disk, so it has to be true. To question the formula verges on irreverence.

The professor's chain of questions hints at an iceberg of issues floating beneath the surface. Questions such as "Why?" and "How did we arrive at this formula?" are part of **epistemology,** the branch of philosophy concerned with the nature and scope of knowledge, its presuppositions and basis, and the general reliability of its claims. How people decide what to call knowledge forms a subtle but central part of their worldview.

One of our main themes in this book has been "the big questions." Epistemology addresses many of these. Here are four:

1. What is knowledge?
2. How is knowledge acquired?
3. What do people know?
4. What confidence does knowledge provide?

In this chapter, we will examine these questions as they apply to mathematical knowledge. Christian belief affirms that God is creator of all things and that Jesus Christ is supreme over creation. Therefore, a Christian perspective must have consequences for the nature and the status of mathematical knowledge. Our answers will lead to an interpretation of mathematical knowledge that places God as creator of and sovereign over mathematics and accounts for the possibility that we can possess mathematical knowledge with complete confidence.

What Is Knowledge Generally?

In the *Theaetetus*, Plato provided a definition of knowledge that remained essentially unquestioned until the twentieth century. He defined **knowledge** as justified true belief—a belief that is true and that can be backed up with an account or explanation. Knowledge requires some form of justification because it should not include situations in which a person believes something that happens to be true only coincidentally. Even using this clear framework, there still remains plenty of room for discussion about each of the terms in the definition—truth, belief, and justification—and how they should interact.

In recent decades, philosophers have devised scenarios that illustrate how Plato's classical definition might not fully describe what we think of as knowledge. However, such examples involve unusual learning processes untypical of how we normally learn mathematics. Consequently, we will set aside this thorny and technical issue and content ourselves with Plato's definition.

How Is Mathematical Knowledge Acquired?

You may not be able to answer the question, "Why is the area of a disk equal to πR squared?" But you probably believe it. So it is knowledge for you: it is true, you believe it, and it is justified for you on the basis of the testimony of trustworthy people—your teachers. But where does such knowledge originate? In this section we will outline the process of the development of mathematical knowledge as it is currently followed by the discipline. We will follow the stages of a mathematician's formation from childhood to contributing member of the mathematical community, and this will give us a personalized perspective on how new mathematical knowledge is generated. The stages occur in the order presented below, although they may overlap.

In a popular book on the nature of mathematics, Keith Devlin evocatively describes the mathematical process as "making the invisible visible." If asked what precisely mathematics makes visible, he replies patterns—patterns of number, shape, motion, reasoning, symmetry, closeness, and frequency. As a running example for the stages, we will consider a famous pattern introduced in chapter 7, the **Fibonacci sequence**. Recall that this sequence is defined as the list of numbers that starts with 0 and 1 and from then on, each term of the list is the sum of the previous two. Hence the sequence is 0, 1, 1, 2, 3, 5, 8, 13, 21, 34, 55, 89. . . . For convenience later, we call 0 the 0th term of the sequence, and we call the first 1 the first term of the Fibonacci sequence.

Fundamental Objects/Patterns

The first stage occurs when a person perceives the fundamental patterns in mathematics. At the early elementary-school level, children are taught the meaning of integers, fractions, operations, and basic geometrical shapes. Teachers expect children to understand a number or a geometrical shape as a pattern and then identify instances or approximations of these patterns in the world around them. In fact, even before kindergarten, most children in modern cultures implicitly learn from their parents that the pattern of three-ness, for example, is independent of the objects being described. In this way, we first conceive of the abstract and universal nature of numbers. However, ever-recurring mathematical questions, which begin as early as pre-algebra, such as "What number satisfies this property?" treat numbers as truly existing abstract objects.

As a student progresses in mathematics, he or she learns about other mathematical objects. These include sets, notions of infinity, functions, sequences, vector spaces, fractals, groups, and countless more. Though these objects are more complicated than integers, understanding what they are requires the same mental activity as perceiving integers.

As regards the Fibonacci sequence, a mental grasp of the integers is the first level of understanding. Also, the concept of a sequence of numbers—that is to say a list that has a first term but is indefinitely long where we provide a method to determine each successive term—is another mathematical pattern that we can understand as an object in its own right.

Epistemology identifies two types of sources of knowledge. Knowledge that is gained independent of experience we call *a priori* knowledge. In contrast, *a posteriori* knowledge means knowledge obtained experientially. A *priori* justification implies reasoning or some direct mental apprehension as opposed to sensory perception. For example, why does 2 + 2 = 4? An *a posteriori* justification would mean directly observing that under every circumstance, a collection of two distinct objects, when grouped with a collection of another two distinct objects, gives a collection of four objects. The problem here is that no one can observe "every circumstance." Instead, an *a priori* justification uses definitions and reasoning independent of the senses. For example, define 2 as the integer following 1, 3 as following 2, and 4 as following 3, and define addition $a + b$ for positive integers as the bth integer after a. Then we have $2 + 2 = 2 + (1 + 1) = (2 + 1) + 1 = 3 + 1 = 4$. This is an *a priori* justification.

Knowledge about abstract objects (such as circles and rectangles) is gained by analogy with patterns in the physical world. Because of this, some modern philosophers contend that mathematical knowledge is at its essence *a posteriori*. However, recent studies in the number sense—how well people directly perceive number—show that most of us cannot look at a group of more than five or six objects and immediately see how many objects there are. We must resort to counting or mentally grouping and counting. However, counting—which is just a means to put word labels on larger and larger numbers—is itself a mental process. Hence, many scholars view any knowledge of numbers beyond (say) six as *a priori* knowledge.

The Variable

A second stage of mathematical development involves understanding the use of variables. Many math teachers can recount anecdotes in which a student shows discomfort over the use of variables. "Why can't you use more numbers?" some students ask. But variables are to mathematics what pronouns are to language. For instance, you might return to your room and your roommate might say, "Someone stopped by an hour ago looking for you." The word *someone* is a variable; it allows us to communicate even when we don't know the noun to which it refers. Similarly, variables allow us to make statements about unknown numbers.

Furthermore, by using variables we can state propositions about all mathematical objects in a given set. For example, we can define the Fibonacci sequence as follows. For each nonnegative integer n, we call the nth term of the sequence F_n. The sequence is the defined by setting $F_0 = 0$, $F_1 = 1$, and then for all $n \geq 0$, $F_{n+2} = F_{n+1} + F_n$. Though doing this may initially seem like just a slick way of defining the sequence, it makes it possible to prove many general results that hold for some or all Fibonacci numbers.

Word Problems / Making Mathematical Models

In chapter 8 we discussed the surprising effectiveness of mathematics in describing quantitative and qualitative relationships in the sciences. Though not directly a stage in the acquisition of abstract mathematical knowledge, the ability to transcribe word problems or physical situations into a mathematical model is a crucial component of mathematical education.

It is interesting to note that people have observed the pattern of Fibonacci numbers occurring in many places in nature, such as how leaves branch from a stem, how florets are arranged in the face of a sunflower, how some insect populations grow, etc. More importantly, if a mathematical model describes relatively well some pattern in nature, there is typically some process in nature that makes the particular model effective.

Doing Proofs

The capacity to prove assertions in mathematics is the core of the epistemological justification for mathematical knowledge. In chapter 6 we discussed the nature of mathematical proof. Here we address a few epistemological facets of proofs.

To review, a proof incorporates definitions of terms, a set of axioms, and other already-established theorems. Sometimes, a proposed proof may not explicitly state at what point one of these is brought in as a hypothesis. How explicitly one states these external hypotheses is a matter of style and expected audience. Nevertheless, every theorem is stated as a conditional, i.e., a statement that says "based on these definitions and these hypotheses, then such and such is true."

We typically first encounter proofs in a formal sense in high-school geometry when asked to prove certain properties of points, lines, or circles. However, every numerical calculation and every correct process of solving an equation is a proof. Some may involve only a few axioms of algebra or a few theorems and are not difficult. The proofs of the Fundamental Theorem of Calculus or theorems of uniqueness and existence in differential equations, however, are significantly more challenging. As a student progresses in learning how to do proofs, it is not uncommon for a professor to hear students bemoan, "I just don't know where to start." This brings us to the crucial issue of intuition and, more precisely, insight.

Suppose you are trying to prove a theorem that is already known to be true, like when you are asked to do a math exercise. It is possible to know all the relevant definitions, to recall many theorems, and to recite all the rules of inference and standard proof techniques and still not know how to start. We can compare this to someone who knows all the rules of chess but does not know how to begin an attack. The difficulty lies in knowing what hypothesis, what axiom, what definition, what corollary of a previously proved theorem to use—and when.

During the act of proving, a mathematician can sometimes immediately "see" what to write to prove a theorem. This insight occurs with varying degrees of confidence. Sometimes, we can think through an entire line of reasoning from the hypotheses to the desired conclusion, similar to a chess player who sees exactly the five moves needed to reach checkmate. Other times, the immediate intuition only provides an educated guess of what might work. At other times, a proof strategy might not come immediately to mind. In this case, we usually work out examples and look for patterns or try to prove less general but related facts. Hopefully, from this work we intuit how to generalize and prove the target conclusion. Of course, reading how other mathematicians prove related theorems provides inspiration.

Helping students develop intuition and insight for how to approach proofs is one of a mathematics professor's hardest roles. Doing proofs is not a routine task for which we can be mechanically trained like typing on a keyboard. Some proofs follow a script dictated either by context or by certain key words in the hypothesis of the theorem. Other times, however, the starting strategy—a key idea, or what to try—simply appears out of our subconscious. However, as with chess or sports or musical improvisation, we can improve intuition and insight with practice, active experience, and study.

We can make an analogy between the process of developing mathematical intuition and the development of spiritual insight. In the letter to the Romans, Paul exhorts his readers with the following: "Therefore, I urge you, brothers, in view of God's mercy, to offer your bodies as living sacrifices, holy and pleasing to God—this is your spiritual act of worship. Do not conform any longer to the pattern of this world, but be transformed by the renewing of your mind. Then you will be able to test and approve what God's will is—his good, pleasing and perfect will" (Rom. 12:1–2). The command to "be transformed by the renewing of your mind" indicates the discipline of renewal of one's spiritual intuition. One cannot read into Paul's exhortation only a progression in mental faculties and ignore the moral dimension, but, as one author put it, "when we change the way we think, we change the way we live."[40] Nonetheless, Paul wants Christians not only to attain factual knowledge of God's will but to develop a sanctified intuition.

Furthermore, since we do not regularly perceive God directly through any of the five senses, acquiring knowledge of his will bears some similarities to the process of gaining *a priori* knowledge, of which mathematics is just one type. Each uses different sources of justification but both involve the development of an intuition toward gaining *a priori* knowledge that profoundly affects our actions.

Hardy and Ramanujan

The collaboration (1914–1917) between G. H. Hardy and Srinivasa Ramanujan stands as one of the most striking vignettes in the history of mathematics. Their groundbreaking work together serves as a living analogy of the interplay between reason and intuition. Hardy excelled through the rigorous British mathematics education. He rose to the pinnacle of academia when he became a lecturer at Trinity College in Cambridge. In contrast, Ramanujan was born into a Brahmin but relatively poor family in southern India. Mathematically speaking, he was primarily self-taught and developed his own methods to arrive at, or guess at, astounding formulas.

The story of how Hardy "discovered" Ramanujan and sponsored him to come to Cambridge is the stuff of lore. In India, the mathematical community recognized Ramanujan as clever but did not realize the full extent of his genius. When no one in India offered him a teaching position, Ramanujan began sending letters to mathematicians in England describing his work. Nearly everyone turned him down or did not respond until a letter reached Hardy. About the formulas in Ramanujan's letter, Hardy later famously wrote that they "must be true, because, if they were not true, no one would have the imagination to invent them."[41]

In 1914, Ramanujan came to work with Hardy in Cambridge, and the pair formed an incredibly fruitful partnership for the next five years. Guided by intuition, Ramanujan would propose thousands of incredible formulas, the likes of which the mathematical community had never seen. When asked for a proof, he supplied evidence, analogy, and some calculations but could not always provide what amounted to a rigorous mathematical justification. Hardy worked with Ramanujan to draw out his ideas and tried to supply the lacking proofs. Once

(continued)

in a while, Ramanujan claimed a formula that turned out to be wrong but even his errors typically evidenced a profound subtlety. When the Indian and British mathematicians worked together, Ramanujan would often provide the intuitive leap and Hardy would fill in the gaps with rigorous proof wherever he could.

To explain the origin and functioning of his own intuition, Ramanujan sometimes appealed to mysticism. He claimed that complicated mathematics would appear to him in his dreams inspired by his family goddess, Namagiri. A hundred years later, mathematicians who understand the content and context of Ramanujan's notes remain dumbfounded by his creative process.

Mathematical Research

The next step in the development of a mathematician involves doing research. In the American educational structure, this begins only occasionally at the undergraduate level but is the principal characteristic of doctoral education.

In many undergraduate humanities and social science classes students are asked to present a thesis representing their own viewpoint and defend it. Not so in mathematics. Undergraduate mathematics students usually confidently accept the content of textbooks and lectures as long-settled justified belief. In doing exercises, a student is aware that he or she does not present potentially new knowledge (a thesis) but simply practices the art of mathematical justification in order to develop skill in exercising it.

Consequently, transitioning to research is sometimes difficult for mathematics students. The researcher must decide what to investigate, what questions to ask, and what tools to try. Research in mathematics immediately raises one of our big questions from chapter 1: Is mathematics invented or discovered? When we prove something new, it seems like a discovery. The mathematician does not create the pattern but observes and confirms (proves) it; the process of "observing" includes the rigorous and intuitive balance of constructing proofs. Some writers claim that the sense of discovery is an illusion and that one is actually creating mathematics. This position, however, seems precarious in light of the deep and unexpected connections between disparate branches of mathematics.

Again referring to our running example, the Fibonacci sequence has historically generated so much interest that there exists a journal called the *Fibonacci Quarterly*. Since 1963, authors have contributed to this journal with papers that investigate sequences, matrices, and many other mathematical objects related in some way to or similar to the Fibonacci sequence. For example, there exist many nice and sometimes surprising results about Fibonacci numbers. Proofs for them range from simple to very challenging. Here are a few examples: 1) every fifth Fibonacci number is divisible by 5; 2) the ratio of successive terms in the sequence tends toward the golden ratio (see chapter 7); 3) a positive integer z is a Fibonacci number if and only if one of $5z^2 + 4$ or $5z^2 - 4$ is a square number. To prove these we'd have to use techniques from different areas of mathematics: proof by induction, limit theorems, and number theory. The topics and theorems in the quarterly often diverge far from the journal's namesake sequence, but someone doing research cannot always predict the direction of their investigations.

Contribution to a Field

The final stage in the development of a mathematician involves contributing to a branch of mathematics. While this takes various forms, our main interest here is in naming and studying new mathematical objects. Typically such objects arise in the study of aspects of the physical world or in the process of clarifying or extending mathematical concepts that are already known.

Even though mathematicians differ on the nature of mathematical knowledge, as we shall see shortly, there is a nearly universal acceptance of what it means for an argument to be valid.

Consequently, a mathematical proof allows for continuity between individual knowledge and communal knowledge. If someone provides a valid proof for a certain mathematical statement, the resulting conclusion is accepted as a justified true belief by everyone. Thus the key to mathematical epistemology is the validity of the proof for a stated claim. For example, one can state with confidence the formula that the area of a disk in the Euclidean plane is "π R squared" and lean on trust in the mathematical community that this result has been proven and verified.

Since mathematical knowledge is independent of any one person, the mathematical community is keenly aware that people may be fallible and make a mistake in a proof. Therefore, it is a regular part of the mathematical process to have mathematicians who are knowledgeable in the particular area check a proposed proof. If they agree that it is correct, the proof is published. Of course, authors and reviewers can miss errors in a proof. However, once published, results are discussed broadly in the mathematical community and are often extended and revised. Eventually a consensus emerges and the new mathematical objects become part of the "canon" or accepted body of mathematical knowledge. Therefore, mathematical knowledge of even a highly technical nature has an extremely high degree of certainty.

What Is Mathematical Knowledge?

We are now in a position to discuss the nature of mathematical knowledge. For nearly two millennia, the **Platonist perspective**, presented in chapter 2, held without question. The perspective that mathematical objects and patterns truly exist in some universe of forms lends itself well to an interpretation where mathematical ideas exist in the mind of God, as believed by many Christians. However, since the Enlightenment, philosophers, mathematicians, and educators have proposed alternative perspectives. In this section, we consider a few common perspectives on mathematical knowledge that are considered in the philosophy of mathematics: realism, formalism, constructivism, intuitionism, social constructivism, and structuralism. So many isms may seem daunting, but we will unpack them carefully.

Recall that by knowledge we mean justified, true belief. All three words in this definition lead to a significant amount of debate but perhaps thorniest of all is the word *true*. As usually conceived, truth indicates a faithful correspondence between a linguistic element and extralinguistic reality. That is, *true* describes statements about reality. However, how people identify statements about reality as true depends on a person's perspective, culture, background, and experience, especially the more detailed such statements become. One could argue that the discussion and discovery of that which is true or beautiful encompasses the entirety of the academic enterprise. Even in mathematics, where **Boolean logic,** a way of doing logic in which every unambiguous statement is either true or false, reigns nearly supreme, there is no consensus on the nature of mathematical truth. Furthermore, as we shall see shortly, there is no approach of which a Christian can say, "This is *the* right approach."

Each of the following perspectives on mathematics hangs on the meaning of mathematical truth and the nature of mathematical objects. Interestingly enough, in most cases, the accepted methods of justification are often structured the same.

Realism

Realism is the position that mathematical objects are real, that they truly exist independently of human minds, and that human minds are able to apprehend them. Thus mathematical knowledge consists of justified, true beliefs about these objects.

Plato first outlined this perspective by affirming that intelligible objects exist in a so-called universe of forms. Tangible objects that try to model geometrical shapes, for example, are at best shadowy reflections of the true form. Plato's brand of realism is called **Platonism**. Gaining mathematical knowledge consists then of observing properties of mathematical objects. The exact meaning of the word *observing* became the key epistemological problem for generations of thinkers.

In chapter 2, we presented Saint Augustine's ontology of mathematical objects; we will discuss it in more detail in the next chapter. We can label his philosophy of mathematics as a Christian realism, where he saw mathematical patterns as truly existing in the mind of God. As Ronald Nash puts it, "[Augustine's] epistemology finds man beginning with sensation but attempting to climb by way of reason to the eternal ideas in the mind of God."[42] As we will see, Augustine's philosophy of mathematics, where a mathematician discovers what is in the mind of God, leads to some theological problems— problems that are not necessarily insurmountable. For example, Paul says to the Corinthians, "no one knows the thoughts of God except the Spirit of God. . . . For who has known the mind of the Lord that he may instruct him?" (1 Cor. 2:11, 16). However, Augustine's is not the only God-centered realist philosophy of mathematics.

The Jewish thinker Philo of Alexandria (20 BC–AD 50), many years before Augustine, proposed a slightly different form of Platonism. Philo contended that God created a "noetic cosmos" of immaterial realities as a precursor to his creation of the sensible world. Mathematical forms exist in this noetic cosmos. Contrary to Augustine, Philo did not argue that these forms exist in the divine reason. Hence, learning mathematics does not imply knowing the mind of God with certainty; rather it involves knowing aspects of this noetic cosmos. In Philo's perspective, one can compare the mathematical enterprise to Adam's role in naming the animals. The mathematician names a pattern, observes its properties, and works out consequences. Obviously, many mathematical objects never get named. Indeed, in any realist position of mathematics, what objects and properties we choose to study and observe is our creative part in the discovery of mathematics.

In response to the question of how humans could perceive anything in the universe of ideas, Augustine proposes his theory of illumination. He wrote, "We must know this [the truth of mathematical statements that go beyond experience] by the inner light, of which bodily sense knows nothing."[43] Many subsequent Christian thinkers held this perspective. For example, Johannes Kepler explicitly understood mankind's ability to perceive geometrical truths as "remnants of natural light," which are vestiges of the perfection of knowledge that existed before the fall. The concept of inner light connects well with the role of insight in finding proofs as we discussed earlier. Unfortunately, as Nash points out, the concept does little to explain in detail how we can perceive this inner light and thereby come to knowledge about mathematics.

Gottlob Frege (1848–1925) was arguably the founder of modern mathematical logic; his life goal was to cast arithmetic purely as a consequence of logic. This led him to pinpoint logical gaps in arithmetic where other writers might refer to intuitive leaps. Frege's view implies that numbers must be thought of as objects, and statements of arithmetic assert nothing of physical objects. His philosophy firmly set mathematical objects as nonphysical realities and any knowledge about them as dependent entirely on Boolean logic.

More recently, though without a reference to divine light, Michael Polanyi, a preeminent twentieth-century philosopher of science, supports a realist view of knowledge. By referring to what he calls tacit knowledge, he carefully analyzes the role of intuition and establishes a language of perception for our awareness of *a priori* knowledge. Though his arguments are too technical to include in this brief survey, they do provide an explanation for how we can know mathematics.

Christian thought provides stronger support for realism than does naturalism (the belief that the physical world is all there is). The concept of the immaterial soul encourages Christians to believe in the reality of entities unperceived by the senses. The soul of a person, though immaterial, produces effects on the material world through its connection with a person's body. Furthermore, the theologian John Calvin argued that every human being possesses a *sensus divinitatis*, that is, an intuition that God exists. If Calvin is correct, this intuition would provide a clear example of *a priori* knowledge.

Formalism

Despite Frege's underlying realist philosophy of mathematics, his emphasis on extreme precision in proofs and the use of a finite list of logical laws inspired a nonrealist approach, the formalist philosophy of mathematics. According to **formalism,** mathematical statements are ultimately nothing more than sentences obtained as consequences to a collection of string manipulation rules. Axioms are one's starting strings and rules of inference are the manipulation rules. From a formalist perspective, mathematics is not "about" anything; it refers to nothing outside of its symbols and inference rules.

At the turn of the twentieth century, David Hilbert proposed a program to identify and codify all axioms and all rules of inference in mathematics that are currently used or could possibly be used. This would provide a consistent method to prove all that can be known in mathematics. Thus for Hilbert "truth" was equivalent to provability. However, Gödel's First and Second Incompleteness Theorems (1931) refuted the very possibility of Hilbert's program. They imply that in *any* formal system in which one can do a certain amount of elementary arithmetic there are statements about arithmetic that cannot be decided in that formal system. That is, if we assume claims in arithmetic are either true or not true, then there are true statements within the system that cannot be proved; hence "truth" is in some sense more than provability.

Nonetheless, some mathematicians retain a formalist perspective. People who study computer proof checking or computer proofs sometimes stand in this camp. In this perspective, mathematics is a game of symbols, and one does not even view mathematical statements as knowledge since they do not qualify as truths or even beliefs.

Constructivism

Constructivism is the position in the philosophy of mathematics that mathematical objects or properties do not exist until they are found or constructed explicitly; from this perspective, mathematical objects do not exist apart from human minds. There are many varieties of constructivism; principally, they differ in what they mean by "constructed explicitly."

For example, consider the following proof that any composite number n (an integer greater than 2 that is not prime) has a factor less than or equal to $\sqrt{n}$. *Proof*: Suppose the contrary, that any time we write $n = ab$ as the product of nontrivial factors ($a, b > 1$), a and b are both greater than $\sqrt{n}$. Then ab is strictly greater than n and we obtain a contradiction. This proves the theorem.

Constructivists would not accept this reasoning as a proof: it does not exhibit a way to find a nontrivial divisor of n less than or equal to $\sqrt{n}$. Though various versions of constructivism exist, the requirement that mathematical objects must be (mentally) constructed or computed is common to many of them. Any theorem that proves the existence of some object must give an explicit means of constructing an object with the desired property. Each brand of constructivism is based first on a particular philosophical stance. Some lay out what basic laws of logic conform to this stance or specifically list allowed proof techniques. The philosophical variants carry names like finitism, predicativism, intuitionism, semi-intuitionism, antirealism, etc. We discuss intuitionism in more detail below.

Some philosophers of mathematics explicitly present constructivism as a response against the view that God is the creator of mathematics. Errett Bishop, for example, insinuates a tight correlation between constructivism and atheism. He writes, "Mathematics belongs to man, not God. We are not interested in properties of the positive integers that have no descriptive meaning for finite man. When a man proves a positive integer exists, he should show how to find it. If God has mathematics of his own that needs to be done, let him do it himself."[44] Not all constructivists are atheists, however. Michael Dummett, one of the foremost modern philosophers of mathematics and an antirealist, is a practicing Catholic. Also, as we will see, the standard interpretation of intuitionism does not speak against God, his creation act, or even a notion of truth.

Intuitionism

The most influential strand of constructivism is L. E. J. Brouwer's intuitionism. Consider the claim "George is a thief." Classical logic assumes that this statement is true or false by virtue of some historical act of larceny that George may or may not have done. However, if we consider the American and British court systems, someone is a thief if he (or she) has been proven (and the jury agrees) that the person committed theft. Debates over what really happened or the definition of theft are irrelevant: all that matters in the eyes of the legal system is the verdict. In the American judicial system, a defendant is "innocent until proven guilty," so there are only two possibilities. But in the British system a jury can return a third alternative—a verdict of "not proven." James Brown characterizes the philosophical stance of **intuitionism** as seeing mathematics as an activity in the mind of the (ideal) mathematician, like a court of law in the (ideal) mathematician's mind. According to Brouwer, "mathematicians do not discover pre-existing things, as the Platonist holds and they do not manipulate symbols, as the formalist holds."[45] Furthermore, mathematics remains independent of sense experience and independent of language. Linguistic communication of mathematics only suggests similar thought constructions to others but does not absolutely guarantee that the thought construction in the listener is the same as in the speaker.

A mathematical intuitionist must utilize a nonclassical logic. According to Graham Priest, the validity of a sentence does not lie in conditions that make it true or false respective to some extralinguistic reality but by conditions under which a proof, i.e., (mental) construction, is given. Hence, the classical meaning of the logic concepts of truth, falsity, conjunction (and), disjunction (or), negation (not), and implication has a different interpretation from classical Boolean logic. Some classical logical equivalences and rules of inference may change or not be accepted. Most notably, as in the example of a person accused of theft in a British court, the principle of the excluded middle, that either p or not p must be true, does not hold in intuitionist logic. Thus for an intuitionist, mathematical knowledge consists of propositions that have been verified via intuitionist logic, not "true" statements that correspond to an independent reality.

Brouwer, his student Heyting, and others labored to extend this logic into various branches of mathematics, trying to establish classical mathematical results through intuitionist logic. Though not held by many mathematicians, intuitionism continues to draw interest mainly because of its well-developed though nonclassical logic. Mathematical works using intuitionist logic are regularly published by the leading publishing firms and in relevant journals. Intuitionism has been particularly attractive to Christian thinkers who regard the Augustinian claim that we can know the mind of God as presumptuous; rather they emphasize that mathematics is a human activity and see intuitionism as a more faithful expression of Christian humility than realism.

Social Constructivism

Paul Ernest, one of the more prolific writers on the philosophy of mathematics education, is an outspoken critic of realism (which he terms *absolutism*). He holds the thesis that mathematics is a socially constructed language. According to Ernest, statements must pass through a sort of formal dialogue within the mathematics community before they can be accepted as mathematical knowledge. His philosophy of mathematics is often called **social constructivism**, though philosophers of mathematics do not usually place this under the rubric of mathematical constructivism as described above.

Though a number of educators who design curricula for elementary and secondary schools ascribe to Ernest's social constructivism, few researchers in mathematics do. Indeed, it is ironic that as Ernest discusses the concept of "creation of mathematics" in *The Philosophy of Mathematics Education* he cites educators, works by the NCTM (National Council of Teachers of Mathematics), or the equivalent bodies in the United Kingdom, but he does not cite any research mathematicians, who purportedly are the people "creating" mathematical knowledge.

The postmodern philosophical tradition affirms truth as individual to each person or as constructed by the power structures in a given society; Ernest's position lies squarely in the latter camp. From this position, the argument that different civilizations or different educational systems present ideas in varying ways but the core objects and properties are the same is not accepted. Nevertheless, mathematics has, for the most part, remained impervious to postmodern trends, perhaps because the effectiveness of mathematics to describe nature underscores its universal character.

Structuralism

Recently, a new strand of philosophy of mathematics has gathered some attention. We could begin by characterizing it as most similar to realism in the following sense. Structuralists hold that arithmetic, for example, is about a truly existing realm of objects and that statements about arithmetic have meaningful true-or-false truth values. However, **structuralism** contends that mathematical objects such as specific integers have no meaning apart from their relation to each other and hence to the structure of the set of integers as a whole. Consequently, what exists fundamentally are not individual numbers like 2 or 72 but the structure of the integers.

As with constructivism, there exist various refinements within structuralism. Discussions about how mathematics relates to God and creation and what mathematical knowledge is would, for structuralism, mirror what we have already said for realism.

What Confidence Does Mathematical Knowledge Carry?

In James Cameron's 1997 movie *Titanic*, when questioned about the possibility the ship might sink, Thomas Andrews, the ship's architect, replies, "She is made of iron, sir. I assure you, she can. And she *will*. It is a mathematical certainty." Perhaps Andrews is thinking of the law of gravity or perhaps he is simply using the word *mathematical* to strengthen his assertion of certainty. Either way, he is drawing on a centuries-old belief that mathematics has served as the bedrock of certainty in the physical sciences. We conclude this chapter with a short discussion on the epistemological status of mathematics, by which we mean the relative strength of certainty accorded to its modes of thought and justification procedures.

Mathematics did not always enjoy its current place of prestige among the sciences. Before the advent of the scientific method, medieval thinkers in western Europe followed Aristotle's inductive reasoning and provided explanations of natural phenomena using metaphysical and theological arguments. Very few, if any, principles of Aristotelian natural philosophy remain in modern science because the methods of reasoning have changed so drastically.

As we saw in chapter 2, a key aspect of Galileo's revolutionary scientific method involved raising the "epistemological status" of mathematics in relation to metaphysics and theology. He maintained that mathematics was the language in which God wrote the book of nature. For him, mathematics was not simply a useful tool for modeling observations but it expressed the essential structure of the universe.

Though Galileo's thesis of raising mathematics above theology for a more certain explanation of physical phenomenon was seen as heretical during his lifetime, the roles are reversed today. The evolution of the expression "the queen of the sciences" strikingly illustrates the point. During the Middle Ages, thinkers called theology the queen of the sciences. Since God created the universe and gives meaning to everything in it, theology should be the primary academic discipline with all other forms of knowledge subordinate to it. In contrast, Carl Friedrich Gauss (1777–1855), certainly aware of the nickname accorded to theology, called mathematics the queen of the sciences because mathematics had become the foundation for explanation of physical phenomenon. This shift in title has remained. Today many scientists do not even know that the expression "queen of the sciences" ever belonged to theology.

Volker Remmert argues that Galileo was not attempting to discredit the Catholic Church and theology entirely. His polemical stance aimed to loosen the Jesuits' iron-grip hold on natural philosophy, which in Galileo's opinion stifled scientific progress. Johannes Kepler, a Protestant contemporary of Galileo and fellow believer in the Copernican model of the solar system, seamlessly merged the conflicting epistemologies: "it is the confidence that God's geometrical plan for the world is accessible through the natural light of reason that underlines the *a priori* demonstration of the structure of the world, and the defence of Copernicus's cosmic scheme."[46]

So for Galileo and Kepler mathematics provided certain knowledge not merely of mathematics itself, but of the physical universe as well. However, the nineteenth-century discovery of non-Euclidean geometry fostered distrust in the confidence of mathematical knowledge and *a priori* knowledge in general. (Recall the example of the triangle on the sphere given at the beginning of chapter 6.) However, this loss of confidence came because some scholars misunderstood the nature of mathematical knowledge. A proper understanding of the discovery of non-Euclidean geometry strengthens mathematical confidence rather than calls it into question, although it does separate that confidence from knowledge of the physical world. As mathematicians worked to clarify Euclidean geometry, they realized that taking alternative axioms to Euclid's Fifth Postulate did not lead to internal contradictions. One can prove many theorems in these new geometric contexts without worrying about a physical interpretation. Indeed, the unjustified sense there could be only one geometry— that which describes the tangible universe—and that this geometry is Euclidean, led to the loss of confidence that accompanied the discovery of non-Euclidean geometries.

Has the pendulum Galileo set in motion swung too far, that is, do we accord too much certainty to mathematical knowledge? In perhaps moralistic terms, do we sometimes treat mathematical certainty as an idol?

Consider the revolutions in physics (e.g., Newtonian gravity, quantum mechanics, and general relativity) and the ongoing research into the basic nature of the universe (e.g., the search for dark energy). The numerous revolutions in science compel a humbler perspective than was held by Kepler and Galileo on the connection between mathematical knowledge and nature. Physicists now view their formulas as mathematical models. Even if these models appear very effective at describing nature, scientists remain aware that they only approximate what we observe. Just because one theory replaces another does not mean that physicists have ceased to value mathematics. Instead, as science progresses, scientists propose more subtle theories with sometimes more complicated mathematics. Older theories typically approximate the newer.

Mathematical knowledge depends on axioms and definitions. An axiom can be defined as a proposition that must be necessarily true and certain for everyone who accepts it. At present, mathematicians rely on a few sets of axioms: Peano's axioms of the integers, Euclid's axioms of geometry (with some revisions), the Zermelo-Fraenkel axioms of set theory, and the Axiom of Choice. Epistemologists call this perspective of mathematics **foundationalist** in that there is a (relatively) unquestioned foundation. There is not an infinite regress of reasons "this is true because . . . and that is true because . . ." The axiomatic foundation is the point where we say "this is just true—no 'because' necessary."

New definitions do not appear out of nowhere. Mathematicians make a value judgment about what patterns are worth looking at, whether for their utility to solve a class of problems or simply for their internal beauty. This judgment determines what collection of objects and properties appear to be fruitful enough to warrant a definition. Some mathematicians have suggested that the choice of definitions is purely subjective; however, this loses sight of the fact that different civilizations have often studied essentially the same objects independently.

Mathematicians as a community make every effort not to define different objects with the same label. This may seem obvious but it is different from many other academic disciplines. For example, try to define *family*. There exist countless definitions of family and each has sociological, political, religious, moral, and poetic consequences. Or consider the word *culture*. In 1952, Alfred Kroeber and Clyde Kluckhohn wrote an entire book on the different definitions of culture. Many words that shape our lives—power, intellect, knowledge, sin, success, and many others—do not enjoy a general consensus on definitions. This simply will not do in mathematics. The strict precision of proofs and the need to communicate results has led mathematicians to make every effort to agree on definitions.

We now come to a point about axioms and definitions that is subtle but important: Sometimes, mathematicians call a definition an axiom. For example, in linear algebra, when presenting the definition of a vector space, mathematicians sometimes refer to the eight operational properties as the vector space axioms. This seems like an abuse of terminology, of the word *axiom*. However, this habit hints that there is little distinction between a mathematical axiom and a definition. A mathematical axiom is not necessarily true in any absolute philosophical sense; it is merely a component in the definitions of the objects/patterns. Zermelo-Fraenkel axioms of set theory define what is meant mathematically by a set; Peano's axioms define what we mean by integer.

Therefore, it is not philosophically inappropriate or theologically unorthodox to ascribe a very high degree of certainty to mathematical knowledge properly justified. At the same time it is essential to remember that mathematical claims are always conditional claims that should be understood as: such and such is true *assuming a list of axioms and/or definitions*. Inflated epistemological confidence occurs when one awards excessively high confidence to the connections between a mathematical model and whatever is being modeled and then transfers that confidence to conclusions that result from the model.

Conclusion

"Soon, we will use integration to prove that the area of a disk is πR squared," the professor says. "We just have to learn how to integrate $(R^2 - x^2)^{1/2}$ over the interval $[0, R]$ to get the area of a quarter disk and then multiply by 4. OK. I'll admit: the formula for the area of a disk was known long before calculus. Archimedes had a clever noncalculus proof in fact. But I think that integration gives us the easiest way to get the formula."

The calculus students can relax. They can take confidence in the collective knowledge of the mathematical community and what educators have taught them. They realize that they can implicitly trust this collective knowledge. Happily, the professor has promised that her lectures will help them develop an intuition and that their continued effort will help them develop insight. By the end they should be comfortable with the proof techniques required for them to construct an acceptable justification for the formula of the area of a disk.

In fact, they can legitimately have a very high degree of confidence in the formula for the area of a disk. They understand it applies perfectly only to an idealized disk, which may only exist as a form, or an immaterial object, or a mental construct. They recognize that the result only makes sense under the hypotheses of Euclidean geometry. It would not surprise them too much when the professor proves (using the surface area formula for surfaces of revolution) that the area of a disk of radius r on a sphere of radius R (where $r < R$) has a different formula: $2R^2(1 - \cos[r/R])$. Indeed, it would simply be a result in a different geometry, with a different set of axioms.

Some students note a secondary theme in the professor's line of questioning: to ask how we know something in mathematics is similar to investigating the grounds of any belief system. Were they to linger on this topic, the Christian students would realize that the philosophy of mathematics and Christian faith share a number of interesting touch points. Indeed, all things exist and have their being through Christ, including mathematical objects.

The calculus students mentally prepare for the professor's introductory lecture on integration. A fly buzzes overhead following a circular pattern. The short moment during which the professor rattled students' confidence (dare we say faith?) in their mathematical knowledge has passed.

Suggestions for Further Reading

Brown, James Robert. *Philosophy of Mathematics*. 2nd ed. New York: Routledge, 2008. A basic book on the philosophy of mathematics; takes a decidedly realist (Platonist) position.

Greco, John. "Introduction: What Is Epistemology?" In *The Blackwell Guide to Epistemology*, edited by John Greco and Ernest Sosa. Oxford: Blackwell, 1999. Contains seventeen essays by leading thinkers on various aspects of epistemology.

Koetsier, T., and L. Bergmans, eds. *Mathematics and the Divine: A Historical Study*. Amsterdam: Elsevier, 2005. This volume includes many interesting essays including Remmert's article on Galileo.

Polanyi, Michael. "The Logic of Tacit Interference." *Philosophy*, XLI, 155 (1966): 1–18. Polanyi writes, "To hold a natural law to be true, is to believe that its presence may reveal itself in yet unknown and perhaps yet unthinkable consequences; it is to believe that such laws are features of a reality which as such will continue to bear consequences inexhaustibly." This landmark article explores this perspective.

Priest, Graham. *An Introduction to Non-Classical Logic*. Cambridge UK: Cambridge Univ. Press, 2001. An excellent introduction to logics that are not Boolean.

EXERCISES

1. Why is epistemology in general important?
2. Name some different ways in which people commonly use the word *prove*. What are the epistemological differences for each instance? What do you think about the claim that axioms are merely definitions? Why does this loss of distinction matter?
3. Do you agree or disagree with the statement that faith and proof should not be viewed as opposites? Explain your position.
4. The text suggested that the belief in the existence of an immaterial soul has consequences for epistemology of mathematics. Why? Do you agree? Why or why not?
5. Assuming God created mathematical forms and in particular the pattern of threeness, what may be some consequences for the doctrine of the Trinity?
6. Using the Internet, look up some differences between the mathematics of the ancient Babylonians and the ancient Egyptians. Some writers point to the different manifestations of mathematics in ancient cultures as evidence that mathematics is socially constructed. Do you agree or disagree with the interpretation of this evidence? Why?
7. Think about mathematical facts that you remember. How many can you prove? What can you conclude about the importance of collective versus individual mathematical knowledge?

8. Suppose that truth is relative to each person and suppose that we are in a situation where only two people converse. The truth-value to each statement could be not just one of two possibilities but one of four: (T, T); (T, F); (F, T); and (F, F), where, for example (T, F) means person 1 consider a statement true and person 2 considers that same statement false. Show that this logic would still include a version of the principle of excluded middle, in that for every proposition p, the compound statement p or (not p) would have the truth value of (T, T). Show that this logic cannot be rephrased as a logic with three truth-values: "agree-true," "agree-false," and "disagree."

Chapter 10

ONTOLOGY

For by him all things were created: things in heaven and earth, visible and invisible, whether thrones or powers or rulers or authorities; all things were created by him and for him. He is before all things and in him all things hold together.

COLOSSIANS 1:16–17

Overview

We've all had the experience of solving a mathematics problem, then looking in the back of the book to check our answer. However, when we look at questions relating to what mathematics is, what it means, or why it is so useful in science, answers are not so easily found. And when we look at mathematics through the eyes of faith, these questions are the ones that are especially important. In the previous chapters, we explored mathematical topics and general aspects of mathematics that relate to Christian belief. In this chapter, we are going to tackle a deeper question: What is mathematics? In particular, we are going to focus on how Christian belief might shape our answer.

The mathematician Keith Devlin has given a partial answer to this question that has been widely accepted: mathematics is the study of patterns. But patterns are not physical objects like comets, chemicals, or chromosomes. They are studied by formulating them abstractly. For instance, the idea of a straight line is an abstraction because we never experience straight lines directly. We envision an edge of a room (where two perpendicular walls meet) as being a straight line. But a close inspection reveals that these edges are not perfectly straight, regardless of how well the house was constructed. Further, lines are one-dimensional; but no physical line is without some width. So the question—what is mathematics?—is part of two larger questions that have occupied the attention of philosophers since Plato: Do abstract objects exist as do physical objects? If so, what are they?

This chapter will present two perspectives on these questions. We begin by discussing something more familiar: abstract concepts. You think about these things on a regular basis when taking a mathematics class. In that context abstract concepts can have surprising properties. They can originally appear to be fictitious entities, but eventually develop into ideas with clear meanings that seem to have a reality greater than mere words or symbols. For example, the complex number $i = \sqrt{-1}$ originally emerged as a fictitious solution to the equation $x^2 + 1 = 0$. As such it was given the name *imaginary number*. Eventually, however, the fiction $i = \sqrt{-1}$ became quite useful in obtaining real solutions to certain types of cubic equations. The concept of $\sqrt{-1}$ solidified further as mathematics developed, and it eventually became accepted as a genuine number with a geometric meaning. To illustrate, consider negative numbers. They can be thought of as numbers in the opposite direction as positive numbers; in a plane -1 is a 180-degree turn about the origin from the number 1. Thus, multiplication by -1 changes the direction of the number—an "about face" so to speak. In similar fashion, multiplication by the number i is associated geometrically with a 90-degree counterclockwise turn about the origin. Multiply the number 1 by i and you rotate that number to line up with the y-axis. Two 90-degree turns amount to a 180-degree rotation. That is, $i \times i = i^2 = -1$. Also, in electronics, this number is used in modeling the impedance of inductors and capacitors.

Not only can mathematical abstractions emerge as profoundly useful with unexpected interpretations, they can also lead to some unexpected connections. Consider two well-used numbers in mathematics: e (≈ 2.71828) and π (≈ 3.14159). The number e was originally given a special label because of its usefulness in calculus: working with exponential functions in base e simplifies calculations of derivatives. The number π relates to a property of circles: it is the ratio of a circle's circumference to its diameter. Nevertheless, it arises in some unexpected places that are not clearly connected to the circle. For example, both π and e appear in the formula for the standard bell curve,

$$y = \frac{1}{\sqrt{2\pi}} e^{-\frac{x^2}{2}},$$

which is fundamental to the whole field of statistics. Also, Leonhard Euler (1707–1783) deduced the remarkable formula $e^{i\pi} + 1 = 0$, which connects five of the most important numbers in mathematics: 0 and 1 (representing fundamental concepts of nothing and unity), e (the base of natural logarithms), π (the ratio of the circumference to the diameter in any circle), and i (the building block for complex numbers). The formula also includes the three primary operations of arithmetic (addition, multiplication, and exponentiation), as well as the essential concept of equality, which is arguably the most important relationship in mathematics. The conjunction of all of these entities, most of which were independently conceived, in a single formula, seems to imply they are real and not merely ideas that someone made up.

In what sense are these concepts real? In what sense does "three" exist? In what sense do triangles and straight lines exist? Questions like these belong to the area that philosophers call **ontology** from the Greek *ontos*, which means "being." So when we investigate the ontology of numbers, circles, triangles, and other mathematical entities, we are looking at their nature. Scholars have thought about the nature of mathematical concepts for over two thousand years and still have not settled on a single "right" account of them.

Many people, including many mathematicians, simply give up when they realize that ontological questions do not easily yield a single right answer. Instead, they typically say something like, "Let's solve the problems we can solve and ignore the rest." Many scholars, however, have studied the nature of abstract concepts. In this chapter we describe two Christian approaches associated with thinkers we discussed briefly in chapter 2: Plato, and (more loosely) Aristotle.

We are not going to present one position as better than the other. Indeed, there are many other approaches that a Christian might adopt, and in many respects these approaches can be held by other theists (people who believe in a God who interacts with the world) as well. If you are to think about mathematics from a Christian perspective, however, we think it is helpful to understand the approaches we have chosen to present. Doing so can increase not only your understanding of mathematics, but your appreciation for God as well. Both approaches take seriously God's sovereignty, God's creation, the fact that human beings are part of the creation, and that human beings are created in the image of God. Furthermore, both lead to powerful motivations for exploring and enjoying mathematics.

Christian Platonism

Could God have made a world in which $5 + 7 \neq 12$? On the one hand, God is sovereign over creation and is free to do as he chooses. On the other hand, denying a basic fact of arithmetic seems to make no sense, and it appears that there is no way such a denial could possibly make sense, at least to us. Could such a denial make sense to God? Is saying that it is impossible for God to come to any other result inconsistent with God's sovereignty? Or, is saying that it is impossible for God to deny this result akin to describing his character? Saint Augustine (AD 354–430) wrote that God could not have made a world in which $5 + 7 \neq 12$. That is, numbers are ideas in God's mind and have been from eternity. Thus, statements like $5 + 7 = 12$ are unchangeable truths. Furthermore, to say God cannot do some things does not contradict God's omnipotence. For example, he cannot lie (Heb. 6:18) and he cannot do things that are logically impossible, like find two integers whose ratio equals $\sqrt{2}$. Thus, God can do all things, but only those things that are logically consistent and compatible with his goodness.

Augustine spent many years reflecting on the book of Genesis. He concluded that the opening words of the Bible, "In the beginning . . ." refer to the beginning of time. That is, God created time. Thus, as we look backwards, time does not extend infinitely, but has a definite beginning. For Augustine, numbers were already present in God's mind at the time of creation. He goes on to argue that the reason we find mathematics so helpful in describing the physical world is that God used mathematics to provide patterns for his creation. He was also concerned with another problem: if numbers existed in God's mind at creation, how then are we able to access them? His answer is that, in creating human beings, God built the capacity to deal with numbers into our minds. Thus, God has given us a kind of "mathematical sixth sense" that serves as the starting point for our thinking about mathematics.

These ideas did not originate with Augustine. As we noted in chapter 2, some nine hundred years earlier the Greek philosopher Pythagoras had noted that if one plucked the string on a musical instrument, then held the string in such that way that just half of it could be plucked, the two sounds seemed alike although one was pitched more highly. He also noted that the sounds from halves, thirds, and quarters of the string blended well. From this starting point he made the leap to the idea that there was an invisible reality underlying the physical world. This reality could be perceived by our minds but not by our senses; the basis of this reality was numbers. Plato, roughly a hundred years later, extended this idea to the notion that there were patterns that he called "forms" underlying the physical world and that these were more real than the physical world itself. He was clear in stating that these abstract entities—the forms—really existed. He located them in what he termed the "realm of being," but it is less clear what exactly this realm of being is supposed to be.

The idea that mathematical entities such as numbers have a real existence independent of human thought is called **Platonism**. Of course, not all Platonists are Christian believers. Further, mathematicians sometimes facetiously comment that they are Platonists except when they are talking to philosophers. Skeptics of the Platonist position often challenge it by citing the "location problem": if mathematical abstractions exist apart from human minds, then where are they? Secular Platonists have a difficult time responding to this challenge; Augustine has provided Christian believers with an attractive answer: numbers (and perhaps more of mathematics) are ideas in God's mind. In making this claim, Augustine does not assume that God has a mind of the same sort that human beings do; rather, it is a way of saying that the ideas are part of God's nature and have been from eternity.

Greek philosophy provided the roots of Platonism, but there have been many branches of it, including some expressed in religious terms. The astronomer Johannes Kepler (1571–1630), best known for showing that the orbits of the planets were not circular but elliptical, argued that geometric shapes were ideas in God's mind that we are capable of understanding in the same way that God does. In other words, we can "think God's thoughts after him." He stated, "the chief aim of all investigations of the external world should be to discover the rational order and harmony which has been imposed on it by God and which He revealed to us in the language of mathematics."[47] Galileo (1564–1642) also thought of the world as being written in the language of mathematics. He thought of revelation from God as being presented in two books: the book of the Bible and the book of creation, both of which had their own language. Isaac Newton (1642–1727) saw his great work on the laws of gravitation as explaining those ideas in God's mind that provided the basis of God's relationship with the physical universe. Gottfried Leibniz (1646–1716), with Newton the founder of calculus, argued that God could not abolish mathematical truths without abolishing himself.

These are astounding claims. If they are right, they mean that the abstract concepts of mathematics have a profound and awesome significance and that in doing mathematics we are dealing with divine things. In the rest of this section, we will take a careful look at the arguments in favor of this position. In the next section we'll look at some arguments for a different approach, the one loosely associated with Aristotle.

Christian Platonists typically produce two classes of arguments for locating mathematics in God's mind: those from revealed theology (that is, from scripture); and those from natural theology (what we can understand about God using only our natural capacities, such as reason and perception).

We begin with revealed theology and four basic scriptural doctrines about God that are relevant to the nature of mathematics: 1) God desires to reveal himself to his people, 2) God is triune, 3) God is omniscient, and 4) God is faithful.

1. God's desire to reveal himself is evident throughout the Old Testament and culminates in the New Testament with the incarnation. The famous prologue to John's Gospel makes this point rather dramatically: "No one has seen God at any time; the only begotten God [that is, Jesus] who is in the bosom of the Father, He [Jesus] has explained Him" (John 1:18, NASB). The Greek word translated as *explained* also means *exegeted*. When biblical scholars *exegete* a passage of scripture, they intend to explain it fully. Thus, in the incarnation God has given us a very good picture of himself. But does this *exegesis*, so to speak, include revealing God's mind to us? Many Christians have been hesitant to speak about our knowing "God's mind" or "God's thoughts," claiming that claims to such knowledge are lacking in humility. Of course, a humble attitude towards claims we make about God is certainly appropriate, and the doctrine of the incarnation does not guarantee that our conclusions about God are always going to be correct. The doctrine can give us some confidence, however, for it tells us that God wants us to understand him.

2. God is triune, and would have been triune even if he hadn't created anything. Thus, the notion of trinity or "threeness" is a numerical attribute that applies to God and would have applied even apart from creation. From this perspective, "numerical laws" are not merely laws of creation. If we think that God is *necessarily* triune, then we may also conclude that at least some numerical ideas necessarily have application to God's reality.

3. Divine omniscience is the doctrine that God knows (and has always known) all that is knowable. For instance, even

though God does not know how to trisect an angle by straight edge and compass methods, God does know (and has always known) that such a procedure is logically impossible. It follows, then, that knowledge of mathematical concepts must have been eternally in God's mind.

4. The **law of noncontradiction** is the claim that an unambiguous proposition cannot be both true and false. Following Augustine, Christian Platonists would typically argue that the law of noncontradiction is part of God's nature. One approach, for example, would be to ground this law in God's faithfulness by appealing to passages such as 2 Timothy 2:13 (NASB): "If we are faithless, He remains faithful, for He cannot deny Himself." But if the law of noncontradiction is indeed applicable to God, then the power of logic originates in God's nature. Furthermore, the logician/philosopher Bertrand Russell (1872–1970) showed that, if we start from the law of noncontradiction and some very elementary ideas of forming sets, we can define the entire collection of natural numbers. Hence, this view also enables us to locate the natural numbers in God's nature.

When it comes to natural theology Christian Platonists also raise four arguments for locating mathematics in the mind of God: 1) the indispensability argument, 2) the argument from universality, 3) the argument from necessity, and 4) the *a priori* argument.

1. Scientific theorizing depends extensively upon mathematics. In fact, mathematics is seen as indispensable for doing science. Not only is mathematics necessary to do measurements and to give formulas for laws of physics and chemistry, but frequently manipulations of these formulas yield surprising predictions that turn out to be true. This close linkage between mathematics and the physical world gives credence to Augustine's idea that God used mathematical ideas to provide patterns for creation. But if he used mathematical ideas to provide patterns

for creation, a natural conclusion is that these ideas were present in God's mind at creation.

2. Another argument refers to the universality of mathematics. While culture does affect the way a people-group develops mathematics, many mathematically similar results have been developed independently by different cultures. Thus, the universality of mathematics can be taken as evidence that mathematics transcends human minds. If mathematical entities are transcendent, where are they located? For a Christian Platonist, it is an easy step to the answer: "In God's mind."

3. Simple statements like $5 + 7 = 12$ and various laws of logic such as the law of noncontradiction are examples of assertions that appear to be necessarily true. Mathematical concepts seem to exist in some necessary and noncontingent way. It is hard to imagine them not being true. Thus it seems that they must be true in any world. This apparent necessity also adds credibility to the notion that mathematical concepts are eternal ideas originating in God.

4. The term *a priori* refers to knowledge that is known independently of experience. We seem to have confidence, for example, that mathematical statements such as $2 + 2 = 4$ are true even in parts of the universe that we haven't experienced. Some people might object, however, and say that mathematical truths such a $2 + 2 = 4$ are known from experience alone: we've just happened to observe that two apples combined with two more apples results in four apples being present. But extending the idea that mathematical knowledge depends on experience alone to all of mathematics may be difficult. For example, Augustine argues that even small children have an intuitive understanding of infinity even though infinity is outside of our experience. Where, then, did such knowledge come from? While there is no universal agreement on this point, many philosophers would stay that such knowledge is *a priori*, and a Christian might well say that it comes from God.

This, then, is the case for claiming that numbers (and perhaps more of mathematics) have existed in God's mind from eternity. Keep in mind that the view we have just presented is simply that: a way of looking at how things might really be. The key idea of this view is that mathematical concepts are part of God's nature.

God as Transcending Mathematics

A Christian approach to mathematics does not have to insist that mathematics is an eternal reality. An alternative view, loosely in the Aristotelian perspective, views mathematics as a human activity dealing with aspects of created reality. Mathematics is about human beings recognizing and abstracting numerical and spatial patterns they find in the world around them, and systematically putting their discoveries into logical and symbolic formulations. This view emphasizes that mathematics is more than pure deduction; the concepts, axioms, and definitions used in mathematics derive ultimately from the human experience of creation. There is always a connection back to the creation, broadly conceived, no matter how far mathematical ideas have been abstracted from their source. Mathematical abstraction is about developing a relatively simple model of certain features we experience, a representation that strips away some properties in order to focus more intently on others. For example, abstracting a straight line ignores minute irregularities and physical context. In so doing, it allows for further analyzing, generalizing, and synthesizing. Thus, this alternative viewpoint sees mathematical theorizing as a human cognitive activity. One might refer to the position just outlined as a type of **mathematical empiricism**.

One classical expression of the Aristotelian tradition (but finding fuller expression in the Middle Ages with thinkers such as William of Ockham) is **nominalism**. This is a view that abstract concepts do not exist in any transcendent way; rather they are linguistic conventions that enable us to communicate effectively with each other. From this perspective, the effectiveness of mathematics does not accord mathematics any special status but is a part of the broader effectiveness of language. Mathematical concepts need not enjoy a higher status than more mundane concepts like "committee" or "highway." This approach was widely studied during the medieval period by many Christian thinkers, but faded into the background during the scientific revolution. Today it is enjoying something of a renaissance. Some secular thinkers use this view to avoid the theological implications of the transcendence of mathematics of the Platonist view.

The mathematical empiricist view presented here draws from the thoughts of the mid-twentieth-century Christian philosophers D. H. Th. Vollenhoven and H. Dooyeweerd, both of whom developed a branch of neo-Calvinism. There are two ideas this view keeps separate when talking about mathematics:

1. There are mathematical patterns and structures present in creation. God established and sustains these regularities.
2. There are mathematical theories developed to account for those patterns and structures. Such theorizing is the work of human beings, part of our responsibility to act as caretakers of creation.

Let's elaborate on this perspective. Regarding the first point, mathematical patterns are not seen as part of God's nature; they are part of the created order. The Genesis story emphasizes that God created the world with order and complexity. Mathematicians seek to understand the numerical and spatial order given in the natural world. This order is seen as divinely ordained, but not as divine. In other words, God is not subject to that order, but transcends it and all things subject to it. Nevertheless, he interacts with it and promises to maintain it, including the numerical and spatial patterns he created. This promise is often described in the Bible as a covenant that God has made, and is exemplified in passages such as Jeremiah 33:25–26 where God declares that he has established a "covenant with day and night and the fixed laws of heaven and earth."

The key difference between this perspective and Christian Platonism is that, for Platonists, some mathematics as well as the laws of logic are part of God's nature; this alternative perspective states that they are created and hence contingent on God's will. They could have been different and God is not constrained to act in accord with them, except as bound by his promises.

Regarding the second point, people develop concepts and theories to try to capture the order that God has made. By interacting with the created order, we recognize and analyze mathematical patterns with the hope of comprehending them in a system of interconnected ideas and propositions. However, we are limited in our theorizing by being a part of the creation. Our ability to conceptualize in creative ways is a gift of God; this gift does not necessarily imply, however, that we understand things as God does. For example, our understanding of number has developed over time. The Romans had a numeration system that was unable to handle arbitrarily large numbers, general common fractions, or negative numbers. Zero was not developed as a bona fide number until after AD 200, though it had been used as an intermediate place holder before then. Complex numbers and other number systems forced mathematicians to reconceptualize what a number can be. In fact, each time new number concepts are developed, mathematicians reconceptualize the notion of number. Different number systems capture various numerical aspects of creation. Thinking of mathematics as a human activity emphasizes that, while God has ordered creation (including its numerical and spatial aspects), humans are responsible to figure out its intricate structure as best they can. In doing so they use the concepts and theories available to them up to that point and recognize that a more refined approach may become standard as knowledge advances further.

Mathematical empiricists present arguments that run counter to the arguments advanced for Christian Platonism presented in the previous section. The first suggests that a divine origin of mathematics does not necessarily imply that numbers (or other mathematical concepts) are part of God's nature. That God is trinitarian does not imply that the properties we experience of numbers apply to God's nature. Likewise, God's omniscience only implies that he knows numbers; God could know them from eternity as he knows trees in the creation but they could still be contingent. Finally, indispensability may simply point to God's ordering of the creation, and not that mathematics is part of God's nature.

A second argument, related to the first, points out that universal properties do not need to be divine and eternal. For example, there is a story of an East Coast farmer who stocked a pond with trout, but had difficulty with osprey diving in. A solution was to insert stakes with wires and netting to protect the fish. A visiting African noted how his people protected their fish in a similar manner. Expressing surprise to his pastor, the farmer got the succinct reply, "Same problem, same God." We are made by the same creator and, although we develop independently, we share the same problem solving skills. Thus, the fact that different cultures make similar mathematical observations does not make such observations divine; the similar observations may simply be due to the similarity of our created minds. In other words, mathematical concepts depend on our God-given ability to think, and the apparent *a priori* quality of some mathematical knowledge can be accounted for by the fact that God gave us the capacity to do mathematics.

A third argument points out that concepts depend on the created order: that a mathematical proposition *seems* to be necessarily true gives no basis to think that it *is necessarily* true in every possible world. When we claim that some axiom in mathematics seems self-evident, we are merely recognizing that we cannot think of it otherwise. Apparent necessity does not imply absolute necessity or independence from this creation. The history of mathematics has examples of faulty claims to "absolute necessity." Since Euclid's time, mathematicians believed that the angles of a triangle summed to 180 degrees. This "fact" was seen as a necessary, noncontingent truth, independent of experience or even the existence of material things. But with the discovery and acceptance of non-Euclidean geometry in the mid-nineteenth century, it was recognized that, in some geometries, triangles can have angle sums different from 180 degrees. This discovery made some thinkers question the nature of truth itself. These events illustrate that we must be cautious when thinking that certain mathematical claims are absolutely certain.

As indicated above, this perspective emphasizes the limits of our ability to develop mathematical concepts and places its emphasis on mathematics as a human activity rather than on the divine nature of mathematics. For example, the work of Kurt Gödel indicates that we cannot prove that our rich mathematical theories are consistent by elementary methods. This result indicates a limitation of our creaturely logic. Furthermore, Imre Lakatos, in *Proofs and Refutations*, demonstrated that the context of mathematical statements gets revised as more knowledge is gained. Describing mathematics as a human activity takes into account the inherent and unavoidable incompleteness of our knowledge and our logic.

The creation mandate discussed in chapter 1 of this book is also a main focus: to exercise dominion over the creation in ways that take good care of it, and to allow for its potential to develop. In Genesis 1, God named objects that he created. To the Hebrews this naming act signified that God ruled over these objects. It meant, for example, that the Hebrews were not to worship the sun as a god, in contrast to the practice of other cultures. In Genesis 2 God asked Adam to name the animals. God asking Adam to name the animals illustrates this understanding; naming demonstrates the caretaker function over creation implicit in the creation mandate. The mathematician's task is like this naming. That is, mathematical theorizing is a human activity and is part of the caretaker function God assigned to us.

From the empiricist perspective, God is not bound by the laws of creation in the same way creatures are subject to those laws. Neither is God bound by human logic. Advocates of this view interpret scripture passages such as Romans 11:33–34—"Oh, the depth of the riches of the wisdom and knowledge of God! How unsearchable his judgments, and his paths beyond tracing out! Who has known the mind of the Lord? Or who has been his counselor?"—as supporting their belief. Roy Clouser states that the creaturely laws "govern our thinking such that we can't form a concept or an idea of what anything would be that is not subject to these laws."[48] A partial analogy would be a flatlander (see chapter 4) considering a sphere; his thoughts are inadequate to capture the full nature of the sphere. The biblical scholar Al Wolters argues along similar lines, claiming that our rationality is limited in application to the created cosmos and that our knowledge of heaven can only be based on the scriptures, not on reasoning that extrapolates from creation. Some who hold this view state along with Clouser that, "Whereas creatures can't break the law of non-contradiction because they're subject to it, God's transcendent being can't break that law because it doesn't apply to God's being at all."[49] This is not to say that God can contradict himself. In interacting with creation, God accommodates himself to that which he created. As an illustration, if there were a three-valued logic by which God operated with respect to certain things, but only two values were realized in the creation, then for us, we would see only a two-valued logic. But God being greater than the created logic would have additional options available to him, outside creation, that are not available to us. Further, the fact that there are additional options available to God does not imply that we cannot trust God or our mathematical representations of creation. The guarantee of our trust in God is God's covenant with the creation and his word revealed in scripture. There is also much evidence for our trust in mathematical representations: the order in creation, God's creational mandate, and the effectiveness of mathematics that we discussed in chapter 8. The effectiveness of the modeling activity is neither a surprise nor an accident. It illustrates that, as image bearers of God in the pursuit of our God-given cultural mandate, we are able to make sense of the created order. It is an illustration of God's faithfulness. As Blaise Pascal (1623–1662) observed, being in God's image, we have the ability to make sense of creation, in order to fulfill our task to care for it, to enjoy it, and to develop it, but the role of logic is limited.

Comparing and Contrasting the Views

The Christian Platonist view has historically been more widely affirmed than the Christian mathematical empiricist view. It provides a simple, clear, explanation of mathematics' universality and usefulness in science. It also provides attractive explanations of the effectiveness of logic in understanding the world and of the apparent necessity

Mathematics: Discovered or Invented?

In its June, 2008 issue, the newsletter of the European Mathematical Society featured two articles on "The Question": Is mathematics discovered or invented? Both were by well-known authors, one by Reuben Hersh, a philosopher of mathematics, and one by Barry Mazur, a mathematician.

Hersh's answer is "invented." Platonism, writes Hersh, "says mathematical objects exist independently of our knowledge or activity, and mathematical truth is objective, with the same status as scientific truth about the physical world. This may be boiled down to the phrase 'out there.' That's where mathematical entities are, meaning, not 'in here.'" But the idea that mathematical objects exist "out there" is, for Hersh, false. He goes on to say that Platonism "is incompatible with the standard view of the nature of reality, as held by the majority of scientists and mathematicians: there is only one universe, one real world, which is physical reality, including its elaboration into the realm of living things, and elaborated from there into the realm of humankind with its social, cultural, and psychological aspects. I have argued that these social, cultural and psychological aspects of humankind are real, not illusory or negligible, and that the nature of mathematical truth and existence is to be understood in that realm, rather than in some other independent 'abstract' reality." So we can see that Hersh is a materialist and his "invented" answer expresses his understanding that mathematics is rooted in human social, cultural, and psychological activity.[50]

For Mazur, the question is intensely real but not as clear cut as it is for Hersh. He says, "If you engage in mathematics long enough, you bump into The Question, and it won't just go away." He acknowledges the "in here" versus "out there" distinction but insists that whichever option we choose, it must be grounded in the experience of doing mathematics. He writes, "The bizarre aspect of the mathematical experience—and this is what gives such fierce energy to The Question—is that one feels (I feel) that mathematical ideas can be hunted down, and in a way that is essentially different from, say, the way I am currently hunting the next word to write to finish this sentence. One can be a hunter and gatherer of mathematical concepts, but one has no ready words for the location of the hunting grounds. Of course we humans are beset with illusions, and the feeling just described could be yet another. There may be no location." He does not take a position as to whether "in here" or "out there" is the correct answer, but he does add clarity to what is at stake.[51]

For Platonists, Mazur writes, "mathematics is the account we give of the timeless architecture of the cosmos. The essential mission, then, of mathematics is the accurate description, and exfoliation, of this architecture." He cautions parties arguing on both sides. The "out there" position, he points out, "has the curious effect of reducing some of the urgency of that staple of mathematical life: *rigorous proof.* Some mathematicians think of mathematical proof as the certificate guaranteeing trustworthiness of, and formulating the nature of, the building-blocks of the edifices that comprise our constructions. Without proof: no building-blocks, no edifice." So, he says, advocates of this position need to provide an adequate account of proof from their perspective. The "in here" position, he argues often uses irrelevant arguments and its proponents need to be more careful. For instance, arguing that mathematics is a human cultural activity has no relevancy to the question; descriptions of the Grand Canyon written by three people would be shaped by their cultures and personal psychology in different ways, but that wouldn't make the Grand Canyon a cultural phenomenon.[52]

What are we to make of these claims? The two positions we have primarily focused upon in this chapter agree that mathematics is "out there," but in different ways. The Platonist places the location in the divine mind; the Christian mathematical

(continued)

empiricist view places it in the creation. The latter position also adds an "in here" dimension by stating that, although God created the patterns of creation, humans identify and conceptualize those patterns. For example, axioms and definitions are not deduced. They are created to model the creation. Thus, there are two different aspects to discovery as well: discovering the patterns in creation, and the discovering the deductive consequences of our models. Further, the "in here" category needs to recognize that this creative work is sometimes individual, sometimes communal. In developing axioms and definitions, the mathematical work is empirical. Mathematicians will often experiment with different formulations of a definition to best capture what they are trying to model.

Thus, as we mentioned above, a Platonist answers the discovered/invented question with an unambiguous "discovered." The Christian mathematical empiricist answer includes more layers. Christian Platonists have a ready response to Mazur's concern with proof. In doing mathematics we are dealing with divine things and we need to treat them with great respect. The empiricist position shares much of this concern, but the urgency is not due to dealing with divine matter. It is more simply due to honoring the creator.

Mazur concludes his article with a statement expressing his reaction when someone begins to influence him to think that The Question is "no big deal": "But someone who is not in love won't manage to definitively convince someone in love of the non-existence of eros; so this mood never overtakes me for long. Happily I soon snap out of it, and remember again the remarkable sense of independence—autonomy even—of mathematical concepts, and the transcendental quality, the uniqueness—and the passion—of doing mathematics. I resolve then that (Plato or Anti-Plato) whatever I come to believe about The Question, my belief must thoroughly respect and not ignore all this."[53]

of numbers, that is, that both logic and numbers originate in God's nature. The second view also provides an attractive account of universality and usefulness. It provides a more extended account of human creativity in doing mathematics. It affirms a significantly stronger sense of God's transcendence than the first view; that is, it assumes that God is not constrained to act in accord with the laws of mathematics outside of creation. Also, by assuming this strong sense of transcendence, it presents God as less comprehensible than the first view.

The two perspectives can also plausibly be associated with two classic doctrines relating to God's nature: immanence and transcendence. The first position stresses limitations on God placed by his goodness and consistency and his desire to be known by us. The second emphasizes God's separation from creation along with his faithful upholding of creation. It affirms revelation but insists that, in revealing himself, God has accommodated the expression of himself to our capacities and finiteness.

Conclusion

This chapter has addressed three of the big questions with which we began this book, focusing primarily on the ontological questions:

1. Mathematical entities like 2, +, =, and 4 are not physical objects like atoms and galaxies, so what are they?
2. Do principles of logic apply only to the natural world or to God also?
3. Is mathematics discovered or invented?

The answers provided by Christian formulations that stem from the Platonist and Aristotelian traditions differ. For the first question, Christian Platonists see mathematical objects as being part of God's nature. The Christian empiricist sees mathematics as a human modeling of patterns found in creation. Regarding the second question, the Platonist sees logic as an expression of God's consistency and part of his nature; the empiricist views it as an expression of God's faithfulness and part of the created order, but asserts that principles of human logic do not apply to God's nature. As for the third question, both answer "discovered," although an Aristotelian answer also includes elements of invention.

The two viewpoints we have presented differ, but there are many commonalities. For both, God is an active participant in creation, sustaining and upholding it. God is faithful and God is good. God is sovereign and we are his creatures, part of creation. We have been given the opportunity to investigate God's good creation, and this understanding motivates our study of mathematics, which has at least a two-pronged purpose: to enable us to be more effective stewards of creation, and to give glory to God. In faith, we can marvel at the beauty, order, complexity, and surprising connections that God has created.

Suggestions for Further Reading

Augustine. *On Free Choice of the Will*. Translated by Thomas Williams. Indianapolis: Hackett, 1993. This is the primary source for understanding the Augustinian perspective on the nature of mathematics. In this book, Augustine discussed mathematics in the context of a proof of God's existence.

Clouser, Roy A. *The Myth of Religious Neutrality*. Rev. ed. Notre Dame, IN: Univ. of Notre Dame Press, 2005. Clouser argues that all disciplines employ underlying presuppositions that are religious in nature. This is the most widely read English-language resource for understanding Dooyeweerd's philosophy. See especially chapters 1, 4, 10, and 11.

Jongsma, Calvin. "Mathematics, Always Important, Never Enough: A Christian Perspective on Mathematics and Mathematics Education." *Journal of the Association of Christians in the Mathematical Sciences* (October 2006). In the context of a letter to his granddaughter, Jongsma presents a view similar to the empiricist perspective on mathematics.

Menzel, Chris. "God and Mathematical Objects." In *Mathematics in a Postmodern Age: A Christian Perspective*. Edited by

R. W. Howell and W. J. Bradley. Grand Rapids: Eerdmans, 2001. Argues for the perspective that mathematics consists of ideas in God's mind, and addresses some challenging problems that arise from set theory for this perspective.

Plantinga, Alvin. *Does God Have a Nature?* Milwaukee: Marquette Univ. Press, 1980. The most complete contemporary presentation of the perspective that abstract concepts are ideas in God's mind.

———. "Theism and Mathematics." *Theology and Science* 9, no. 1 (February 2011). A brief and highly readable paper arguing that the effectiveness of mathematics and the existence of abstract concepts are better explained by theism than by naturalism.

Wolters, Al. "Dutch Neo-Calvinism: Worldview, Philosophy and Rationality." In *Rationality in the Calvinian Tradition*. Edited by H. Hart, J. Van den Hoeven, and N. Wolterstorff. Lanham, MD: University Press of America, 1983. An essay providing various arguments for making a sharp distinction between human rationality and divinity, focusing on the thoughts of both Dooyeweerd and Vollenhoven, in a book that presents various views of the relationship of God and rationality.

EXERCISES

1. For each of the following mathematical entities, do you see it as discovered, invented, or some combination of both? Explain.
   a. The Pythagorean theorem
   b. The equation $i^2 + 1 = 0$
   c. Boolean arithmetic $(1 + 1 = 1)$
   d. A random sample taken by the Gallup poll
   e. A mathematical model of the waiting line in a bank
2. How do you assess the two views described above? Do you favor one of them over the other? Why?
3. Here are some critiques that have been made of the two main views of this chapter. For each, say whether you think it is a sound critique and explain why.

    a. Of Christian Platonism: If God created the world according to some preexisting eternal patterns as described by the phrase "God used mathematics in creating the world," then this is inconsistent with the doctrine that God created the world out of nothing.

    b. Of Christian Platonism: This position elevates a created aspect to the level of divinity, which can be seen as a form of idolatry. It puts a confidence in God's goodness on something other than faith in God's word.

    c. Of Christian mathematical empiricism: This position emphasizes a sharp distinction between God and creation. Some in this position also assert that the law of noncontradiction does not apply to God. But making such a sharp distinction uses the law of noncontradiction. So this assertion is inconsistent.

    d. Of Christian mathematical empiricism: If we cannot trust that our mathematics and logic are eternal and if God transcends these, then God can contradict himself. Hence, this position provides no basis for trusting in God's goodness. It can only affirm that God has promised to act according to his covenant, but it cannot affirm that goodness is part of God's nature.

4. The two positions presented in this chapter appealed to scriptural passages to support their beliefs. Do you agree with their interpretation of the following passages? Explain your reasoning.

    a. Second Timothy 2:13 (used by Christian Platonists to support a belief that the law of noncontradiction is part of God's nature).

    b. Romans 11:33–34 (used by Christian mathematical empiricists to support a belief that God's nature is not bound by human logic).

5. Some neurophysiologists are currently trying to understand how human brains do mathematics. Barry Mazur has argued that even if they succeed, their results will shed no light on the

question of whether or not Platonism is true. Is he right? Why? Does his assertion also apply to the arguments for Christian mathematical empiricism?

6. A supporter of mathematical empiricism might assert that the first view only argues for divine origin of mathematics, not for mathematics being part of the divine nature. Test if you agree with this assertion on each of the eight arguments for Christian Platonism.

7. What do Christian Platonism and Christian mathematical empiricism have in common? How do they differ? Are they more alike or more different?

8. The nineteenth-century mathematician Leopold Kronecker quipped "God created the integers. All the rest is the work of Man." Evaluate this assertion in the light of the ideas presented in this chapter.

9. Chapter 9 introduced you to the schools of thought known as formalism and structuralism. The focus was on their approach to mathematical knowledge. Do their proponents have anything to say about the nature of mathematical objects? Write an essay that investigates this question, including your assessment of the various positions.

Chapter 11

AN APOLOGY

> *But in your hearts set apart Christ as Lord. Always be prepared*
> *to give an answer to everyone who asks you to give the reason for*
> *the hope you have.*
>
> 1 PETER 3:15

The English word *apology* can be used in two ways: to express regret, and to offer a justification. If the title of this chapter seems odd to you, it may be that you are thinking of the first meaning and are thus wondering why we are apologizing for writing this book!

Well, we are going to offer an apology, but it will be in the second sense. That is, we are going to map out a justification for the pursuit of mathematics, whether that pursuit be a casual investigation or a lifelong career. In doing so we will pull together some of the main ideas of this book, but many of our comments will apply to other fields of study as well. Thus, our discussion should be helpful to you even if your main area of interest is far removed from mathematics.

We begin by taking a cue from a person you read about in chapters 7, 8, and 9, the famous British mathematician G. H. Hardy. In 1940 he published *A Mathematician's Apology*, where he formulated answers to two questions that all mathematicians should deem important: whether the pursuit of mathematics is a worthy effort in general, and why, regardless of the value of mathematics, they are engaged in it.

We will modify Hardy's questions so that they become relevant to all educated people. First, should you bother with the study of mathematics? In other words, is the discipline of mathematics worthy of your attention, even if you do not plan on pursuing it or a related field as a career? Second, assuming you have sufficient interest and talent, is the pursuit of mathematics something you should consider as a worthy calling?

Should Every Educated Person Study Mathematics?

We have stated in this book that the capacity we have as humans to engage in mathematical activity is a good gift from God. But not everyone has the same degree of mathematical interest or talent, so are those with less interest or talent exempt, so to speak, from seeking to develop it? After all, Paul himself says, with reference to spiritual gifts, "All are not apostles, are they? All are not prophets, are they? All are not teachers, are they? All are not workers of miracles, are they? All do not have gifts of healings, do they? All do not speak with tongues, do they? All do not interpret, do they?" (1 Cor. 12:29–30, NASB).

Of course, Paul is asking rhetorical questions to point out that different gifts are given to different people. It hardly follows from this train of thought that a person with minimal interest or talent in mathematics need not bother devoting some serious time in studying it. Indeed, we maintain that the study of mathematics is important for every educated person, and especially for a Christian. In fact, a good argument can be made that such study will not only make people more effective in their Christian calling; it will also enrich their lives in personal ways, and in ways that will make them more effective as they work to bring about peace, wholeness, and harmony in our world.

Effective Service

The famous British historian Arnold J. Toynbee (1889–1975) lamented his decision not to pursue a minimal study of mathematics. Note the end of the following quotation where he indirectly indicates that, in making this decision, he was subsequently a less effective citizen than he would have been otherwise.

At about the age of sixteen, I was offered a choice which, in retrospect, I can see that I was not mature enough, at the time, to make wisely. The choice was between starting on the calculus and, alternatively, giving up mathematics altogether and spending the time saved from it on reading Latin and Greek literature more widely. I chose to give up mathematics, and I have lived to regret this keenly after it has become too late to repair my mistake. The calculus, even a taste of it, would have given me an important and illuminating additional outlook on the Universe, whereas, by the time at which the choice was presented to me, I had already got far enough in Latin and Greek to have been able to go farther with them unaided. So the choice that I made was the wrong one, yet it was natural that I should choose as I did. I was not good at mathematics; I did not like the stuff. . . . Looking back, I feel sure that I ought not to have been offered the choice; the rudiments, at least, of the calculus ought to have been compulsory for me. One ought, after all, to be initiated into the life of the world in which one is going to have to live. I was going to have to live in the Western World . . . and the calculus, like the full-rigged sailing ship, is one of the characteristic expressions of the modern Western genius.[54]

This is a powerful statement, but we can take Toynbee's thoughts even further. It is not just the Western world, and not just a study of calculus that is important for living in today's global society. As the British mathematician Ian Stewart observed, "We encounter mathematics everywhere, every day, but we hardly ever know it."[55]

Stewart goes on to list concrete examples, claiming that, most of the time, the use of mathematics is invisible to us. He asks us to imagine what the world would look like if everything that relied on mathematics displayed a sticker saying, "Maths inside." There would be a sticker on every computer, every credit card (transactions are encrypted using mathematical algorithms), every car, every airplane, every communications device, every movie, and every vegetable.

Every vegetable? Yes. Virtually every vegetable or dairy product you buy comes through a very intricate commercial breeding program. These programs require sophisticated mathematical analyses. Even DNA sequencing makes use of techniques that involve statistical sampling of incomplete data.

The list goes on and on, but while the above examples may be good illustrations of the use of mathematics in daily life, a lingering issue remains. You might happily grant that mathematics is important. After all, we devoted chapter 8 of this book to explain how mathematics might even be considered to be unreasonably effective. You still may think, however, that (so long as there are others who enjoy mathematics and are good at it) there is no reason that you yourself would directly benefit from its study, Toynbee's comment notwithstanding. How—practically, and in a direct way—might even a cursory study of mathematics, such as the reading of this book, help you be an effective "kingdom-citizen" in today's complex society?

As one example imagine that as a school board member you are involved in an acrimonious PTA meeting. Loud voices are clashing over the issue of the teaching of evolution. You are asked for your opinion. How do you react? Regardless of your view on the subject we'd like to think that your reading of chapter 5 would enable you to have a more nuanced view of the nature of chance and how a Christian might appropriately dialogue with others on topics that involve a deep understanding of this issue.

Indeed, the study of mathematics promotes important thinking habits of all sorts: analyzing carefully the implications of one's statements, being careful with the meanings of words, imagining alternative interpretations or possibilities for action, and recognizing that the mere declaration of your opinion on an issue does not render it true. These qualities are no doubt what Stanley Hauerwas had in mind when he wrote, "In truth I suspect the best moral training that occurs in the contemporary university is in the sciences. At least in those disciplines the student is disciplined to acquire habits necessary to participate in ongoing research. . . . That the highest praise one mathematician can give to another mathematician is that the work they do is 'deep' is a lovely indication of the moral character of mathematics."[56]

Think back to some of the chapters you read in this book, and to some of the exercises listed for you to consider. Would you agree that they contributed to the kind of thinking Hauerwas applauds? To be more specific, recall your study of the nature of proof in chapter 6, of the nature of mathematical knowledge in chapter 9, and the nature of mathematics itself in chapter 10. These are very abstract chapters, but with practical benefits. Chapter 6, in its discussion of mathematical proof, commented, "mathematical proof does more than tell us something *is* true; the best proofs give us a feeling for *why* it is true." That kind of thinking, when translated into different contexts, can be of enormous value. For example, a popular negotiating technique, known as "principled negotiation," asks that negotiation leaders focus on four tasks: 1) separating the people involved from the problem at hand; 2) concentrating on the ultimate interests of the respective parties (and not necessarily their current positions); 3) creatively suggesting options for mutual gain; and 4) requiring objective criteria. In a very real way these are the tasks one must take up when creating or understanding a mathematical proof.

Chapter 10 introduced different ways that thinkers have come to view the nature of mathematical objects. Likewise, chapter 9 raised important issues relating to how knowledge is acquired, and introduced you to some different schools of thinking about that question within the mathematical community. Being aware of these different approaches, and understanding them, can help promote a more disciplined, effective, and humble attitude in dialoging with those who may have views different from yours. Mathematics has been accused of being objective and dogmatic. While we do not dispute that the conclusions of mathematics may be so labeled, a real understanding of the mathematical enterprise should produce in those who study it the opposite of dogmatism: respect and understanding of the other.

Personal Enrichment

A classic justification for a liberal arts education is that a person so educated has been enriched. The use of such language, however, should not be taken as referring only to personal satisfaction. It also has to do with fully actualizing one's potential for service. Many Christian institutions have labeled this quality as being educated for *shalom*. *Shalom* is a Hebrew word that connotes wholeness and harmony in the world.

Chapter 7 discussed beauty in mathematics. It pointed out that aesthetic contemplation gives us a foretaste of the joy of shalom and that such contemplation helps us see more clearly the beauty of God and his creation. In fact, the deeper one goes into mathematics, the more one is able to see deeper aspects of beauty. Ian Stewart discusses this fact in terms of more fully appreciating a rainbow. He describes at length the joy one gets in understanding the geometry involved in the refraction of light rays, and in understanding that different viewers actually see different rainbows. He closes his illustration with an important point.

> Some people think that this kind of understanding "spoils" the emotional experience. I think this is rubbish. It demonstrates a depressing sort of aesthetic complacency. People who make such statements often like to pretend they are poetic types, wide open to the world's wonders, but in fact they suffer from a serious lack of curiosity: they refuse to believe the world is more wonderful than their own limited imaginations. Nature is always deeper, richer, and more interesting than you thought, and mathematics gives you a very powerful way to appreciate this. . . . I'd say that my understanding of the geometry of the rainbow adds a new dimension to its beauty. It doesn't take anything away from the emotional experience.[57]

It is important not to fall into the trap of thinking that disciplined, careful reasoning must somehow be detached from emotional fulfillment. Those who understand the beauty of a mathematical proof or the breathtaking display of mathematical ideas experience emotion joined with analysis on a daily basis.

Chapter 4 discussed, from a Christian perspective, how nature might be deeper and richer than you thought. In it you learned about a variety of dimensions and connected them with spiritual ideas. It illustrated, for example, what *flatlanders* (beings living on a two-dimensional surface) who were visited by a three-dimensional object would see. It then applied this thinking to give one possible model of the incarnation. The physicist Hugh Ross has used similar dimensional ideas to explain God's ability to answer the prayers of millions of people who are simultaneously petitioning him. While such ideas can be useful metaphors in helping to understand mystifying spiritual realities, it is important to understand that these models do not necessarily correspond with reality. They can be helpful guides for understanding, but can be dangerous if pressed beyond their natural limitations.

Chapter 3 explained the amazing fact that there are different sizes of infinity. It is hard to imagine Christians learning and understanding this mathematical result without also realizing that their thinking of God as being infinite must now take on a new, expanded, and richer meaning. The chapter also demonstrated a result that is shocking when set against two curious facts:

1. between any two *irrational* numbers lies a *rational* number;
2. between any two *rational* numbers lies an *irrational* number.

The shocking part came from a result due to Georg Cantor: there are more irrational numbers than rational numbers. The word *more* in this context means that the two sets cannot be put into a one-to-one correspondence with each other, but even that clarification leaves Cantor's result as a paradoxical issue given the two facts stated above. We should take comfort from the fact that there are paradoxical ideas in a carefully defined, logically precise system such as mathematics. As we saw earlier, mathematics can help explain some of the paradoxes in our Christian faith. Ironically, being filled with paradoxes itself, mathematics can help remove the angst when we find paradoxes in our faith.

Thus, not only can mathematics help create shalom, not only can it help you as you seek to be salt and light to a lost world, it can also contribute in meaningful ways to an enriched understanding of your Christian faith.

Mathematics as a Vocation

G. H. Hardy gives two reasons why a person might reasonably choose the pursuit of mathematics as a career. His argument, you'll note, applies to any career: "I do what I do because it is the one and only thing that I can do at all well. I am a lawyer, or a stockbroker, or a professional cricketer, because I have some real talent for that particular job."[58] Hardy's second reason is similar: "There is *nothing* that I can do particularly well. I do what I do because it came my way. I really never had a chance of doing anything else."[59]

Hardy was an atheist. Because of his religious views Christians could erroneously be dismissive of his more eccentric remarks. Lest we fall into that trap it would be wise to take a closer look at them. At first glance Hardy's second reason seems to describe a depressing situation. The person he depicts appears to be stuck in a certain career. It is important to remember, however, that Hardy had extremely high standards, and for him there were very few people who were "world class" at anything. But that fact should not surprise us. That is more or less what being world class means. The more relevant question for a Christian is not how good we are at something relative to others; it is how, given whatever talents we possess, we should use them.

We'll discuss the question of using our talents in a moment. First we need to say a few words about relative comparisons. Vernon Grounds (1914–2010), who served at Denver Seminary for over sixty years, was fond of pointing out the danger in making them. He often quoted from the closing portion of the Gospel of John, where Jesus indicated to Peter that he was going to suffer an unpleasant death. Peter, upon hearing these words and seeing John the disciple, said to Jesus, "What about this man?" Jesus responded, "If I want him to remain until I come, what is that to you? You follow me!" (John 21:21–22, NASB). According to Grounds the lesson from this passage is clear: we are to focus our energies on following our Lord and not let relative comparisons to others—who may seem much better than us at a variety of tasks—distract or discourage us.

What about Hardy's first remark? Should you do something because you are good at it (even in a lesser sense than Hardy intended)? Well, no, and yes. The Presbyterian writer Fredrick Buechner helps with both answers in his book *Wishful Thinking: A Theological ABC*, when he says, "The place God calls you is the place where your deep gladness and the world's deep hunger meet."[60] In other words, say no to a career in something you excel at if the world is in no need of your developing that talent. To illustrate, the world probably does not need a plethora of world-class tiddlywinks players. So, your ability to trounce everyone you've ever played in that game is probably not a good reason for developing that gift into a career.

If, however, the gifts you have correspond to something you can do for which there is a real need you may very well say yes. Indeed, the Bible teaches that you should use your God-given gifts to the fullest extent:

> Since we have gifts that differ according to the grace given to us, each of us is to exercise them accordingly: if prophecy, according to the proportion of his faith; if service, in his serving; or he who teaches, in his teaching; or he who exhorts, in his exhortation; he who gives, with liberality; he who leads, with diligence; he who shows mercy, with cheerfulness. (Rom. 12:6–8, NASB)

Thus, if you have talent in some area, you should take that as *prima facie* evidence that God would be pleased if you engaged in a vocation whose primary purpose was to use that talent.

Notice that we've just made a linguistic switch. Up until now we've been referring to an occupation as a career. Just now we used the word *vocation*. It comes from the Latin *vocatio* and literally means "calling." It is often used to designate an appointment to a particular business or profession. The theologian Kathryn Kleinhans states that, prior to Martin Luther, the word "typically referred to a special calling to religious life, as a priest or as a member of a vowed order. Such vocation was understood as a higher calling, set over against life in the household and in civil society."[61] According to Kleinhans, Luther's ability to see a (secular) vocation as a Christian calling was one of the great contributions of the Reformation.

Let's recast Kleinhans's comment with the language of chapter 5, which discussed how God may use secondary agents to accomplish his purposes. When viewed in the context of trying to bring wholeness to the world, Christian mathematicians may very well see themselves as those secondary agents, and thus have a career that is also a vocation.

Thus, whether you choose to use your gift in mathematics—or any field—as a vehicle for your Christian vocation depends on several factors. Do you like it? Are you good at it? Does the world need it? Do others encourage you in it? If your answer is yes then you might very well be near the junction between your deep gladness and the world's deep hunger. We hope, in some small way, that this book will help you arrive at that junction. Shalom!

Suggestions for Further Reading

Buechner, Fredrick. *Wishful Thinking: A Theological ABC*. San Francisco: HarperSanFrancisco, 1993. An alphabetical look at various theological concepts.

Hardy, G. H. *A Mathematician's Apology*. London: Cambridge Univ. Press, 1967. A classic defense of the mathematical enterprise by one of the greatest mathematicians of the twentieth century.

Kleinhans, Kathryn. "The Work of a Christian: Vocation in Lutheran Perspective." *Word and World* 25, no. 4 (Fall 2005): 394–402. A scholarly essay exploring the nature of Christian vocation.

Stewart, Ian. *Letters to a Young Mathematician*. New York: Basic Books, 2005. A modern version of Hardy's *A Mathematician's Apology*, Stewart's book is a series of letters addressed to a fictitious student (but who is a compilation of all his students) as she progresses from high school to college to a professorship in mathematics.

EXERCISES

1. Hardy gave at least two justifications for the value of mathematics: (1) Whatever a mathematician creates is *permanent*, unlike the fruit of almost any other profession (such as a painting one creates, a garment one makes, or a building one constructs). (2) Mathematics does absolutely no *harm*. How do you react to this analysis? When you think about Hardy's second reason keep in mind that he first published his book in 1940.

2. Write your own apology for mathematics or for any other discipline you find attractive. Be sure to justify the worth of the discipline as well as your possible involvement in it.

3. What vocation might you pursue? Answer this question with reference to some of the guidelines outlined in this chapter.

4. Take any single chapter in this book and discuss how the ideas presented in it can be of help to you in your Christian walk, regardless of what field of study occupies your primary area of interest.

BIBLIOGRAPHY

Abbott, Edwin A. *Flatland: A Romance of Many Dimensions.* 1884, Sealy & Co., London. Available in several subsequent editions.

Achtner, Wolfgang. "Truth and Proof in Mathematics and (Philosophical) Theology." *Theology and Science* 9, no. 1 (March 2011): 75–89.

Adamson, D. "Pascal's Views on Mathematics and the Divine." In *Mathematics and the Divine*, edited by Koetsier and Bergmans, 405–21.

Aigner, Martin, and Günter Ziegler. *Proofs from The Book.* New York: Springer, 1998.

Augustine. *On Free Choice of the Will.* Translated by Thomas Williams. Indianapolis: Hackett, 1993.

Baggert, David, Gary R. Habermas, and Jerry L. Wallis, eds. *C. S. Lewis as Philosopher.* Downers Grove, IL: InterVarsity, 2008.

Bartholomew, David. *God, Chance, and Purpose: Can God Have It Both Ways?* New York: Cambridge Univ. Press, 2008.

Bishop, Errett, and Douglas Bridges. *Constructive Analysis.* New York: Springer, 1985.

BonJour, Laurence. *In Defense of Pure Reason.* New York: Cambridge Univ. Press, 1998.

Bradley, James. "An Augustinian Perspective on the Philosophy of Mathematics." *Journal of the Association of Christians in the Mathematical Sciences* (November 2007). Available online at http://www.acmsonline.org/journal/2007/Bradley-Augustinian.htm.

———. "Theology and Mathematics: Key Themes and Central Historical Figures." *Theology and Science* 9, no. 1 (February 2011): 5–26.

Breger, H. "God and Mathematics in Leibniz's Thought." In *Mathematics and the Divine*, edited by Koetsier and Bergmans, 487–98.

Brown, James Robert. *Philosophy of Mathematics.* 2nd ed. New York: Routledge, 2008.

Buechner, Fredrick. *Wishful Thinking: A Theological ABC*. San Francisco: HarperSanFrancisco, 1993.

Burkert, W. *Lore and Science in Ancient Pythagoreanism*. Translated by Edwin L. Minar, Jr. Cambridge, MA: Harvard Univ. Press, 1972.

Byl, John. "Indeterminacy, Divine Action and Human Freedom." *Science and Christian Belief* 15, no. 2 (October 2003): 101–116.

Cantor, Georg. "On a Characteristic Property of All Real Algebraic Numbers." Originally published in 1874. English translation by Ewald in *From Immanuel Kant to David Hilbert: A Source Book in the Foundation of Mathematics*, 840–43. New York: Oxford Univ. Press, 1996.

Casullo, Albert. *A Priori Justification*. New York: Oxford Univ. Press, 2003.

Charrak, A. "The Mathematical Model of Creation According to Kepler." In *Mathematics and the Divine*, edited by Koetsier and Bergmans, 363–74.

Chihara, Charles. *A Structuralist Account of Mathematics*. Oxford, UK: Clarendon, 2004.

Clouser, Roy. *The Myth of Religious Neutrality*. Notre Dame, IN: Univ. of Notre Dame Press, 2005.

Cohen, Daniel. *Equations from God: Pure Mathematics and Victorian Faith*. Baltimore: Johns Hopkins Univ. Press, 2007.

Darwin, Charles. *On the Origin of Species by Means of Natural Selection*. London: J. Murray, 1859.

Dauben, J. W. "Georg Cantor and the Battle for Transfinite Set Theory." *Journal of the Association of Christians in the Mathematical Sciences* (2004). Available online at http://www.acmsonline.org/journal/2004/Dauben93.htm.

———. *Georg Cantor: His Mathematics and Philosophy of the Infinite*. Princeton, NJ: Princeton Univ. Press, 1979.

Dawkins, Richard. *River Out Of Eden: A Darwinian View of Life*. New York: Basic Books, 1995.

de Pater, C. "An Ocean of Truth." In *Mathematics and the Divine*, edited by Koetsier and Bergmans, 461–81.

Devlin, Keith. *The Language of Mathematics: Making the Invisible Visible.* New York: W. H. Freeman, 1998.

Dirac, Paul. "The Evolution of the Physicist's Picture of Nature." *Scientific American* 208, no. 5 (May 1963): 45–53.

Dunham, William. *Journey Through Genius: The Great Theorems of Mathematics.* New York: Wiley, 1990.

Edwards, Jonathan. "The Nature of True Virtue." In *The Works of Jonathan Edwards.* Carlisle, PA: Banner of Truth Trust, 1974.

———. *The Nature of True Virtue.* 1749. Reprinted with a foreward by William Frankena. Ann Arbor: Univ. of Michigan Press, 1960.

Engeler, Erwin. *Foundations of Mathematics.* New York: Springer-Verlag, 1983.

Ernest, Paul. *The Philosophy of Mathematics Education.* Basingstoke, UK: Falmer, 1991.

Fearnley-Sander, Desmond. "Hermann Grassmann and the Creation of Linear Algebra." *American Mathematical Monthly* 86 (1979): 809–17.

Flint, Thomas. *Divine Providence: The Molinist Account.* Ithaca, NY: Cornell Univ. Press, 2006.

Gilson, Etienne. *The Christian Philosophy of Saint Augustine.* London: Victor Gollanz, 1961.

Gingerich, Owen. "Kepler's Trinitarian Cosmology." *Theology and Science* 9, no. 1 (February 2011): 45–51.

Grassmann, Hermann. *The Theory of Linear Extension, a New Branch of Mathematics.* 1844. English translation by Lloyd Kannenberg. Chicago: Open Court, 1995.

Grattan-Guinness, Ivor. "Christianity and Mathematics: Kinds of Link, and the Rare Occurrences After 1750." *Physis: Rivista Internazionale di Soria della Scienza, Nuova serie* 37, no. 2 (2000): 26, 30.

———. "The Scope and Limitations of Algebras: Some Historical and Philosophical Considerations." *Theology and Science* 9, no. 1 (February 2011): 137–147.

Greco, John. "Introduction: What Is Epistemology?" In *The Blackwell Guide to Epistemology*, edited by John Greco and Ernest Sosa. Oxford: Blackwell, 1999.

Greene, Brian. *The Elegant Universe: Superstrings, Hidden Dimensions, and the Quest for the Ultimate Theory.* New York: Vintage Books, 2000.

Hamming, R. W. "The Unreasonable Effectiveness of Mathematics." *American Mathematical Monthly* 87, no. 2 (February 1980): 81–90.

Hauerwas, Stanley. *The State of the University.* Blackwell Publishing, 2007.

Hardy, G. H. *A Mathematician's Apology.* Cambridge: Cambridge Univ. Press, 1967.

Harrison, Peter. *The Fall of Man and the Foundations of Science.* New York: Cambridge Univ. Press, 2007.

Heller, Michael. *Creative Tension: Essays on Science and Religion.* Philadelphia: Templeton Foundation Press, 2003.

Hersh, Reuben. "On Platonism." *European Mathematical Society Newsletter* 68 (June 2008): 17–18.

Hilbert, David. "Konigsberg Address." 1930. Available in English translation at http://math.ucsd.edu/~williams/motiv/hilbert.html.

Hovis, R. Corby, and Helge Kragh. "P. A. M. Dirac and the Beauty of Physics." *Scientific American* 268, no. 5 (May 1993): 104–9.

Huntley, H. E. *The Divine Proportion: A Study in Mathematical Beauty.* New York: Dover, 1970.

Jongsma, Calvin. "Mathematics, Always Important, Never Enough: A Christian Perspective on Mathematics and Mathematics Education." *Journal of the Association of Christians in the Mathematical Sciences* (October 2006).

Kanigel, Robert. *The Man Who Knew Infinity: A Life of the Genius Ramanujan.* New York: Washington Square Press, 1991.

Kant, Immanuel. *Critique of Judgment.* Translated by Werner Pluhar. Indianapolis: Hackett, 1987.

Katz, Victor J. *A History of Mathematics: An Introduction.* New York: Harper Collins, 1993.

Kepler, Johannes. *Defundamentis Astrologiae Certioribus.* Thesis 20. 1601.

Kleinhans, Kathryn. "The Work of a Christian: Vocation in Lutheran Perspective." *Word and World* 25, no. 4 (Fall 2005): 394–402.

Koetsier, T., and K. Reich. "Michael Stifel and his Numerology." In *Mathematics and the Divine*, edited by Koetsier and Bergmans, 291–310.

Koetsier, T., and L. Bergmans, eds. *Mathematics and the Divine: A Historical Study.* Amsterdam: Elsevier, 2005.

Kroeber, Alfred, and Clyde Kluckhohn. *Culture: A Critical Review of Concepts and Definitions.* New York: Vintage Books, 1963.

Lessl, Thomas. "The Galileo Legend." *New Oxford Review* (June 2000): 27–33. Available online at http://www.catholiceducation. org/articles/apologetics/ap0138.html.

Lewis, Albert C. "The Divine Truth of Mathematics and the Origins of Linear Algebra." *Theology and Science* 9, no. 1 (February 2011): 109–120.

Lewis, C. S. *The Weight of Glory.* New York: HarperCollins Publishers, 2001, 25–46.

———. *Miracles.* London: Fontana Books, 1960.

Lindberg, David C. "Galileo, the Church, and the Cosmos." In *When Science and Christianity Meet*, edited by David C. Lindberg and Ronald L. Numbers. Chicago: Univ. of Chicago Press, 2003, 33–60.

Livio, Mario. *The Golden Ratio.* New York: Random House, 2003.

———. *Is God a Mathematician?* New York: Simon and Schuster, 2009.

Lowe, Ivan. "An Algebraic Theory of English Pronominal Reference (Part I)." *Semiotica* 1, no. 4 (1969): 397–421.

Lowe, Ivan. "Christian Mathematicians, Where Are You?" *Translation.* (January–March 1971).

Mazur, Barry. "Mathematical Platonism and Its Opposites." European Mathematical Society Newsletter 68 (June 2008): 19–21.

McDowell, Josh. *Evidence That Demands a Verdict.* Nashville: Thomas Nelson, 1992.

McGrath, Alister. *The Open Secret: Renewing the Vision for Natural Theology.* Malden, MA: Blackwell, 2008.

Mendell, Henry. "Aristotle and Mathematics." *Stanford Encyclopedia of Philosophy.* Edited by Edward N. Zalta. March 26, 2004. http://plato.stanford.edu/entries/aristotle-mathematics/.

Menzel, Chris. "God and Mathematical Objects." In *Mathematics in a Postmodern Age: A Christian Perspective.* Edited by R. W. Howell and W. J. Bradley. Grand Rapids: Eerdmans, 2001.

Merton, Thomas. *The Living Bread.* 1956. New York: Farrar, Straus & Giroux, 1980.

Methuen, Charlotte. "The German Reformation and the Mathematization of the Created World." *Theology and Science* 9, no. 1 (February 2011): 35–44.

Moo, Douglas J. *Romans.* The NIV Application Commentary. Grand Rapids: Zondervan, 2000.

Morris, Simon Conway. *Life's Solution: Inevitable Humans in a Lonely Universe.* New York: Cambridge Univ. Press, 2005.

———. *The Deep Structure of Biology: Is Convergence Sufficiently Ubiquitous to Give a Directional Signal?* Philadelphia: Templeton Foundation Press, 2008.

Mueller, I. "Mathematics and the Divine in Plato." In *Mathematics and the Divine,* edited by Koetsier and Bergmans, 99–121.

Murphy, Nancey. "Divine Action in the Natural Order: Buridan's Ass and Schrödinger's Cat." In *Chaos and Complexity: Scientific Perspectives on Divine Action,* edited by Robert John Russell, Nancey Murphy, and Arthur R. Peacocke. Berkeley: Center for Theology and the Natural Sciences, 1996, 325–357.

Nash, Ronald H. *The Light of the Mind: St. Augustine's Theory of Knowledge.* Lexington: Univ. Press of Kentucky, 1969.

Netz, R. "The Pythagoreans." In *Mathematics and the Divine,* edited by Koetsier and Bergmans, 77–97.

Neuhouser, David L. *Open to Reason.* Upland, IN: Taylor Univ. Press, 2001.

Nicolle, J. M. "The Mathematical Analogy in the Proof of God's Existence by Descartes." In *Mathematics and the Divine,* edited by Koetsier and Bergmans, 387–403.

Noonan, Harold W. *Frege: A Critical Introduction.* Cambridge, UK: Polity, 2001.

Norris, Kathleen. *Amazing Grace: A Vocabulary of Faith*. New York: Riverhead Books, 1998.

Outram, D. *The Enlightenment*. New York: Cambridge Univ. Press, 1995.

Philo. *On the Creation of the Cosmos According to Moses*. Introduction, translation, and commentary by David T. Runia. Boston: Brill, 2001.

Plantinga, Alvin. *Does God Have a Nature?*, Milwaukee: Marquette University Press, 1980.

———. "An Evolutionary Argument Against Naturalism." *Logos: Philosophic Issues in Christian Perspective* 1.

———. "Theism and Mathematics." *Theology and Science* 9, no. 1 (February 2011): 27–33.

———. *Warrant and Proper Function*. New York: Oxford Univ. Press, 1993.

Plato. *Theaetetus*. Translated by M. J. Levett. Indianapolis: Hackett, 1992.

Polanyi, Michael. "The Logic of Tacit Interference." *Philosophy* 41 (1966): 155.

Polkinghorne, John. "The Metaphysics of Divine Action." In *Chaos and Complexity: Scientific Perspectives on Divine Action*, edited by Robert John Russell, Nancey Murphy, and Arthur R. Peacocke. Berkeley: Center for Theology and the Natural Sciences, 1996, 147–156.

———. *Quantum Theory: A Very Short Introduction*. Oxford University Press, 2002.

———. *Science and Providence: God's Interaction with the World*. Philadelphia: Templeton Foundation Press, 2005.

Pollard, William. *Chance and Providence: God's Action in a World Governed by Scientific Law*. New York: Scribner, 1958.

Polya, George. *How to Solve It: A New Aspect of Mathematical Method*. Princeton, NJ: Princeton Univ. Press, 1945.

Posamentier, Alfred, and Ingmar Lehmann. *The (Fabulous) Fibonacci Numbers*. Amherst, NY: Prometheus Books, 2007.

Priest, Graham. *An Introduction to Non-Classical Logic*. Cambridge, UK: Cambridge Univ. Press, 2001.

Ptolemy, C. *The Almagest*. Vol. 15 in *Great Books of the Western World*, translated by R. Catesby Taliaferro. Chicago: Encyclopedia Britannica, 1952.

Remmert, Volker R. "Galileo, God, and Mathematics." In *Mathematics and the Divine*, edited by Koetsier and Bergmans, 347–60.

Reppert, Victor. *C. S. Lewis's Dangerous Idea*. Downers Grove, IL: IVP Academic, 2003.

Richards, Joan L. "God, Truth, and Mathematics in Nineteenth Century England." *Theology and Science* 9, no. 1 (February 2011): 53–74.

Rucker, Rudy. *Infinity and the Mind*. Princeton, NJ: Princeton Univ. Press, 1995.

Russell, Bertrand. "The Study of Mathematics." In *Mysticism and Logic: And Other Essays*. New York: Longmans, Green, 1918.

———. *Mysticism and Logic*. Nottingham, England: Spokesman Books, 2007.

Schroeder, Chad Matthew, ed. *Cygnifiliana: Essays in Classics, Comparative Literature, and Philosophy*. New York: Peter Lang, 2005.

Shapiro, Stewart. *Philosophy of Mathematics: Structure and Ontology*. New York: Oxford Univ. Press, 1997.

———. "Theology and the Actual Infinite: Burley and Cantor." *Theology and Science* 9, no. 1 (February 2011): 101–108.

Steiner, Mark. *The Applicability of Mathematics as a Philosophical Problem*. Cambridge, MA: Harvard, 1998.

Stewart, Ian. *Letters to a Young Mathematician*. New York: Basic Books, 2006.

Stover, David, and Erika Erdmann. *A Mind for Tomorrow: Facts, Values, and the Future*. Westport, CT: Praeger, 2000.

Strobel, Lee. *The Case for Christ: A Journalist's Personal Investigation of the Evidence for Jesus*. Grand Rapids: Zondervan, 1998.

Sylla, E. D. "Swester Katrei and Gregory of Rimini: Angels, God, and Mathematics in the Fourteenth Century." In *Mathematics and the Divine*, edited by Koetsier and Bergmans, 249–71.

Tapp, Christian. "Infinity in Mathematics and Theology." *Theology and Science* 9, no. 1 (February 2011): 91–100.

Tonietti, Toni. Axiomatic versus Constructive Procedures in Mathematics. *Mathematical Intelligencer* 7, no. 4: 10–17.

Toynbee, Arnold. *Experiences.* New York: Oxford Univ. Press, 1969.

Troelstra, A. S. "A History of Constructivism in the 20th Century." Univ. of Amsterdam, ITLI Prepublication Series ML–91–05, http://staff.science.uva.nl/~anne/hhhist.pdf.

van Inwagen, Peter. "The Place of Chance in a World Sustained by God." In *God, Knowledge, and Mystery.* Ithaca, NY: Cornell Univ. Press, 1995.

Voltaire, Francois-Marie Arouet. *Candide: or, All for the Best.* Penguin Classics editorial, London, 2005.

Ward, Keith. *God, Chance, and Necessity.* Oxford, UK: Oneworld, 1996.

Wigner, Eugene. "The Unreasonable Effectiveness of Mathematics in the Natural Sciences." *Communications in Pure and Applied Mathematics* 13, no. 1 (February 1960): 1–14.

Wolters, Al. "Dutch Neo-Calvinism: Worldview, Philosophy and Rationality." In *Rationality in the Calvinian Tradition.* Edited by H. Hart, J. Van den Hoeven, and N. Wolterstorff. Lanham, M.D.: University Press of America, 1983.

Wolterstorff, Nicholas. *Art in Action: Toward a Christian Aesthetic.* Grand Rapids: Eerdmans, 1980.

NOTES

Chapter 2: Historical Context

1. Volker R. Remmert, "Galileo, God, and Mathematics," in Koetsier and Bergmans, eds., *Mathematics and the Divine: A Historical Study* (Amsterdam: Elsevier, 2005), 355.
2. D. Outram, *The Enlightenment* (New York: Cambridge Univ. Press, 1995), 3.
3. Ivor Grattan-Guinness, "Christianity and Mathematics: Kinds of Link, and the Rare Occurrences After 1750," *Physis: Rivista Internazionale di Soria della Scienza, Nuova serie 37*, no. 2 (2000): 26.
4. Daniel Cohen, *Equations from God: Pure Mathematics and Victorian Faith* (Baltimore: Johns Hopkins Univ. Press, 2007), 108.
5. Bertrand Russell, *Mysticism and Logic* (Nottingham, England: Spokesman Books, 2007), 91.
6. David Hilbert, "Konigsberg Address," Fall 1930, available in English translation at http://math.ucsd.edu/~williams/motiv/hilbert.html.

Chapter 3: Infinity

7. Kathleen Norris, *Amazing Grace: A Vocabulary of Faith* (New York: Riverhead Books, 1998), 72.
8. Quoted in Rudy Rucker, *Infinity and the Mind* (Princeton, NJ: Princeton Univ. Press, 1995), 43.
9. Letter written by Cantor to Grace Chisholm Young, June 20, 1908, as quoted in J. W. Dauben, *Georg Cantor: His Mathematics and Philosophy of the Infinite* (Princeton, NJ: Princeton University Press, 1979), 124.
10. Thomas Merton, *The Living Bread* (1956; New York: Farrar, Straus & Giroux, 1980), 51.

Chapter 4: Dimension

11. Hermann Grassmann, as quoted in Albert Lewis, *The Divine Truth of Mathematics and the Origins of Linear Algebra, Theology, and Science,* February 2011.
12. Desmond Fearnley-Sander, "Hermann Grassmann and the Creation of Linear Algebra," *American Mathematical Monthly* 86 (1979): 809–817.

Chapter 5: Chance

13. David Stover and Erika Erdmann, *A Mind for Tomorrow: Facts, Values, and the Future* (Westport, CT: Praeger, 2000), 37.
14. Richard Dawkins, *River Out Of Eden: A Darwinian View of Life* (New York: Basic Books, 1995), 133.

Chapter 6: Proof and Truth

15. William Dunham, *Journey Through Genius: The Great Theorems of Mathematics* (New York: Wiley, 1990), 2.
16. Ian Stewart, *Letters to a Young Mathematician* (New York: Basic Books, 2006), 79.
17. As quoted in Owen Gingerich, "The Censorship of Copernicus' De Revolutionibus," *Journal of the American Scientific Affiliation* (March 1981): 58–60.

Chapter 7: Beauty

18. Bertrand Russell, "The Study of Mathematics," in *Mysticism and Logic: And Other Essays* (New York: Longmans, Green, 1918), 60.
19. G. H. Hardy, *A Mathematician's Apology* (Cambridge: Cambridge Univ. Press, 1940), 85.
20. Quoted by Toni Tonietti (editor), Letter written by Hermann Weyl to Freeman Dyson, *Mathematical Intelligencer* 7, no. 4 (1985): 8.
21. Paul Dirac, "The Evolution of the Physicist's Picture of Nature," *Scientific American* 208, no. 5 (May 1963): 47.
22. Hardy, *A Mathematician's Apology*, 85.
23. Jonathan Edwards, *The Nature of True Virtue* (1749; repr., Ann Arbor: University of Michigan Press, 1960), 14.
24. William Shakespeare, *Love's Labors Lost*, act 2, scene 1.
25. Edwards, *Nature of True Virtue*, 132.
26. Quoted in Chad Matthew Shroeder, ed., *Cygnifiliana: Essays in Classics, Comparative Literature, and Philosophy* (New York: Peter Lang, 2005), 50.
27. Nicholas Wolterstorff, *Art in Action: Toward a Christian Aesthetic* (Grand Rapids: Eerdmans, 1980), 169.
28. C. S. Lewis, *The Weight of Glory* (New York: HarperCollins Publishers, 2001): 30–31.
29. Abraham Kuyper, *Lectures on Calvinism: The Stone Lecture of 1898.* (Eerdmans, 2000): 143.

Chapter 8: Effectiveness

30. Ivan Lowe, "Christian Mathematicians, Where Are You?" *Translation.* (January–March): 2.

31. Eugene Wigner, "The Unreasonable Effectiveness of Mathematics in the Natural Sciences," *Communications in Pure and Applied Mathematics* 13, no. 1 (February 1960): 9.

32. Wigner, "Unreasonable Effectiveness," 2.

33. Wigner, "Unreasonable Effectiveness," 14.

34. R. W. Hamming, "The Unreasonable Effectiveness of Mathematics," *American Mathematical Monthly* 87, no. 2 (February 1980): 89.

35. C. S. Lewis, *Miracles* (London: Fontana Books, 1960), 21.

36. Charles Darwin, *On the Origin of Species by Means of Natural Selection* (London: J. Murray, 1859), 315–16.

37. Brian Greene, *The Elegant Universe: Superstrings, Hidden Dimensions, and the Quest for the Ultimate Theory* (New York: Vintage Books, 2000), 374.

38. John Polkinghorne, *Quantum Theory: A Very Short Introduction.* (Oxford University Press, 2002), 72–73.

39. Keith Ward, *God, Chance, and Necessity* (Oxford, UK: Oneworld, 1996), 73.

Chapter 9: Epistemology

40. Douglas J. Moo. *The NIV Application Commentary—Romans* (Grand Rapids, MI: Zondervan Publishing House, 2000), 398.

41. Kanigel, Robert. *The Man Who Knew Infinity: A Life of the Genius Ramanujan.* (New York: HarperCollins Publishers, 1993), 168.

42. Ronald H. Nash, *The Light of the Mind: St. Augustine's Theory of Knowledge* (Lexington: Univ. Press of Kentucky, 1969), 5.

43. Augustine, *On Free Choice of the Will,* trans. Thomas Williams (Indianapolis: Hackett, 1993), 46.

44. Errett Bishop and Douglas Bridges, *Constructive Analysis* (New York: Springer, 1985), 4–5.

45. Quoted in James Robert Brown, *Philosophy of Mathematics,* 2nd ed. (New York: Routledge, 2008), 121.

46. Quoted in Peter Barker and Bernard Goldstein, "Theological Foundations," in Peter Harrison, *The Fall of Man and the Foundations of Science* (Cambridge: Cambridge Univ. Press, 2007), 104.

Chapter 10: Ontology

47. Johannes Kepler, *Defundamentis Astrologiae Certioribus*, Thesis 20, 1601.
48. Roy Clouser, *The Myth of Religious Neutrality* (Notre Dame, IN: University of Notre Dame Press, 2005), 230.
49. Clouser, *Myth of Religious Neutrality*, 229.
50. Reuben Hersh, "On Platonism." *European Mathematical Society Newsletter* 68 (June 2008): 17.
51. Barry Mazur, "Mathematical Platonism and Its Opposites," *European Mathematical Society Newsletter* 68 (June 2008): 19–21.
52. Mazur, "Mathematical Platonism," 19.
53. Mazur, "Mathematical Platonism," 21.

Chapter 11: An Apology

54. Arnold Toynbee, *Experiences* (New York: Oxford Univ. Press, 1969), 12–13.
55. Ian Stewart, *Letters to a Young Mathematician* (New York: Basic Books, 2006), 2.
56. Stanley Hauerwas, *The State of the University.* (Massachusetts: Blackwell Publishing, 2007): 131.
57. Stewart, *Letters to a Young Mathematician*, 8–9.
58. G. H. Hardy, *A Mathematician's Apology* (Cambridge: Cambridge Univ. Press, 1940), 67.
59. Hardy, *A Mathematician's Apology*, 73.
60. Fredrick Beuchner, *Wishful Thinking: A Theological ABC* (San Francisco: HarperSanFrancisco, 1993), 119.
61. Kathryn Kleinhans, "The Work of a Christian: Vocation in Lutheran Perspective," *Word and World* 25, no. 4 (Fall 2005): 395.

INDEX

Page numbers of illustrations appear in italics.